If Your Dream Doesn't Scare You, It Isn't Big Enough

A solo journey around the world

by

Kristine K. Stevens

SUBTEXT
PUBLISHING

For more information, contact Subtext Publishing LLC, 510 E. 64th St., Savannah, GA 31405.

Author's disclaimer: All of the events in this book are true. The sequence may be tweaked for better storytelling and a few names have been changed to reduce gossip.

First Edition
First Printing 2013

ISBN 13: 978-0-9882529-1-2

Printed in the United States of America

Dedications

To Larry Maxwell and the mealy bugs,
which will die very, very soon.

To Gene Beeco, a man of confidence and dignity:
"The luggage isa founda!"

To John Ruskin, who wrote,
"Your art is to be the praise of something that you love."

A note to the reader

Thank you in advance for reading this book! Want to be more involved?

- **Visit** kristinekstevens.com to see photos from the trip.
- **Share** what you think about the book on Amazon.com, GoodReads.com and LibraryThing.com.
- **Like** Facebook.com/IfYourDreamDoesntScareYou.
- **Post** comments on Twitter using #DreamBigBook.
- **Contact** me via Facebook.com/IfYourDreamDoesntScareYou if you would like to arrange a book signing.

I can't wait to hear what you think of my journey!

May you have good travel karma,

Kristine K. Stevens

Gratitude

MY HEARTFELT THANK YOU to all the people who made my journey possible, who shared portions of it with me, and who helped me make this book a reality, including but not limited to: Aimee Petkus and Greg Patselas, Allen Furr, Allen Landers, Andrea le Roux, Amanda Wetherhold, wordsmith Amy Paige Condon, Barbara Fertig, Becca Hillburn and Joseph Coco, Beth Concepcion, Bill Metz and Timmy Welter, Blake Thornton, Bradley Layfield, Brandi Cockram, Brett Gilleo, Caila Brown, Carl Feldman, Cayce and Mark Girardeau, Chad Faries, my parents Charles and Gerry Stevens, Charlie and Kim Slosson, Cheryl G. Edenfield, Christina Waddell, Cynthia Hotvedt, Dave Malouf, David Dolezel, Dawn Chrisman, Dawn Tarter, Don Holloway, Don Senior, Doug Stein, Eddie Ball, Eddie Edenfield, Libby and Tommy Hersch, Elizebeth and Tyme Tong, Eric Von-Duyke, Erin Cramer, Esther Robbins and Carl Stevens, Francis Allen and Leslie Lovell, Geir Haukursson, Genna Matson Trombley, Geoff Stead, Gerry and Sandy Sokolik, Ginger McDevitt, Graeme and Ott Bolger, Hartford Gongaware, Hash House Harriers, Holly Barrett, Hunter Cattle Co., Ian Leslie, Jamee Parsons, author James Caskey, mentor James Lough, Jamie Marie Smith, trainer Jane Ogle, migratory Janna and Peter Belau, Jason Parker, Jennifer Morris, Jennifer West, Jillison Parks, Jim Johnston, Jim and Mariana Tuten, Jo Collins, Joel Wenham, John Brown, Joleen nd Rachel Lewis, Jon Gump, Jon Kaplan, Judy Beckett, Karen O'Brien, Kate Fitzpatrick, Katherine Hanzalik, Kathy Levine, Katie Campbell, Keith and Maggie Bullock, Kirk Hutchins, patron Kristi Majni, Laura Swanson, Linda Zettler Boeko, Lisa Owens, Lis Miller, publisher Liz Wiglesworth, Malissia McGinnis, Mary Stewart, Melissa Meyers, Michael Jordan, Michael Stanton, BFF Michael Wrachford, Philippe Chanelet Dardenne, Rachel Allgood, Rachel Leigh Oliver, Richard Koch, Rick Basdeo, Robert Richards, Ryan Shaver, Sarah Leadbeater, BFF Scott Meeker, Servane Pierre, Shannon Davis, Shannon Detro, Shawna Allen, Shelley Murphy, Sherrie Cockram, Sloane Kelley, Steve Bowman, Tamara and Todd Rasmuson, Thomas Harrison, Todd Williams, Tom Schmitendorf, Travis Walters, Vijay Prabhakar, Vinh T. Dang, Virginia Bedford, Weihua Zhang, Lis Miller, Wim van Hoek, and Zack Jones.

Table of Contents

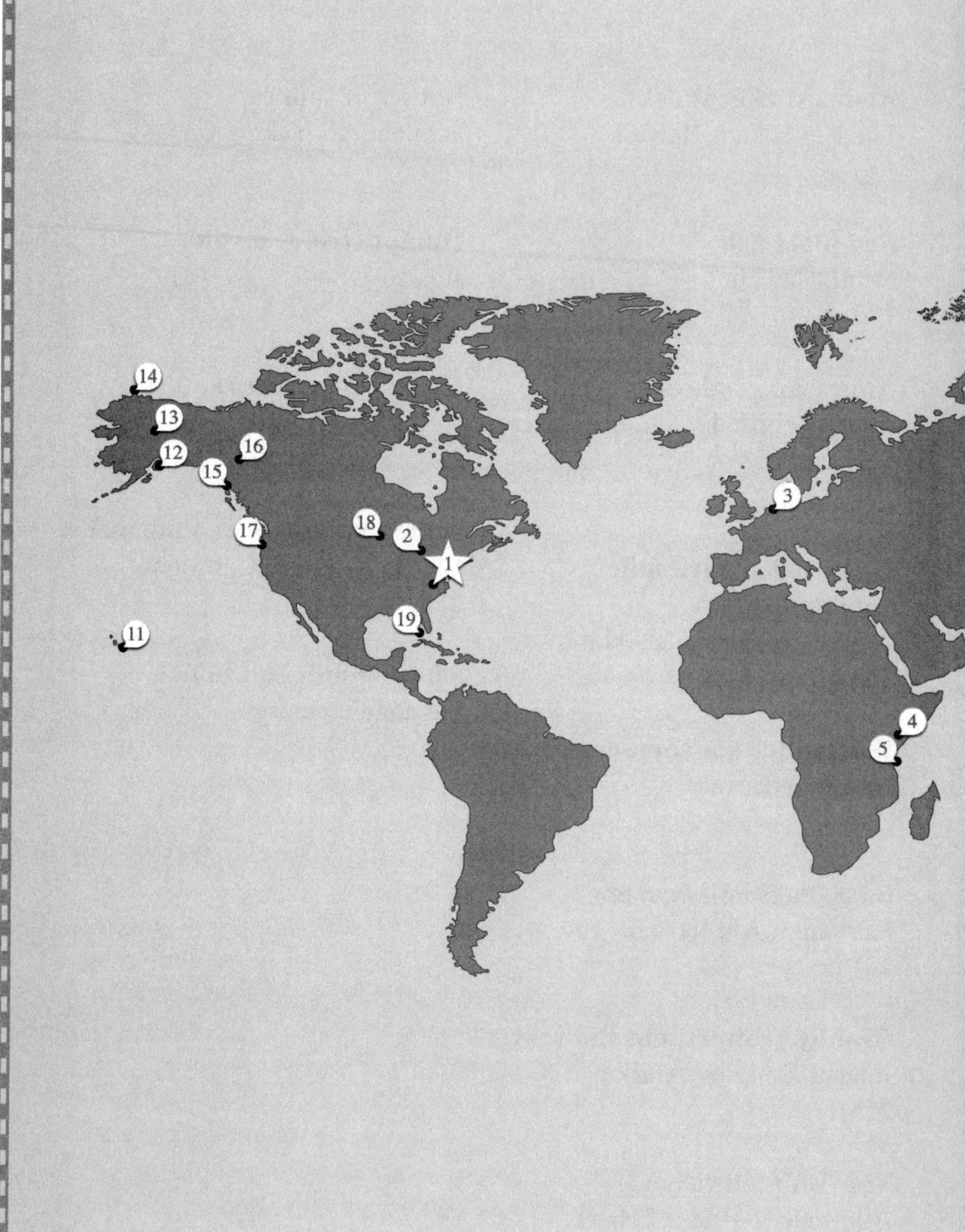

14
13
12
16
15
17
18
2
1
19
11
3
4
5

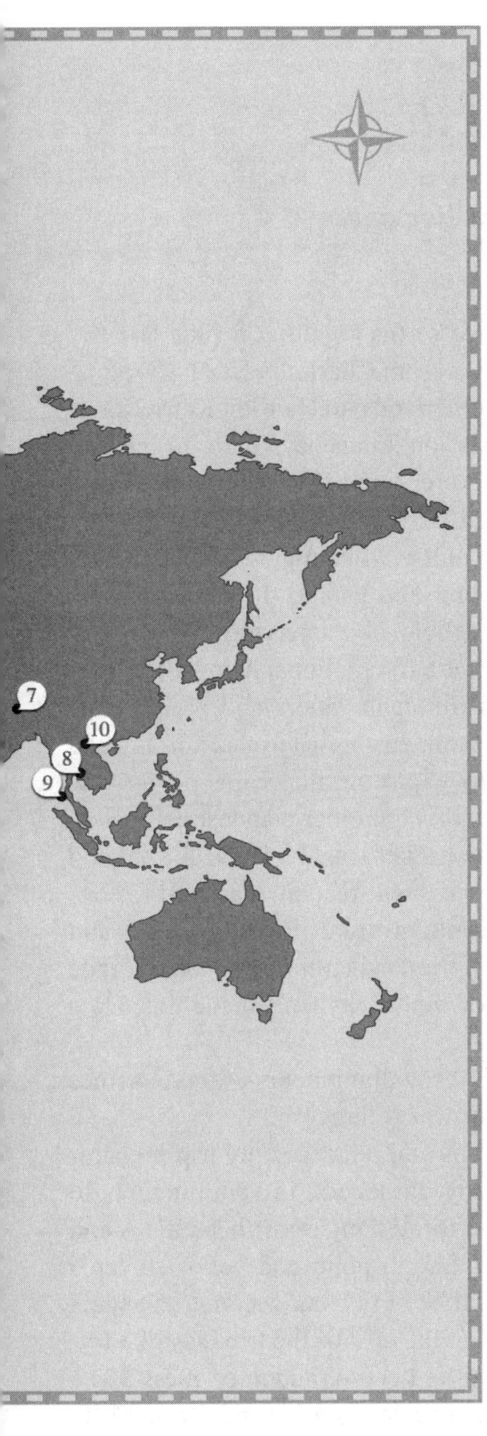

Itinerary

1. Charlotte, North Carolina
2. Detroit, Michigan
3. Amsterdam, Netherlands
4. Nairobi, Kenya
5. Dar es Salaam and Zanzibar, Tanzania
6. Mumbai, India
7. Pokhara and Kathmandu, Nepal
8. Bangkok, Thailand
9. Phuket, Thailand
10. Vientiane, Vang Vieng and Luang Prabang, Laos
11. Oahu and the Big Island, Hawaii
12. Seward, Alaska
13. Fairbanks, Alaska
14. Barrow, Alaska
15. Juneau, Douglas and Admiralty Island, Alaska
16. White Horse, Yukon, Canada
17. Seattle, Washington
18. Minneapolis, Minnesota
19. Key West, Florida

I prey to thee

Dar es Salaam, Tanzania

WAITING FOR MY FLIGHT was worse than waiting for the last day of high school to end. I had already flown from Charlotte, North Carolina, to Detroit, Michigan, to Amsterdam, Netherlands, to Nairobi, Kenya. Now I was up at 4 a.m. to fly on to the coast on Tanzania. There, in the city of Dar es Salaam, I had no plans. No driver waiting to shuttle me to and from the airport. No knowledge of the city beyond the brief listings in my *Lonely Planet East Africa* guidebook to hint at what might lay ahead. After a heavily structured childhood, schooling and career, the upcoming six months of travel around the world felt deliciously unnerving.

The waiting room in the Jomo Kenyatta International Airport was boringly practical, with bare white walls, linoleum floors and hard plastic chairs. Beyond the wall-long window facing an empty tarmac, nothing had moved since I arrived. I passed time by exploring the seams of my new forest green North Face jacket and found yet another clandestine pocket, a perfect home for 26 plane tickets. The packet was thick and formal and pungent with an inky smell. It bulged as if such freedom was hard to contain. People dream. They talk about escaping from it all. Their friends and family diligently listen and politely ignore it when the ruminations fade into oblivion. So, quite a few eyebrows went up when I made this trip a reality.

Now I was 8,569 miles away, 37 butt-numbing hours of travel across seven time zones in the last two days, or was it three?

I crunched through a bag of Combos and pondered my trip preparations. Yellow Post-it Notes feathered my guidebook in vain attempts to make a to-do list. Vaccination marks perforated my arms: hepatitis A and B, tetanus, measles, mumps, rubella, typhoid, polio and yellow fever. I had squirreled away enough money to make my bank account balance a chubby five digits wide. Trying to predict the cost of the trip was like trying to predict how long I was going to live. I could randomly guess $50 a day for a total of $9,000 for six months, but a day in Africa might cost $10, compared with a day in Hawaii that might cost more than $200. I finally decided to adopt guidelines rather than set a budget. If it could be done at home, skip it. If I had done it before, skip it. If the odds were that I would never have another chance to do it, do it. Scrimp on meals, transportation and accommodations.

By the time I finished off a York Peppermint Pattie, drama erupted in the security screening area by the waiting room entrance. Two solidly built uniformed guards detained a young couple who looked innocent enough. The man had a blond buzz cut and was wearing a white T-shirt and jeans over his lanky build. His companion looked like a fair-skinned model dressed in a gauzy peasant shirt and skirt. The guards glared at them and pointed to the poster on the wall. Not good. It listed laws about endangered animals and illegal transportation of animal-related products.

The couple's expressions ranged from surprise to confusion to submission during the confrontation. Finally, the guards dismissed them into the waiting area. Once they settled into chairs and I heard them speak English, I approached them for details. Maybe they knew something that would help me later on.

"When I emptied out my pockets, there was a lion's tooth," Thomas explained after we introduced ourselves. No problem for me there. "I bought it from a Maasai man I met on safari."

The guards had danced along a fine line of intimidation, suggesting the couple might face large fines or possible prison time, though not outright demanding a bribe on the spot.

"Bastards," said Thomas' girlfriend, Venke.

The Norwegian couple said they eventually wore the guards down with claims of ignorance and poverty.

THE PLANE HEADED SOUTHEAST toward the coast of Tanzania. As it descended, a brilliant rainbow arched across the sky. I could not remember the last time I had seen one. By spending so much time indoors—working so many hours in offices and stores—I had unknowingly stripped them from my life.

The savanna below appeared unmanaged, lightly forested and marred by few roads. The cloudless blue sky seemed to go on forever. Tinsel-bright sunlight baked the cool morning air into a sweltering soup. Along the landing strip, glistening, bare-chested men cut down spring grass with rhythmic sweeps of their machetes.

Thomas and Venke were taking a taxi to the inexpensive YWCA in the central part of Dar es Salaam, so I asked if I could join them. A swarm of taxi drivers jockeyed for our business. Thomas negotiated the deal because, as a man, he commanded more authority than Venke or me. It was annoying but not unexpected. Before Thomas agreed on a price within the guidebook-recommended range, he asked the driver to show us his car. Its cleanliness implied that it was fairly safe. So many tiny lessons for me to learn.

After we settled in the vintage, white four-door Toyota, the driver headed down the road. Pockmarks full of rust-colored water disguised teeth-rattling dips and bone-jarring drops. We three were silent as we took in our surroundings. The view of the open landscape soon funneled into a corridor of one-story, cinderblock buildings with metal roofs, and shacks cobbled together with scraps of wood and plastic sheeting. There were no sidewalks, just crusty red dirt. Bits of litter tumbled by in the breeze. Most cars and trucks looked "rode hard, put away wet," while closer to town, some newer, cleaner cars joined the mix. Where traffic stopped, men with trinkets—plastic toy trucks, neon-colored scrubby pads, boxes of cigarettes dangling from strings tied to their arms—wandered through sooty clouds of exhaust to find buyers. Their income came one hard-earned shilling at a time.

As we entered the heart of downtown, traffic backed up. Battered white minivans called *dallah-dallahs*—the local public transportation—joined the melee in the narrow streets. Buildings of various sizes crowded up against each other. In the dirt strip across the street from a polished granite high-rise building, men fried potato wedges and roasted ears of corn over charcoal fires. Down the block, men sold cucumbers, bananas and pineapples from carts. Others sold playing cards, lighters, hair clips and chewing gum on battered metal TV trays.

Within this hodgepodge of urban life, black mold shadowed most of the walls, and many were crowned with broken bottles and swirls of barbed wire. Some business owners not only barred their windows, but also posted armed sentries at their front doors. I expected to see new things on my trip, but I had not expected these blatant displays of defense. When I saw uniformed men, each with a rifle slung casually over a shoulder, guarding an ATM machine, I questioned why I was here in the first place.

This trip was not my idea to start with. Traveling around the world was my former boyfriend's dream. It was so daringly beyond anything I could have imagined, but he convinced me we could do it together. When

I figured out he was not the right man for me and that it was time to let him go, I asked myself if I had to let go of the dream as well. Could I do it by myself?

That question and my impending 40th birthday forced me to evaluate my life. The results were financially solid, but lackluster. There was no sense of adventure and accomplishment. I was not one to climb a corporate ladder, raise a family or join a church. My job producing newsletters for a healthcare system for the last seven years had become as easy as tying my shoes. I had always dreamed of travel, but I had passively waited until others brought trips into my life. The only thing I had to look forward to was a comfortable retirement. I had stopped growing.

It was time to give quality of life priority over fiscal responsibility. And as I overcame each obstacle to make the trip real, my resolve grew. I was pushed toward the trip as much as I was lured by it. Author Anaïs Nin neatly summed up my feelings when she wrote: "… and then the day came when the risk of remaining tight in a bud was more painful than the risk it took to blossom."

What I did not realize was that I also hoped to have an epiphany, to discover a cause to devote my life to, a location where I thrived, a man to love, a life that would give me more fulfillment than the meager amount I had been living on for years.

The trip was supposed to start with a month living in a rural Tanzanian village with my missionary cousins, Tamara and Todd, but visa problems forced them to leave the country a couple of weeks before I arrived. Faced with this sudden change in plans, I decided to visit the Tanzanian coast for 10 days before traveling north to Kenya where my cousins had temporarily relocated. I had the visa and the time, so why not?

On the corner of Maktaba Street and Ghana Avenue, we walked through a wrought iron gate and a pair of massive wooden doors and into the modest hallway of a 1950s YWCA. A matronly woman, sitting in a closet disguised as an office, checked us in. A sign declared that we were permitted to stay no more than one week. We must leave our door keys (each attached to a block of wood the size of a chalkboard eraser) at the desk in return for pink receipts if we left the building.

The guest rooms were up one flight of stairs. My concrete-floored room was annoyingly teal, the corporate color of the hospital system I had worked so hard to leave behind. Teal walls. Teal bed sheets. Teal pillowcase. Thankfully, the curtains broke stride with navy blue batik.

The screenless windows had louvered slat-glass panes, like vintage

Ranch houses in Florida. But there were no white sandy beaches outside. The view featured a road, a dingy high-rise apartment building with laundry hanging off the balconies, and a patch of lush grass inside the high cinderblock walls of the YWCA's compound.

The room's porcelain sink, wooden table and chair were impressively small, as if they had been built for children. There was a latch on the wardrobe so I could padlock my backpack inside it. A tent of mosquito netting hung over the single bed. I was not thrilled to see that its holes were patched with less-than-fresh looking Band-Aids. But what more could you ask for when the room, with complimentary breakfast, cost less than $5 a night?

The communal toilets and showers were down the hall. In the women's bathroom there were two stalls—one with a Western sit-down toilet, though no seat, and one with a squat-over-a-ceramic-trough design. Neither had toilet paper. The shower, with a metal sunflower-shaped nozzle, had plywood walls and a concrete floor that sloped down to a drain. I forgot to pack a towel, so later that day I bought a navy blue turtle-print sarong from a street vendor. It became my towel, my swim cover-up and, soon enough, my security blanket.

Before Thomas, Venke and I went for a walk, I sneaked a peek down the off-limits hall on the third floor where local women lived. Orderly rows of worn canvas shoes and flip flops trailed along the wall from each door. Only the first pair of each row was adult sized. The rest were for children.

PINK RECEIPTS IN OUR POCKETS, we walked the streets, mindful that pedestrians had no rights whatsoever. We rarely spoke to each other as we got our bearings. Sadly, this area was drab inner city. It lacked the intricate architecture, foreign clothing and spicy smells I expected from a city that had been influenced for centuries by Arab, German and British occupations.

We passed rows of open-front cinder block shops, a spired mosque, a building filled with stacks of tires and a seamstress shop no bigger than a parking space. Random things caught my attention. Odd patches of tropical overgrowth. The smell of hot grease and leaf mold. Trees I could not name and words I could not understand, though most people spoke English because Tanzania had been a British colony for about four decades before it gained independence in 1961.

The people on the sidewalks wore resigned expressions and modest clothes that jarringly mixed textures, fibers, prints and styles. East-meets-West combinations were common. One woman wore a trendy logo T-shirt with a traditional geometric print sarong. Another proudly wore a multi-colored head wrap with an emerald green satin, full length, bridesmaid dress complete with puffy sleeves and a V-neckline.

The styles reminded me of a time when shoulder pads and pastel-colored, *Miami Vice*-inspired linen jackets were the rage. My cousins later explained that unwanted Salvation Army and Goodwill clothes from the U.S. were often baled and shipped to East Africa for sale in the public markets.

The few smartly dressed people I did see would be trendsetters in New York City. No doubt I would have seen more fashionable clothing if I had stayed at the local Movenpick Royal Palm Hotel. According to its website, it offered "East African culture and tradition combined with international standards and Swiss quality." One of its finest suites would cost more per night than 200 nights at the YWCA.

The locals immediately sized me up as a *mzunga*, a foreigner. Even in a chambray shirt and khaki pants, with no guidebook in hand or camera hanging from my neck, I was still a 6-foot-tall oddity with copper red hair, jade green eyes and pale white skin. Most people stared at me. Some scowled. Others approached me to sell something. It made it tough to welcome truly kind gestures because I quickly became skeptical of strangers and their motives.

"Hello, madam. Would you like to buy some rat poison?" The man at the street corner held out a packet featuring a black silhouette of a rat against a blood red background. The rest of his packets were neatly arranged in a cardboard box on top of a plastic milk crate.

"No, thank you." I said. It was just enough words for him to peg my nationality.

"Oh, but this poison is strong enough to kill American rats. Take some with you." He held the packet closer to me. If he could just get it in my hand, he would be one step closer to making the sale. "You can use it when you get home."

"No, thank you," I said again as I walked away.

He was a dedicated man on a mission. I would be, too, if my family and next meal depended on it.

At a corner convenience store, the young cashier handwrote a receipt for my juice box-sized container of Foma laundry detergent and a packet of Tabisco glucose biscuits (an impressive name for cookies). Imagine an employee hand-writing a receipt for a cart full of groceries at a Walmart.

A block from the YWCA, we explored the Imalesko Supermarket. It had no meat, a few wilted fruits and vegetables, and a large selection of nonperishable goods, like soap, dried grains, noodles, canned goods and cookware. Canned sodas were almost twice as expensive as soda in glass bottles that could be recycled. In most cases, the store offered only one or two brands or sizes of anything. Toilet paper was either bleached white or unbleached gray, yet there were more than a dozen kinds of ketchup and about thirty brands of cookies. I approved of their priorities.

"That's the president of Tanzania," Thomas explained as we walked out the door, past a large portrait of a distinguished looking black man in a suit. I had seen them many times during our walk. "Businesses are required by law to display it."

For lunch, we sat at a linen-covered table on a restaurant's first-floor porch. Yards away, cars and trucks whizzed around a traffic circle. For less than $3, I dined on curried chicken, white rice, French fries and a Fanta Orange soda. While I certainly appreciated the tasty meal, I soon learned there was no comparison between the succulent D-cup chicken breasts in America and the tough A-cup chicken breasts in Dar es Salaam.

"So what was it like, starting this big trip?" Venke asked after I explained why I was in Dar es Salaam. She and Thomas were on a three-week holiday.

"It was like that first drop on the roller coaster—exciting and scary all at the same time," I said. Every day my mood swung up and down, from exhilarated and wired with anticipation to panicking over the unknown and questioning my sanity for pursuing this trip. And then it got complicated.

"When I gave my two-week notice at work, I didn't know my cousins were being forced to leave Tanzania," I said. "I had also planned to spend some time in Lebanon, but Middle East politics went from smoldering to flash-fire status. Syria had moved its army of 20,000 soldiers out of Lebanon just to play it safe. There were violent demonstrations in front of the U.S. Embassy. I had no interest in wandering around in a war zone."

"What did you do?" asked Thomas.

"I decided to come see Tanzania anyway. And my friend Kathi—she was going to travel with me in Lebanon—we talked about Egypt and Madagascar, but picked Nepal," I said. "We wanted to go trekking, and I could get a visa at the airport when I got there."

"We want to go there some day," Thomas said as he lit a cigarette for Venke and himself.

"So that safari company you used, Primetime Safaris, would you recommend them?" I asked.

"Yes, they were very good," he said.

"And cheap," Venke added. "Only $50 a day and you can go for three, four or seven days."

When I had looked into safari pricing, I found most were around $300 a day—too expensive for me.

"And you get a free place to stay the night before the safari."

"That sounds too good to be true. What's the catch?" I probed.

"They're new," Thomas said. "They want people to talk about them so they will get more customers. That was how we found out about them."

The company's plan was working.

Back at the YWCA, Thomas, Venke and I parted company. They wanted some down time and were leaving early in the morning to travel inland. They were the first of many people who influenced my trip, and I did not have to wait long, or go far, to cross paths with other travelers.

Walking over to the combination dry cleaner and Internet cafe, I took a seat in one of the cubicles with beige fabric-covered walls and ergonomically correct chairs. This was a time before surfing the Web had became a part of my life, before Google and Wikipedia were mainstream, before travel websites were as common as gas stations. But I was using email to keep in touch with people back home, making sure someone had an idea of where I was, without admitting to myself that there was nothing they could do if I needed help. For 63 cents an hour, it was cheap. But it was not easy. The Internet connection kept crashing.

Before I could send three emails, the café closed down for the day, two hours early, due to loss of power, but not before tiny black ants trailed up the wall and swarmed the plastic bag of fresh popcorn I had set next to the monitor. These unexpected quirks were amusing at first but had great potential to become annoying.

THE CITY WAS CHAOTIC and intimidating during the day, so I was not ready to go out at night alone. Fortunately, I met two women in the YWCA canteen who asked me to join them for dinner.

Servane (who lived up to my expectation that all French women were petite and lively) was on her fourth month of a year-long trip zigzagging around the world, mostly in Africa. Her plan was impressively daring and footloose, yet fortified with a comfortable ending. She would reclaim both her apartment and professional marketing job when she returned to Paris. I wondered how different my trip would be if I had such a structured ending. Would it be less thrilling, like knowing how a movie ends before watching it?

Our other dinner companion, Julia, was a bubbly, athletic woman from Finland who had just completed her work on a humanitarian project for college. I was jealous. I do not remember opportunities like that when I went to the University of Georgia and Purdue University. However, I was not confident (or mature) enough at that age for that kind of challenge. But I was going to make up for it with this trip. I felt brave and daring and unique. These were new feelings, and I liked them.

Julia, Servane and I dashed through the dark streets in a warm rain, jumping a moment too late to avoid a wave of street muck created by a passing truck. At Chicken Tikka Restaurant, our dinner topics ranged from favorite authors to hallucinogenic dreams, a common side effect of the Lariam medicine we all took once a week to help prevent malaria. One night I dreamed that I was riding in a limousine that seated 100 people to my parents' house where a U.S. Army general and Mr. French from the TV show *Family Affair* were dumping fireplace ashes into the indoor swimming pool. When I woke up, I could make no sense of these multi-sensory experiences as they teetered between dreams and memories.

Servane and Julia talked to me about being solo women travelers.

"I lie a lot," Julia said nonchalantly as she ate chicken biryani.

I could lie too.

"I tell them I'm married, that my husband is back home, and I'm on my way to see him," she continued.

"Me, too. I even brought a gold band to wear," said Servane, taking dainty bites of sautéed cabbage and carrots. "And do not use one of those under-your-waistband safety pouches."

Like the one I was wearing.

"I met a woman here who wandered into an alley in the bad part of town."

Every part of town I had seen so far looked equally sketchy to me.

"A couple guys cornered her. They lifted up her shirt and pulled down the top of her skirt. They were looking for one of those pouches. Everyone knows tourists use them. At least they didn't hurt her when they didn't get what they wanted."

As I struggled to keep my jaw from dropping, Julia lifted her pants leg to show me how she had modified a security pouch so that it strapped around her upper calf. While it was inconvenient to casually access, it was far more discreet and discouraging to thieves.

At the end of the meal, the waiter dropped off a handwritten bill. I thought the total was laughably small, but Servane scrutinized it and confronted the waiter.

"These are not the prices listed on the menu," she said as he feigned innocence. "Fix it or bring me the manager."

Though his attempted crime was petty, it showed me that I should never let my guard down.

By the time we got back to the YWCA, it was 10 p.m. We had missed the 9 p.m. curfew. A uniformed guard was sleeping in a hardwood chair tilted back against the closed lobby doors. We had no choice but to wake him up and hand over our pink receipts. After signing in, we giggled our way up the stairs like young girls defying their parents.

Before going to bed, I hand-washed my muddy pants in the sink. The plastic lid to my face wash container worked as a sink stopper. I strung a nylon cord between some of the oddly placed bent nails in the walls around the room. It created a web directly under the ceiling fan. Obviously, I was not the first person to dry clothes this way.

Later, with the light out and the mosquito netting tucked around the bed, I listened to the ticking of the rain and marveled at my adventurous new world. My life had never been this unpredictable. There were a gazillion new details to take in and so many things to learn that I did not know what to make of it all. But one thing was for certain—I was not bored.

DESPITE WEARING EAR PLUGS, I woke up early to the sounds of screaming cats and slamming doors. The sky was gray and threatening more of the rain that had fallen through the night. Water covered about thirty feet of the road below my window.

The YWCA canteen had an airy dining room that opened on one side to a communal courtyard, home to a metal jungle gym and a tree shaped like a giant broccoli floret. Women in blue uniform dresses managed the canteen and brightened the Formica tables with aluminum foil-wrapped bowls filled with flowers. To deter flies, they covered the trays of tea cups with linen towels and stored clean silverware in pots of hot water.

Besides travelers, most of the canteen patrons I saw were men in uniforms, most likely security guards. One wore a black uniform trimmed with gold braid along the shoulder and gold stripes down each pant leg. He could have been a marching band leader if it were not for the billy club.

My complimentary breakfast featured a white bun, a banana, margarine and a sweet yellowish jam I could not identify. I passed on the make-it-yourself coffee—just add boiling water to the dark sludge poured from a can. For about a dime, I could add a hard-boiled egg or some fried dough strips or a beef samosa (think pyramid-shaped pastry filled with minced onion and ground beef).

I met up with Servane, and between downpours we walked to a French photography exhibition hosted by the Alliance Française, a nonprofit association subsidized by the French government. Servane had tried to see the exhibition a couple of days earlier, but the staff asked her to come back when they had found the key to its locked door.

This was the first of many times when my American expectations were flicked aside by the local, organic sense of time. In Dar es Salaam, people seemed to accept that things happened when things happened. A schedule had no more authority than a silent birthday wish.

To get to the museum on Ali Hassan Mwinyi Road, we walked down Ohio Street, past a swanky hotel that backed up to a golf course, past a cemetery with gravestones from World War II, past a rubbish pile picked over by blue-black colored crows, and down a dirt road edged with lush foliage and banana and papaya trees. High concrete walls topped with barbed wire surrounded the Alliance Française complex. Stepping through its wrought iron gate was like stepping out of the city and into a world of elegant simplicity with pristine white walls, arched doorways and slate floors. The focal point was a square pit full of white coral rocks in an open-air courtyard surrounded by offices, a library and exhibition rooms.

We stepped into the now open rectangle-shaped exhibition room that had a black ceiling, polished concrete floors and stark white walls. Track lighting shined on 66 photographs that gave stunning glimpses into the raw, vibrant faces of the African continent—from portraits of wrinkled tribal elders to aerial views of mint green savannas silver-veined with tributaries. My favorite one captured a caracal (a feline sometimes called an African lynx because of its ear tufts) in mid-pounce on a kangaroo rat in the desert night. How many nights did the photographer wait to capture that precise moment?

On the way back home, we passed the only familiar business I ever saw in town—Subway restaurant. Servane believed that the founder of the sandwich franchise came from Africa, but I later learned that it was really started by two guys in Bridgeport, Connecticut, in 1965.

As we walked along the waterfront market, vendors keenly appraised us as we looked at the wares they sold along both sides of a paved sidewalk. It was a perfect time for Servane to share some more travel advice.

"Don't carry your passport when you can leave it secured in your room," she said. "Carry a photocopy of it. Legitimate people won't mind waiting for you to get the real one. This way, your passport is less likely to get lost or stolen."

A man wearing a red Maasai blanket like a toga was selling string-tied bundles of twigs stacked on a wooden crate. Another was selling unlabeled, cork-topped vials filled with pale powders.

"Don't tell people your plans," Servane sighed. "Taxi drivers will hound you, follow you around and try to get you to take overpriced rides."

When we saw a destitute-looking man trying to sell worn flip-flops, I vowed never to complain about a job again. When I considered the steady paycheck and quality of life it provided, most of my past gripes—primarily about unproductive meetings, back-biting office politics and panty hose—were just whining.

"Always know what and who is around you," she said. I had lost that awareness after years of driving in the same city, working in the same office, living in the same house and hanging with the same friends. It all blurred into a false sense of security.

"If your instincts tell you to be wary of something," Servane cautioned, "take the feeling seriously even if you can't explain why you feel that way."

This last point was the most valuable advice I heard during my entire trip.

No sooner had we completed this talk than we reached the edge of Kivukoni Forest. From what I could see it looked like a grassy park with groupings of trees along the waterfront. It was, however, a known dangerous area, so we turned around. So did a man with bloodshot eyes, ratty clothes, twitchy shoulders and a shuffling walk. Tailing us, he avoided our eyes but held his ground when we stopped to stare at him. To be safe, we darted down the stairs on the muddy bluff to an open-air restaurant. We chatted with the hostess until the man lost interest in us and wandered away. Servane shrugged the experience off, but I found it unsettling.

When we arrived back at the YWCA, the electricity in the building was out. Again. Servane did not mind; she was leaving town in an hour to travel westward across the continent.

"Would you like to go with me?" she asked casually.

I tried not to laugh. Who did she think I was? Before I left home, I set up my trip by playing dot-to-dot with places where I knew someone because, I sheepishly admit, I have a control issue. Dropping that plan and traveling across Africa with her, a person I had known for a day, was inconceivable.

"Thank you for asking," I said, "but I'm meeting up with my cousins in Kenya in about a week."

After we said our goodbyes, she left and I went down to the YWCA canteen for dinner. I ordered a piece of fried chicken, a *chapati* (an unleavened flat bread) and a pile of sautéed cabbage and carrots. Wanting just a little more food, I also ordered what I thought was a side dish of potatoes. Incorrect American thinking. I ended up with an entire dinner plate stacked with boiled new potatoes. Not one to waste food, I forced myself to eat it all as the uniformed ladies watched to see how much the big American woman could eat.

AT BREAKFAST, I MET MY FIRST Americans, Kate and Celeste. They had been in Ethiopia for the last three months as part of a college course. With her hair pulled back by a blue kerchief, Kate wore a T-shirt with a gold and brown sarong. Celeste had on a faded pink oxford shirt and jeans.

"We're heading home in a few hours," Kate said, "so we gave away all of our other clothes a couple days ago."

"Why?" I asked.

"They were pretty worn out," she said. "We'd throw them away back home, but here people will still value them."

"Won't the people sitting next to us on the airplane love us," Celeste laughed as she sniffed at her shirt to see how bad it smelled.

I joined them for a walk to the Kariakoo Public Market. With the last of their shillings and a bed sheet to trade, they wanted to buy traditional, geometrically patterned fabric to take home as presents. I laughed when we passed a bottle-shaped Coca-Cola stand selling soft drinks in front of a huge Pepsi billboard. Nothing like brand recognition in action. We passed a bare-chested black man in trousers and red flip-flops who was pulling a two-wheeled trailer stacked high with boxed goods. Like us, he was headed toward the noisy swarm of people ahead. We had reached the hive of commerce.

Vendors who sold perishables—fruits, vegetables, rice, nuts, fish, meat—created a jostling, 30-foot wide ring around the exterior of an open-sided, two-story concrete building. Inside vendors sold things like bicycles, sewing machines, baskets, cooking pots, vegetable seeds and sewing patterns in orderly stalls. The hot, humid air smelled of fresh produce and the occasional acrid armpit.

I bought a bottle of Spar-letta soda from one vendor. Its light, citrusy taste was pleasing as I walked around looking at chicken feed and gardening tools. I was halfway through the bottle before I realized that a young woman was quietly following me. She was waiting to get the bottle back. It was worth more than the soda.

When it was time to head back to the YWCA, we formed a single line to squeeze through the outside crowd. Kate led the way, but she soon fell to her knees. It took Celeste and me a few confused moments to realize what had happened.

Throughout this part of town were foot-deep concrete troughs for gutters. Most were covered with flag stones. Kate had unknowingly stepped where one of the stones was missing. I was surprised when two kind men gently took her by the elbows, helped her up and gave her a rag to wipe the dark filth off her knees. Fortunately she was not hurt, and no skin was broken. Kate was nonchalant about it and said to me, "You have to learn to expect the unexpected here."

"I also need to learn that not everyone is a bad guy," I thought.

Around noon at the YWCA, the rain fell as if the sky was a giant broken faucet. Several times I went down to the lobby to marvel at the rising water. Soon it lapped against the YWCA front step. Two young white women left the building wearing only spaghetti-strap tank tops, knit shorts and flip-flops. They were laughing and giggling and playing in the warm rain, oblivious to the blatant stares from the local people who found their revealing clothes offensive.

The guard at the YWCA entrance looked at me to see what I thought of their apparel. I shook my head and silently scolded them by striking my right index finger down my left index finger. The doorman laughed and nodded in agreement.

BY THE TIME THE RAIN STOPPED and I had bought a liter of water at the Imalesko Supermarket, it was too dark to cut through an unlit alley to get back to the YWCA, so I headed the long way around the block. As I rounded the corner onto Maktaba Street, I was startled by the bustling crowd catching *dallah-dallahs*. Without the benefit of a streetlight to illuminate the melee, people pushed, horns blared and headlights broke the scene into fragments. Touts yelled destinations and collected money from boarding passengers.

I waded into the crowd, shoulders back, trying to appear casual and indifferent. People looked me over and then went about their business. Except one.

It was impossible not to bump up against people as I made my way, a shoulder nudge here, an elbow poke there, yet one bump felt different. It was more of a full body rub against my side. And in that instant, my nylon pants pocket had been unzipped. Amazing. Terrifying. The spare change deep in my pocket was still there, but I felt violated nonetheless.

Clutching the water bottle in the crook of my arm like a football, I saw a small opening in the crowd up ahead and rushed toward it. Big mistake. It was a stray plot of grass, about the size of a sidewalk square, surrounded by shin-high strands of barbed wire. Metal sliced my pants and raked across my knees. I caught myself from falling forward, but the water bottle slipped free and bounced to a stop on the grass.

As I leaned over to pick up the bottle, a man grabbed my arm and started shaking it. He chastised me in clipped British English for my outrageous damage to the grass, as if I had purposely defiled a national treasure and disrespected his country.

Speechless, I yanked my arm away from him. I grabbed the water bottle. My white-knuckled hand gripped the top of my unzipped pocket. Only 10 more feet of crowd between freedom and me. And then another person body-rubbed me. A strange hand knocked mine as it tried to slip into my pocket. I shoved it away and pushed past people until I could break into a run.

I dashed through the entrance of the YWCA, grabbed my key off a hook, took the stairs two at a time, locked myself in my room, jumped into bed and dropped the mosquito nets around me. Muttering every obscenity I knew, I checked my bloody knees. The scrapes were not deep. I was lucky. And scared.

"What have you gotten yourself into?" I said, dabbing Neosporin on the cuts with a shaky finger. I had not taken this city, or my place in it, seriously.

"This is not a jaunt around a Disneyland theme park," I scolded myself. "No one's watching out for you. You have to make better decisions. This. Is. Serious."

When I planned my trip, Dar es Salaam was just a dot on the map, a few descriptive pages about cultural sites and historical notes in a guide book. I had worried more about germs than the people. How naive. Hopefully my mistakes would not cause permanent damage as I learned to make my way.

"This is the deep water of travel, Kristine," I thought, wrapping the turtle sarong around my shoulders. "Swim hard or go home."

My tick with time

Zanzibar, Tanzania

WITH A HIP-SWAYING PIRATE SWAGGER, I happily teetered up the wooden gangplank to the Flying Horse Ferry. Rain gushed from the morning sky, but my spirits remained crisp.

Happy to be leaving behind all the barbed wire, barred windows and armed guards, I was going to spend a few days exploring Unguja (the largest island of Zanzibar), east of Dar es Salaam across the Zanzibar Channel. During the eighth century, traders from the Arabian Peninsula and Persia (now Iran) came to Zanzibar with glassware, ironware, textiles, wheat and wine. In return, they fueled a demand for ivory, tortoise shell, rhino horns and slaves. Up to 30,000 Africans were sold every year—more than 80 men, women and children a day—for most of the 19th century. The Arabs remained in control of the coast until the British and Germans arrived in the late 19th century.

"Madam," said the man who was taking tickets from passengers. He gestured for me to go upstairs, away from the locals who sat on plastic benches on the main deck. As a *mzunga*, a foreigner, I had to pay $20 for the ticket. Only local residents were allowed to pay in Tanzanian shillings, and they were charged a much lower fare. As a tall white American, I knew I would not blend in with the local people, but I did not expect to have to pay for being different.

I also had to stay on the upper deck that had red velour cushioned benches, two 19-inch color TVs mounted in the front corners of the room and royal views of the surrounding waters. When others arrived in the *mzunga* section, a group of men and women with black hair and dark skin, they pulled fabric-wrapped pads from the cabinets under the window seats and settled into groups on the floor.

Lightning flashed on the horizon as the ferry lurched away from the shoreline. We soon passed a long wooden boat full of men playing a challenging game of balance. All of them were standing, jumping up and down, yelling and waving at the ferry as their boat bounced over small waves.

"They are happy," said the man standing next to me at the railing. "They had a good day of fishing."

After the shoreline disappeared from view, I settled into a corner bench and updated my journal. Writing was the only way I could keep track of the last experience before a new one came along and erased the old one from my thoughts. I also jotted reminders, expense notes and translations in the margins. *Karibu* meant welcome, and *jambo* meant hello in the common African language of Swahili. Over time, the journal pages would become thick with amusing candy wrappers, receipts, postage stamps and ticket stubs.

When the ferry started rocking too much to write, I put away the journal to watch the Jean-Claude Van Damme movie on the TV and my fellow passengers. While the men in short-sleeve shirts and slacks showed no outward sign of their religious beliefs, the young women kept their hair and bodies covered with black scarves and purple satin gowns. One woman ruined the shimmery beauty of her outfit when she threw up on it during the rough crossing. I was close to puking myself, and the next movie's dreadful plotline did not help. It featured a skinny American heroine in a Madonna leather jacket who took revenge on the villains who killed her Bruce Lee-looking soccer-hero lover.

Thankfully, before a third movie could start, the port in historic Stone Town came into view. Behind the docks were canyons of two-story, metal storage buildings and a maze of rusted cargo containers.

"Hello, I am Jimmy. May I be your guide?" The sinewy man tilted his head back so he could look up at me. Servane had explained that escorts like Jimmy were free and legitimate. He earned commissions from guest houses when he delivered paying customers.

"Yes, please," I said. "I'd like to go to the Princess Guest House."

As I strapped on my backpack, Jimmy snatched my day pack, making me nervous not to be in control of it. I stayed on his heels as he elbowed his way through the departing crowd and into the drizzling rain. Soon we were ahead of the other passengers.

"Let's go this way," Jimmy said, pointing to a dark opening between two buildings. "It's a short cut." The short cut was a perfect place to get mugged, while the flow of people kept to the road.

"Let's stick to the road," I said.

Jimmy shrugged as if he had heard this many times before. When we arrived at the small row of immigration offices, I saw his short cut was legitimate. I thought about apologizing for not trusting him, but remained quiet. I had made the safest decision for me.

Once the immigration officials checked my passport, we walked into town. I would not have found the guest house without Jimmy's help. We zigzagged along puddle-filled, shadowy alleys that bent around coral stone buildings, canvas-shaded bazaars, minaret-spiked mosques, angular cathedrals and narrow shops with upstairs apartments.

I expected Indiana Jones to come racing around a corner at any moment. Many of the colonnaded buildings from Colonial times had seen better days, though scaffolding and plaster work implied restoration projects were underway.

The rain petered out by the time we arrived at the Princess Guest House. It looked like a plain three-story townhouse. My new $8 room—including breakfast—was a 6-by-8-foot cell with a bare light bulb hanging from the ceiling. There was no chair, table, sink or wardrobe.

The single-wide, wooden bed frame lacked mosquito netting. The high-density foam mattress was impressively firm, like a giant rubber eraser. There was an oscillating fan mounted above the barred window, but the electricity was out. And the color of the walls? Teal.

I did not mind the simplicity of the room, but I found the slip-rod latches on the solid wood door disconcerting. When I checked in I received a chunky padlock. As easily as I could lock myself out of the room, someone could lock me in.

The door to my room faced a small social area full of Persian rugs and tasseled floor pillows. A color TV sat on a rolling cart by the wall. (When electricity was available, it was always set to CNN.) On the other side of the social area were two small, white-tiled washrooms. One contained a Western toilet with a hose and nozzle for guests who wanted to go the bidet route.

I was pleased to see that the toilet had a seat, but decided to use the toilet paper I brought rather than the rose-colored toilet paper provided. Servane had warned me that the harsh dyes in them sometimes caused rashes in delicate places.

The other washroom had a sink and a showerhead. Both drained straight onto the tile floor that was sloped so that the waste water flowed into the floor drain. This lack of plumbing seemed practical, but probably made the bathroom harder to keep clean.

It took me three excruciatingly painful whacks to my forehead to learn to duck before passing through the low doorways of either washroom.

AS THE AFTERNOON WANED, I wandered around the neighborhood, mindful to remember how to find my way back to the guest house. The streets were quiet as shopkeepers closed their businesses for the evening. At a busy intersection, two men in crisp white uniforms kept wary eyes on the motor scooter and bicycle traffic that whizzed past. Behind them, a billboard promoted Fanta Jisikie Free soda. On the far side of an unkempt field full of flooded low spots, young men played basketball on an unfenced court near a series of concrete apartment buildings.

I was happy to note that few locals paid much attention to me, and no one tried to sell me anything. I hummed "Bohemian Rhapsody" by Queen and wondered if my favorite musician Freddie Mercury had walked these streets; he was born here in 1946.

For about a dollar's worth of shillings I bought a small loaf of bread, a bunch of finger-size bananas and two green apples. Afterwards I realized I should not eat the apples because of the standard traveler adage, "If you can't cook it or peel it, don't eat it." The apples became the first of my random acts of giving.

The first apple I gave to a legless man propped against a wall along a sidewalk. He rewarded me with a toothless expression of great happiness and said something I could not understand. I smiled and walked away. He may not be able to eat the apple, but perhaps he could trade it for something he needed.

When I returned from my walk, three guests were talking in American English on the second floor landing of the Princess Guest House. The young blonde woman in a blue jean jumper dress had a heavy Southern accent.

Playfully imitating her, I said, "Ya'll look like you're having fun."

The woman squealed in excitement. The two men, with Brawny paper towel man good looks, faded polo shirts and khaki pants, stood to shake hands with me. After a round of introductions, I learned that Susie was from Texas. Mike and Steve were from Minnesota. They were all Peace Corps workers on vacation, and they were leaving in the morning to go back to their various rural villages.

"We're going to Forodhani Gardens for dinner," Mike said. "Want to come with?"

"Sure." I was loving the "we are instant friends because we have something in common" aspect of travel.

I made a quick stop in my room before going out, but there was no "getting ready" for dinner. I wore no make-up. I kept my hair pulled back into a ponytail. I had no dress clothes. Because I was a foreigner, I felt no pressure to fit in. Graphic designer Stefan Sagmeister had it right when he said, "Trying to look good limits me." My focus was on what I saw, not how I looked.

As I padlocked the door to my room, a radio played Patsy Cline singing "Crazy" until the electricity abruptly went out.

The Peace Corps volunteers knowingly guided the way through the dark alleys. What little light there was came from second-story windows. I stopped to watch the silhouette of a monkey as it ambled across a power line between buildings, the way squirrels did back home. At one point we passed through a courtyard packed with people of all ages, yelling, cheering and gesturing at a soccer game on a TV set on a wooden table. They noted our passing only because we had to walk in front of the TV to get by.

Forodhani Gardens was a food market along the waterfront. Dolphins frolicked by the pier. Squids the size of footballs darted about the concrete sea wall. Boys raced off a bastion to see who could cannonball the farthest out into the water. Within the temporary market of blue plastic tarps and hissing kerosene lanterns, vendors set out tables laden with crab claws, fish, squid and shellfish. The seafood was not kept hot or packed on ice, but it was selling at a brisk pace.

After checking out the options, I bought a baseball-sized lump of curry-spiced mashed potatoes, a charcoal-grilled barracuda kabob and a Krest soda, each from a different vendor. When I returned to the group, Mike asked what had taken me so long.

"I didn't have exact change for the man selling soda."

Mike started laughing. "What else was he selling?"

"Jewelry."

"And did you buy some?" he asked with a knowing smile.

"No. Why?"

"She broke his heart," he said to Steve.

"What do you mean?" I asked, concerned that I had committed a cultural faux pas.

"The man was slow to get your change because he wanted you to spend more time looking at his jewelry," Mike said. "He wanted you to buy jewelry, not walk off with your change."

Clever. Another tiny lesson learned.

We took our food over to a rickety wooden picnic table. More than two dozen stray cats gathered nearby like pigeons hoping for breadcrumbs. Some had the glossy coats of good hunters. Others, with ripped ears, mangy coats and runny eyes, were down on their luck. The cats made me think about my own cat Roxanne. She had just turned 16 years old when I dropped her off at a friend's house for the duration of my trip. Leaving her behind was the hardest separation I made before I left. I did not know if she would be alive when I got home.

Roxanne's death, whenever it came, would be the end of an era. The queenly, ample-bodied orange tabby was the last vestige of my short-lived, first and only marriage. Since the amicable divorce 15 years before, my sense of failure had faded and the underlying reason for its demise had been revealed. I had been too young. I had not known who I was, so I did not know what I wanted or needed or how to tell the difference between the two. I had just finished college and getting married was the next logical step in adulthood. It was easy to be who my husband wanted me to be, for a while. It was a heartbreaking learning experience.

"So what's it like being in the Peace Corps?" I asked.

"I really feel like I'm making a difference, helping people dig a well and plant fruit trees and learn to read and write," said Susie, eating a crepe full of scrambled eggs with onions and green peppers. "But it's hard, too, seeing them struggle with stuff we take for granted back home—clean water, electricity, medicines, indoor plumbing, phones …."

Susie disappeared into her thoughts for a moment, then continued softly. "I have a watchman. He sleeps on the ground outside my hut every night, but he's gotten very sick. No one has been able to help him. I don't know what to do."

Mike and Steve both nodded with understanding. Medical resources were scarce in the countryside. We ate quietly until Steve switched to a happier topic. "I miss barbecued ribs."

"And broccoli and snow pea pods," added Mike.

Susie declared with a loving sigh, "Dairy Queen Blizzards."

I knew I was going to miss Ben & Jerry's Heath Bar Crunch ice cream. I had a tender parting moment with a pint just before I left.

"Do you know about Listerine Breath Strips?" I asked. "They're the rage back home right now."

All three shook their heads.

"They're like little pieces of tissue paper that dissolve in your mouth. They taste like mouthwash." I fished a packet, a parting gift from former co-workers, out of my pocket. The threesome had a good laugh when I opened it. The humidity was so high that all of the strips had melted together into one aqua blue, gummy block.

As we were eating grilled crepes folded around Hershey's chocolate syrup and bananas, two young women from another Peace Corps group walked by.

"Hi, Tiffany, Megan," Mike called out to the petite brunette and her friend.

"Hello," she said, scanning the closest row of vendor tables. "Anything good tonight?"

"Barracuda kabobs are good," he said between bites. "You just get to town?"

"Yeah. We took a safari with that new company, Primetime Safaris."

"I've heard of them," I said eagerly. It was the same company Thomas and Venke had used. "Did you like them?"

"They were okay," Tiffany shrugged. "We did the four-day trip. Saw some animals. Camped out a couple nights. We should have taken the three-day trip. The roads were awful. We spent most of the time bouncing around inside the truck or stuck in the mud."

"Thank God we didn't take the seven-day trip," Megan whined.

So much for my impression that Peace Corps volunteers were undaunted by all obstacles and discomforts.

THE NEW DAY WAS FULL of learning experiences. The first was served at breakfast. When I was ready to eat, I had to walk downstairs to notify the front desk. Then I had to wait back upstairs as the woman in the kitchen prepared the meal. She served it at the small table where I had met the Peace Corps threesome.

Compared to the modest YWCA offering, the Princess Guest House breakfast was a bounty. The plate featured slices of banana, mango and papaya, three slices of whole wheat toast, and a green pepper and tomato omelet. Even though there was cream in the spiced tea, I drank it because I could not resist its chai-like aroma. It would not be long before all of the dietary guidelines I had memorized were forgotten.

The second learning experience was late to arrive. When I signed up for a spice plantation tour the day before, the receptionist asked if I wanted to be picked up at 8 or 9 a.m. I said 8 a.m. thinking that I would be taking an earlier tour. Wrong. Reaffirming the irritating flexibility of East African timing, the driver showed up at 9:30 a.m., and then I waited another thirty minutes by the tour office for the other participants to be picked up.

This last delay gave me a chance to enjoy the cool sea breeze and the grassy plaza along a seawall. The scene would have been idyllic if I had not seen a syringe and three razor blades in the grass.

"Always wear shoes, no matter how inviting a place looks," I warned myself.

When the tour pickup truck finally arrived, an older, energetic Belgian couple, a stout young man from Ireland and a Filipino-American from New York huddled on two long benches in the back under a blue plastic canopy. It started to rain.

Between intermittent showers and short rides on dirt roads, we stopped to walk through wild tangles of forest or plantings in odd-shaped clear cuts. By pulling down branches, digging up roots and peeling strips of bark, our guide introduced us to breadfruit, jackfruit, cardamom, vanilla, cinnamon, star fruit, coffee, cocoa, turmeric, ginger and nutmeg.

At one point in its history, Zanzibar produced 90 percent of the cloves traded around the world, the guide noted. The aromatic dried flower buds were cooked in food, smoked in cigarettes or administered as a medicine. At times they were worth their weight in gold because of the high demand and the cost of shipping them to distant ports.

We stopped at a grove of young trees, their trunks scarred as if constantly attacked by carrot peelers. The guide picked a peel off the ground for us to smell. Locals harvested the inner tree bark to make cinnamon sticks.

Just as fascinating as the spices were some of the creatures we encountered. A millipede as big as a cigar. Snails the size of tangerines. When the Belgian couple asked if the snails were good to eat, the guide looked at them with great disbelief that anyone would want to do such a thing. I sided with the guide. One culture's food was another culture's garden pest.

Part of our tour included a visit to a rural hamlet of mud-and-bamboo huts with thatched roofs. Only foot traffic kept the forest from overtaking the small clearing. No adults were to be seen as we took photographs, but young children came out to watch us and smiled if we did something they found silly. I was surprised to see the little girls wearing new cotton print dresses.

The spice tour stopped for lunch at a one-room white cinderblock building on a paved street lined with randomly spaced similar buildings. I could not tell which were homes and which were businesses. One building was distinctive with a white satellite dish perched on its roof.

The lunch room had counters and benches running down the two side walls. By the back wall was a glass refrigerated case of sodas, a white porcelain sink for hand washing and a serving counter. Men took the orders, cooked the food on the back porch and served the meals.

Lunch was rice pressed into an upside-down bowl-shaped mound. On top of it was a piece of stewed beef the size of an ice cube. A boiled new potato and a clump of sautéed onions and cabbage rounded out the meal. Sodas, not part of the tour package, cost about 50 cents.

"Do you have Orange Crush?" I asked.

"No, madam."

"OK." I walked to my seat without buying a soda. One of the men left the building. When he returned 10 minutes later, he set the desired bottle next to my plate. I was impressed and humbled by the amount of time and effort he spent to make such a small sale. I had never worked that hard for so little money in my life, even when I worked as a babysitter for a couple of dollars an hour.

After the tour, I wandered around Stone Town and passed through Forodhani Gardens. Without the bustle of vendors, the yellow glow of kerosene lanterns and the beautifying cloak of darkness, it was just a bunch of rickety plywood tables in a muddy lot. The romance was gone.

I stopped by a shop the size of a walk-in closet. It offered the contents of a single man's cupboard—tubes of Pringles potato chips, Snickers bars, Kodak film, Gillette razors and Marlboro cigarettes, but it also had what I wanted: Internet access for about a dollar an hour.

That night, the fan took the edge off the hot, humid air as I tried to sleep. My feet ached but were slowly getting used to all the walking. My belly had mild rumbles but nothing to be concerned about. All in all, I had a sense that I was unwinding, slowly finding my own pace, one not dictated by an alarm clock. My last thought before sleep was that I hoped no one noticed that my clothes were starting to smell sour from being damp for so long.

DAWN ARRIVED COOL, GRAY and rain-soaked. If I were back home, it would have been a perfect day to wear sweat pants, cook chili, make love or watch old movies from deep in the couch. The best I could do here was flip slowly through my mini photo album of the friends I had left behind.

My farewell party in Charlotte, with four kegs of beer and 500 Jell-O shots, was a night of merriment. Some out-of-town friends even camped in the back yard. I was stunned by everyone's well wishes.

"We are celebrating your escape from the daily grind," one friend said. With a conflicting sense of boldness and trepidation, I felt like an astronaut.

The day after the party, I had two weeks to fill before I left for my trip. I decided to go to Charleston, South Carolina, for a week to hang out with friends and compete in the 25th Annual Cooper River Bridge Run 10K along with 14,338 other participants. It was the first time I had ever attempted a race of that distance. The fact that I had run all of it without walking boosted my confidence. I was not humbled by the fact that a 98-pound, 29-year-old woman ran it twice as fast as I had.

My friend Annette, who was a few years older than me, also lived in Charleston. Even though she was from Denmark, she felt like the big sister I never had.

"Welcome to your 40s," she noted. "It's a wiser, more accepting phase of womanhood."

We bonded during retail therapy, kayaked through waterways along the salt marsh, and flirted with sailors for beers.

It took a while to adjust to the lack of routine. Sometimes I did nothing until noon on a week day just because I could. I took naps after lunch. I went running midday. I stayed up late reading books and watching movies with no fear of repercussions.

Each day I expected it all to end—to be yanked back behind a desk. But slowly all the days became Saturdays, full of more sunlight than I could remember seeing in a long time.

I SCHEDULED A MORNING TOUR of Changuu Island, also known as Prison Island. At the shoreline, I met the captain of a hardy wooden boat with an orange awning. He wore cut-off shorts and a shirt that read Reebok in faded red letters. He jumped into the shallow water and tried to steady the boat as I waded to the bow and swung myself aboard.

As we motored away, the coastline looked like the kind of place where people drank glistening bottles of Corona beer in a commercial, but I could not forget the syringe and razor blades in the grass.

When we arrived at the small island, the captain dropped me off at a spit of sand.

"I will be back in two hours," he said as he motored away. I noticed he was not wearing a watch.

Abruptly discovering my tour was self-guided, I headed inland without fear. I knew I could walk all the way around the island in a few hours.

I checked out the remains of a slave prison and some empty field hospital buildings from a former leper colony, but what I wanted to see most were the Aldabra giant tortoises. The males could weigh more than 500 pounds and live for more than 200 years.

A British governor sent the first tortoises to Changuu as a present from the island of Aldabra. Since then, the tortoises had thrived, been decimated by poachers and made a promising comeback with the help of conservationists. Young tortoises huddled to form a cobblestone patch in a nursery pen. Even younger ones lived in a restricted access building.

In a tree-shaded pasture, seventeen adult tortoises randomly stood around. As I fed them spinach leaves sold by an opportune vendor, they tolerated my gentle strokes to their boney skullcaps and the warm black skin on their necks. It was as thin and delicate as the skin on a grandmother's hand. Their obsidian black eyes gleamed with deep wisdom and patience—Dalai Lamas on the half shell.

Back at the shoreline, I was grateful when the captain returned to pick me up, only 90 minutes late.

THE TOUR GUIDE'S MOOD WAS AS FOUL as the weather when we left for an afternoon visit to the Jozani Chwaka Bay National Park, home to a rare population of red colobus monkeys.

After we drove away from Stone Town, the landscape turned into tropical forest with random clearings around cinderblock homes. Most were surrounded by piles of plastic bags, wrappers and bottles. I felt guilty that I was throwing away disposable cameras (farewell party gifts). One conscientious cleaning woman gave me back an empty one I had left in a trash can. When I tried to explain why I threw it away, she wanted to keep it and put new film in it. I did not think that would work, but I was not going to dash her hopes.

About 10 minutes outside Stone Town, the tour guide mumbled something about turning back. Ahead, the road disappeared under water. What had once been two small ponds on each side of the elevated road had become one murky lake. A crowd of men and boys gathered at the water's edge, pushing trucks through the water for tips or scurrying to catch rides to the other side.

"That truck made it across." I pointed to a pick-up truck like ours on the far side of the lake. "He must be a skillful driver."

I fought back a smile as the tour guide rose to the manly challenge. Scowling, he gently pressed on the gas pedal and upshifted to second gear. The truck slowly entered the muddy water as a couple of boys hopped onto the tailgate for a ride. The engine held steady. A gentle wake formed behind us. I watched to see if water would leak in under the passenger side door, but it never came. The boys hopped off as we pulled out of the water on the far side.

"Well done," I said, but the tour guide did not respond.

At the park entrance, I learned I had been swindled by the tour company again. The driver was only a driver, not a tour guide.

"You have to learn to ask better questions," I told myself as I paid an additional fee to enter the forest and to hire Mufta, a knowledgeable young guide who carried a red- and white-striped golf umbrella. As we walked along, he explained in clipped British English ways to use the plants around us as food or medicine and pointed out signs of animals.

"There are tree hydrax in this forest," Mufta said, going on to describe an animal that might look like a raccoon without a mask and stripes. "They have four toes on each of their front feet and three toes on each of their back feet."

It was calming to walk along leaf-carpeted paths under a high canopy of branches. To smell the forest's earthy cologne. To trail my fingers along moist fern fronds. To pick up a pebble and roll it around in the palm of my hand. According to Alain de Botton's book, *The Art of Travel*, William Wordsworth suggested that, "regular travel through nature was a necessary antidote to the evils of the city." Indeed.

When I was a young girl in Columbia, Missouri, I thrived in the forest by our house. My friends and I spent endless hours there, roaming the woods, cracking hickory nuts, building crude forts and damming creeks. This forest tapped into those memories. It comforted me with the same lullaby. Then Mufta grabbed my arm and pulled me backwards.

Three days ago, the man protecting the grass in Dar es Salaam had grabbed my arm, and I had panicked. Now, I was just pissed off. I turned a hostile face toward Mufta.

He just smiled and pointed to the ground. My foot was about to smash down on a four-inch wide freeway of ferocious army ants. The survivors of my misstep would have swarmed my sandal and attacked me with skin-piercing bites.

"Good call," I said.

We continued our walk along a puddle-filled access road, then onto a raised wooden boardwalk that looped over a mangrove swamp. I peered when he peered. I listened when he listened. But still no monkeys. We headed back to the park entrance. The impatient driver waved at me to get in the truck so that we could leave. The sprinkling of rain had not stopped since we arrived. The flood waters covering the road would be even higher.

Of course, that was the moment Mufta pointed out a red colobus monkey with a young one clutched to her chest. They looked like pale gray animals wearing red Santa Claus jackets with black trim. Their crinkly, septuagenarian-looking faces were surrounded by an Eskimo hood of long white hairs.

While *National Geographic* magazines images had given me a taste of the world, the three-dimensional details of this moment—the tickle of the rain drops, the squishing sound of my sandals in the mud, the challenge of getting a photograph of the monkeys, and my immature urge to make the driver wait even longer because he was annoying—would feed me for years to come.

After I finally got back into the truck, the ride across the lake and back to Stone Town was uneventful until we reached the Princess Guest House.

"You must pay me," the driver demanded.

"I already paid."

"I have not been paid." He held out a callused hand.

"I paid." I pulled out my receipt, but he did not relent.

It was payback time, and he was challenging me. Would I spend about $10 to get on my way to dry clothes and a hot meal, or would I spend time proving him wrong? I called his bluff.

We drove to the tour office where they confirmed I had paid. The driver shrugged and drove me back to the Princess Guest House in silence. I was nothing more than a potential sucker to him.

FOR THE REST OF MY LIFE, Zanzibar will be the Swahili word for rain. At breakfast, the pitter-patter was mixed with the sing-song of tropical bird calls. By the end of the meal, the rain was heaving in big orgasmic waves. During my three-day visit, the rain would drizzle, spit, mist, downpour, shower, torrent, gust, deluge and blast. At one point it hit the ground so hard it created a haze as it bounced up a foot off the ground and fell a second time.

Servane had warned me that the rains were worse on Zanzibar. How bad could they be? I thought with dry ignorance.

This was what I got for traveling off-season during the "long rains" (mid-March through May). It had been one thing to read average monthly rainfall statistics (14 inches in April, the wettest month). They were just a bunch of numbers with no tangible meaning to me. I came to learn that the numbers meant washed-out plans, disappearing roads and moldy clothes.

RIDDLE ME THIS: If the ferry ride from Dar es Salaam to Stone Town took about four hours, why did my evening ferry ride from Stone Town to Dar es Salaam take about three times as long? Because the captain sailed the ferry across the Zanzibar Channel and then waited offshore until 6:30 a.m. to dock when the Dar es Salaam immigration office opened in the morning for business. That was just the way it was.

When I arrived in Dar Es Salaam the second time, I knew where I was going and how to get there. I knew the cost of things. I had bargaining tactics.

"I want to go to the YWCA," I said to the taxi driver.

"1,000 shillings."

"No, 500 shillings," I replied even though I had paid 1,500 shillings for the same trip three days before.

"1,000."

"No, thank you. I will ask someone else."

"Wait. 500. OK."

One step toward becoming a strong traveler. So many miles ahead.

I checked my backpack into the YWCA storage room where it would stay until I left for my flight to Mombasa, Kenya, later that afternoon. In the meantime, I walked over to the National Museum.

While crossing the museum's inner courtyard, I saw an elderly man meticulously pulling out each weed that grew in the sidewalk cracks and picking up each leaf that littered the ground. He moved in slow but determined way.

"Jambo," I said holding out my second green apple for him to take.

Again, another a toothless yet beautiful smile. He remained silent, so I waved goodbye and went into the museum, more grateful than ever that I had all my teeth.

Water dripped from the ceiling in a few places, so some glass-enclosed displays had been moved to odd positions. A few walls were just wire and glass slats open to the outside grounds. In one wing, I startled a peacock who had wandered in from the street.

There was one display among the tribal artifacts that made me laugh. It featured little animal figurines in crude lovemaking positions. The sign stated that they were used by the Wapare tribe during initiation ceremonies, and it listed the following dialog to explain the rhythm method of birth control:

"Give me what I want."

"I cannot do it. I have non."

"Tortoises are very noisy when they cohabit, and they fight first. This is bad. Do not pester your wife if she refuses you; she has her reasons, and she counts the days. Do not make a noise in your house at night like the tortoise."

As I walked on, a small group of boys dressed in tattered clothes swarmed me.

"Please buy our postcards," one of them said as they all held postcards out for me to look at. "The money helps orphans."

I was irritated because even in a museum I was a target. And I did not know if I should believe them, but they were all so skinny and unwashed.

"Are you orphans?" I asked.

"Oh no, we have families."

That detail made matters seem even worse. I had no more apples to give, but I could not just walk away. It was a sucker thing to do, but I used up my loose change to buy a postcard from each of them.

Outside the museum a man with deformed legs crawled by on his hands and knees. He protected the palms of his hands with flip-flops, but only thick pads of scar tissue covered his kneecaps. I looked away.

In my journal that night, I wrote, "There's such a big difference between knowing that there are people in the world struggling with great hardships and deformities—and actually seeing them. I can't ignore them. I can't change the channel or flip the page. It feels personal, like I need to do something about it, but there are so many people that need help. It's overwhelming. And I feel guilty because I can just leave them all behind."

I PAID VALENCIA THE TAXI DRIVER to take me to the airport for a 4 p.m. Air Tanzania flight. After passing through security and waiting in line to check in, I learned that I had gotten my days mixed up. My flight was tomorrow.

Irritated, I caught another cab back to the YWCA, much to the puzzlement of Valencia and the YWCA matron who checked me into a room. It was a sunny day, but I did not know what to do with my time. I had explored everything in walking distance. I did not understand what the *dallah-dallah* touts were yelling to beckon potential riders or where the vehicles were going. There were no set schedules or convenient color-coded route maps. Worried that I would get stranded somewhere, I gave up exploring the city. I showered, washed clothes, read, snacked, wrote in my journal and slept until it was time to go to the airport the next day.

Days later, it dawned on me that I should have hired Valencia to take me on a tour of the city. This idea had not occurred to me that afternoon because, back home, taxis were expensive. The few times I had used them was to efficiently go from point A to point B. Here they were cheap. I needed to recalibrate the way I considered options and made decisions.

On my second trip to the airport, I learned that Valencia supported a wife and nine children with his fares.

"Men will give me much money to marry my four daughters," he said, "but my five sons will need money to get wives."

I arrived at the airport early to avoid the stampede through security, yet there were no other passengers around. The security guard would not let me enter the building. So I fussed in a shady courtyard until the ticket office opened a couple hours later. The woman behind the thick pane of glass delivered the crushing news.

Yesterday's ticket agent had neglected to tell me that my 4 p.m. flight had been rescheduled to 8 a.m. this morning, and there were no more flights scheduled to Mombasa today. And her good news—that I could transfer my ticket to tomorrow's 8 a.m. flight—was worth as much to me as a cigarette butt. I stomped over to the taxi stand yet again.

When Valencia saw that I had returned yet again, he jokingly asked if I really wanted to leave. At least my difficulties would help his sons get married.

IN THE YWCA CANTEEN that evening, I met a young German brother and sister, Dieter and Martina, who spoke German, English and Swahili. They asked me to join them for some live music, so off we went under a starry sky. On the steps of the soon-to-open Hard Rock Café, we met a barefoot Maasai warrior. The narrow black leather belt with silver studs around his waist kept his red blanket in place. Tradition with a touch of punk. A long wooden spear lay by his side. He recommended Club Bilicanas around the corner.

The club seemed familiar with its long backlit bar and a mirrored disco ball dangling from a black ceiling. A DJ played music from a sound booth high above a dance floor surrounded by tiers of booths. The two wide-screen TVs featured boxing and motorcycle dirt racing.

"What do you think about her?" I asked my companions after we bought Kilimanjaro beers from the bartender and settled into a booth. A woman milled around by the bar. Her succulent figure threatened to pop out of her sky blue tube top and white short shorts as she moved.

"Prostitute," they both agreed. It was jarring to see so much of her body when all the women I had seen so far had not shown more than their heads and lower extremities.

Before we finished our second round of beers, the place filled up with patrons, and the live music started. The five-member band kicked off with some discordant jazz-type music, then moved on to a funky, playful version of "The Lion Sleeps Tonight." Two performers competed during the band's final song. A curvaceous woman in an orange cotton dress, her hair in corn-row braids, swayed through a sensual dance, then challenged her male counterpart to do something more impressive. He did, with a series of struts and hip thrusts.

In response, she bent over with her hands on the drum stage and ground her hips toward the audience in a way I thought physically impossible. The crowd went wild.

Not to be outdone, the man let loose with a macho version. We all felt like having a cigarette by the time he was done.

Resorting to a fortified oasis

North of Mombasa, Kenya

MY THIRD TIME at the Dar es Salaam airport, I noticed an older man at the immigration counter in front of me. He did not blend in with the other dark-skinned passengers any more than I did. His white hair and beard were neatly trimmed, and he wore a pressed white shirt, blue tie and dark slacks.

Mr. White Shirt and the two grim immigration officers were not getting along. They pushed papers back and forth at each other. Their tense voices flipped between English to Swahili. Finally, an officer stamped a paper and gave Mr. White Shirt a dismissive wave toward the waiting room.

When I stepped up to the counter, the offices gave a cursory look at my visa to enter Kenya and waved me on.

"Hello," I said as I walked past Mr. White Shirt.

"Hello, how are you?" he said.

"Fine, thank you." I sat two chairs away from him.

"What's taking you to Mombasa?" he asked as he organized the papers in his briefcase.

"I'm going to visit my cousins. They're missionaries. You?"

"Business." He shut the case and turned to give me all of his attention. "I work for a company based in Nairobi that makes steel cable."

I nodded.

"Moving anything in Africa is so much harder than it sounds," he sighed. "Between the roads, shipping schedules, weather and government agents, there are always problems."

"You must be a very patient person," I said. "Did you grow up speaking Swahili?

"Yes. I'm South African. You?"

"Only English," I admitted with some embarrassment. "I have a really hard time with other languages. I studied French in school for years, but it wasn't a part of my everyday life so I've forgotten most of it."

He appraised me for a moment, then asked, "Are you an American?"

"Yep."

As our flight was announced, Mr. White Shirt introduced himself as Geoff, and we walked in the milky morning light across the tarmac to board a 12-seater prop plane. A giraffe emblem gleamed on its tail fin.

During the flight up the coast, the views were spectacular—amoeba-shaped reefs and azure water speckled with white triangular sails. There was not a rain cloud in sight. I would not miss Tanzania, but my short time there would always make me smile proudly as if I had graduated from travel boot camp.

I FOLLOWED SERVANE'S ADVICE about trusting my instincts and accepted Geoff's offer of a ride from the airport to the Voyager Resort to have drinks with him. Afterward, I would catch a shuttle to the resort where my cousins were staying.

At the Moi International Airport, we walked over to his car parked near a massive tree that shaded trap boxes made of chicken wire.

"They feed the crows caught in those traps to alligators that locals raise for hides and meat," Geoff explained. He could not explain why the birds liked to hang out at the airport.

Before we drove through Mombasa, Geoff made sure all the car windows were rolled up, and the doors were locked.

"The bastards will just reach in and grab things and run away," he said bitterly, looking warily at any people we passed. "They'll even open the car doors if they think they can get away with it."

The armpit stains on my shirt grew slightly larger.

VOYAGER RESORT WAS A FORTIFIED OASIS of immaculate, first-class civilization amid a sea of squalor. Shanties lined dirt roads. Men hoed rows in small fields. Goats ambled about, one standing king of the hill on a trash pile. A man pedaled by on a hardy black bicycle with a milk crate of leafy greens strapped to the back fender.

"I have some calls to make," Geoff said before heading to his room. "How about we meet at the bar in about an hour?"

I wandered along polished hallways that opened onto manicured gardens and sparkling swimming pools. Two 4-foot-long mahi-mahi fish, with giant foreheads and yellowy-green skin with blue freckles, lay dead on the grass next to the booth where guests could book fishing trips. On the beach, guests could rent sailboats, kayaks and pedal boats. They could buy trinkets that vendors displayed on blankets. Or they could do nothing.

I was unfamiliar and uncomfortable with the resort's white-glove treatment. It looked like an all-black staff served the all-white guests.

Geoff and I met up at a thatched roof, open-air bar built on a promontory. The vast blue Indian Ocean spread before us and disappeared into the far horizon. The sunlight was warm. The breezes were cool. The lapping of the surf was soothing. The bar could host a lot of happy hours every day.

Geoff and I shared our experiences with travel, relationships and work. He had been happily married for more than 20 years to an independent woman, and they had raised four daughters. He was particularly keen about my trip because his wife and daughters were also globetrotters.

"They would like you," Geoff said as the bartender placed drinks made with fresh citrus juice and dark rum in front of us. "Too bad they're visiting family in South Africa right now. I would love for them to meet you."

"Thank you."

"Where else have you been?" he asked.

"A lot of places in the U.S., Paris, a few weeks in Japan when my brother lived there, and a month roaming around Costa Rica with a boyfriend," I said before eating the pineapple garnish off the edge of my drink.

"Going from those trips to this one was a big leap of faith," Geoff noted. "It goes with our family motto—if your dream doesn't scare you, it isn't big enough."

"Then my dream is big enough." We laughed and toasted the moment before I counted my pre-trip fears on my fingers. "First, there were primal fears, like what if I got sick or hurt 'out there?'"

I raised a second finger. "There were practical fears, like what if I ran out of money before the end of the trip or before I get another job?"

Geoff smiled and nodded. I must have looked foolish recollecting my fears of a trip that currently had me sitting at a tiki bar, sipping drinks served by a man wearing a starched white shirt and a black vest.

"The egotistical fears were the worst," I said quietly raising my third finger. "What if I got out here and didn't like it? What if I gave up everything only to quit the trip early and go home a failure? Who am I to think I could actually pull off something like this?"

"Those were all reasonable fears," Geoff concluded. "Good job overcoming them."

I gazed out at the undulating blueness of the water. "I'm not religious, but it seemed like for every problem that came up, the solution appeared right after it, as if this trip was inevitable, my destiny."

AFTER I HUGGED GEOFF GOODBYE, I caught a shuttle to Club Sun and Sand Resort, another first-class oasis of pampering and indulgence. As one of Kenya's largest all-inclusive resorts, it had 285 rooms spread out over 18 acres. The resort gave missionaries discounts during the off-season, so this was where my cousins and other members of their displaced group had gathered to consider new directions for their energies.

I noticed the uniformed guards carrying rifles patrolled its perimeter as I stepped out of the shuttle by the lobby. A greeter welcomed me with a chilled moist washcloth and a glistening shot of fresh fruit juice on a silver tray.

When I checked in, the front desk attendant strapped a blue plastic band around my wrist to be worn at all times. For the next five days, I was B16945.

I was escorted to a teal-free room with two double beds, a private bathroom, an air conditioner, and a balcony with a view of palm trees and sparkling water that zigzagged down to the beach through a series of man-made pools and waterfalls. Each day, a housekeeper made the bed, swept the tile floor and folded the end of the toilet paper into a sharp little point.

While I was content with the simplicity of my previous abodes, I confess this level of comfort was a pleasing change, but never gloriously enough to make me forget the people who lived on the other side of the wall.

At the center of the resort was a large outdoor plaza with a thatched roof shading groups of comfy couches and chairs. The panoramic view included a palm-fringed shore and an outdoor snack bar where glossy black crows swooped down to steal undefended food. The plaza was the perfect place to just be on an unmeasured afternoon.

"Hello," I said when I saw the familiar face of my cousin, Tamara. She was two years older than me, but looked 10 years younger. The rewarding quality of her life and her Swedish heritage had served her well.

"*Jambo*," said her husband, Todd. He was a willowy man who approached the world with a great calmness. I did not recognize their young sons, Jacob and Daniel, who had both grown more than a foot each since I last saw them, when they were but a tow-headed boy and toddler. We shared hugs all around.

"So how are you doing?" I asked after we settled around a coffee table and got past the pleasantries.

Tamara and Todd had been living with their missionary group in Bariadi, a town of about 15,000 people. Only the main road was paved. There were no street lights or stop signs. The main food staple was *ugali*, a stiff corn porridge.

After about seven years of service, the group learned that an official had decided not to renew the group's visas. No explanations were given. They were forced to leave the country with little time to prepare for the exodus. Perhaps they were pawns in a power play.

"We're okay," said Tamara.

Todd sighed. "We miss our friends."

"Can you go back and visit them sometime?" I asked.

"Probably, but first we need to figure out where to go from here," Todd said.

"Got any ideas?"

"We might go to England, and I could go to grad school," Todd said. "We're also looking at other places to serve in Africa or we could go back to the United States."

"Those are some very different options."

He nodded. "Do you know what you'd like to do after your trip is over?"

"I only know I don't want to go back to Charlotte. It doesn't feel right to me any more," I said. "But I've got lots of options because I'm unemployed and homeless."

"Perhaps just home-free for now," Tamara suggested.

"It's weird," I said. "In one way I feel almost crushed by all the freedom, but the longer I travel, the more I feel like I'm exhaling after holding my breath for years. It's like I'm breathing normally again."

"That's wonderful," Tamara said.

Todd added, "God will lead us where we need to be."

I agreed. I had never warmly embraced an organized religion, yet if I swapped around keywords like fate, karma and God, I shared many sentiments with my cousins.

"It does seem like doors of opportunity are magically opening and closing—sometimes not so gently—to make me go a certain way," I said.

For the next couple of hours, as the two boys played in the nearby pool, Todd and Tamara talked about the challenges of living for the glory of God in Tanzania. Their faith was often tested as they embraced a new culture where life seemed so fragile.

One time, Todd loaned his bicycle, a precious commodity in the rural area, to his friend Mayoke, but someone stole the bike from him. Three days later, police in a neighboring district confiscated the stolen bike.

Mayoke's friend Johni went to retrieve the bike and slept on the floor of a relative's house until he could pick it up from the police. While he waited, Johni became sick and died.

The rest of our conversations were lighthearted. Todd had forced himself to eat goat parts—liver, kidney, stomach lining, intestine and testicles—presented to him as an honored guest. There were also memorable language bloopers.

"I meant to tell the man who was carving a tray for us to put flowers all over the wooden handles because my wife would like that," Todd said. "But what I said was, 'Please put snot all over the wooden handles. My wife would like that.'"

DURING MY STAY at Club Sun and Sand, the staff served a variety of curiosities in its dining rooms. Sometimes the dishes looked familiar but tasted bland, like cream fillings and chocolate frostings made with a meager amount of butter and sugar (two of my favorite things). Sometimes the food was incomplete, like waffles and pancakes served without syrup. Sometimes the food was deceptive. The barbecue sauce was just a soup of ketchup, crushed pineapple and minced green peppers. Sometimes the food was plain foreign, like Vitmo soda that tasted like a mix of Dr. Pepper and Vicks cough syrup.

Something they served one day picked a fight with me, and I lost. My stomach started churning as the "Kenyan Express" arrived. Thankfully, I did not have to grab the toilet paper, lock my door and run down the hall whispering fervent prayers that a toilet was available. Odd that on this trip so far I had no big stomach troubles, had eaten a variety of questionable foods and never remembered to use the hand sanitizer I had packed. Yet, at the resort, where I thought the food would be most safe, I got sick.

ONE DAY I WALKED ABOUT a quarter mile out into the ocean. The full moon deserved the credit for this lowest of low tides. In the distance, I could see waves crashing against a long jagged rock ledge where deep water began.

I wandered from one coral formation or another, each the size of a monster truck tire and bustling with life. Short- and long-spined sea urchins. Chunky, five-sided starfish that looked like decorative brick paperweights. Darting schools of neon blue, nickel-sized fish.

A local man in a short sleeve shirt and shorts waded out to me and struck up a conversation. He asked the usual questions about where I was from and why I was here. He pointed out animals in the water that I would not have noticed without his help. This went on for about 10 minutes when he asked if I was familiar with the local services, if I knew that there was a nice massage place down the beach.

"Thanks, but no thanks." I did not like the direction the conversation had turned. "That's my husband's job."

"I can give you a massage, no charge."

"My husband wouldn't like that." I moved to the other side of a coral formation until it was between us.

"It could be a secret, just between the two of us." He winked.

"We don't lie to each other. That's why we have a happy marriage." Enough already. "Time for you to go away now. I want to be alone."

He scowled as I waved him away. We both knew that an armed guard was watching from the seawall and waiting for the slightest sign that I needed help. The water licked the backs of my knees as I straddled the two worlds. One was the false perfection of the resort. The other was the harsh reality of the local people. I did not feel comfortable or confident in either.

I SPENT THE AFTERNOON with Tamara and three of her friends at a marine park. To get to the site, we rode in a pickup truck through a landscape of poverty until we reached a swanky neighborhood with stucco mansions and perfect lawns. We could have been in California. We walked behind one of the mansions and down the steep stairs to a dock. Before we could leave in the basic wooden boat that looked like the *African Queen* in the Humphrey Bogart movie, our guides had to install its outboard motor. They had to remove motor and lock it up every night or someone would steal it.

The visibility in the water was only about 10 feet, but it was still fun to snorkel around. We saw colorful clownfish, tangs and pufferfish. Clams the size of footballs slammed shut when our shadows passed over them. A crown-of-thorns starfish slowly devoured a bank of coral.

When we returned to the resort, I made travel plans for the upcoming week. To make long distance telephone calls, I filled out a paper at the cashier's office and then waited in a telephone booth off the main lobby. They placed the call, but only if outgoing telephone service was available.

First, I called Primetime Safaris to see if I could book a trip. Because it was the rainy season and I was booking for just one person, my only hope was to join someone else's trip. The travel gods winked at me. A foursome had already booked a seven-day safari, and I could take the remaining seat in the truck for an all-inclusive $350 if I arrived at their Nairobi office in two days. The itinerary included game drives, flamingos at Lake Nakuru, and visits to Maasai Mara and Samburu villages. Fate had lined up a better safari than I could have planned.

Next, I bought a one-way plane ticket to Nairobi. The Mission House travel agents, whom my cousins often used, could not take Visa payment over the phone, but they would let me pay them when I arrived in Nairobi. This unbelievable show of trust had to be due to my cousins' reputation.

My third call was to Geoff, Mr. White Shirt from my last flight. He had left a message for me at the front desk.

"Hello, Geoff. This is Kristine at Club Sun and Sand."

"Hello, how do you like the resort?"

"It's very nice, and it's great to see my cousins," I said.

"Well, my plans have changed, and I'll be in Nairobi for the next week. Will you be coming this way?"

"I just booked a trip with Primetime Safaris. I fly to Nairobi tomorrow and then we leave the next morning."

"Right then, well, I can put you up for a night, give you a tour around and drop you off at the tour office Tuesday if you like."

"That would be wonderful. Thank you very much," I said flipping through my papers. "Let me give you my flight number and arrival time."

"No need. Just call me when you get off the plane," he said before giving me his phone number and ending the call.

At dinner that night, I told Tamara and Todd about my fortuitous plans while I ate grilled kingfish.

"We may be living in Nairobi by the time you get back from the safari," Tamara said. "Hopefully we can see you again before you travel on to Nepal."

The after dinner music and dancing oddly ranged from Kenny Rogers to Lionel Richie as a full moon rose brilliantly white above the ocean. As I walked back to my room under the watchful eye of the guard by the sea wall, I stopped to laugh at the sign that read, "Pool closed—please avoid swimming."

WHEN IT WAS TIME FOR ME to leave the resort, I paid for my room at the cashier window. The front desk receptionist cut off my blue wristband and my access to all services. It was time to journey back into the real world, ready or not.

Let me pet your ossicones

Nairobi, Kenya

IT WAS ANOTHER PUZZLING East African moment. I could not get on the plane in Mombasa without a ticket, but they did not print tickets at the airport. The woman behind the counter finally called the travel agent and verified I was supposed to be on the flight to Nairobi.

After everyone boarded the plane, an attendant offered us digestion biscuits (a bland cookie with a bale of fiber kneaded into it). The man sitting next to me was reading the *Daily Nation* newspaper. The headlines whipped me home and back. There was an article about the Charlotte Hornets basketball team on page 35. Another article reported that a woman had been killed and two more seriously injured by rogue elephants.

I laughed when I read in *Msafiri*, the Kenya Airways in-flight magazine, that "any Swazi man can exercise polygamy, providing he has the means to support his wives."

I bet that East African wives were far less expensive to support than American wives.

My allotment of poor flight karma continued when one of the passengers looked out into the rain and said we had just landed at the wrong airport in Nairobi. So that was why Geoff said it was better for me to call him when I arrived rather than for him to wait there for me.

"Sirs and madams, we have landed at the Jomo Kenyatta International Airport because we can only land at the Wilson Airport in good weather," the pilot said over the intercom. "You may wait for the weather to clear and then we will fly over to the Wilson Airport, or you can take the shuttle that we have arranged."

Everyone, including me, got off the plane and boarded the shuttle.

When I finally arrived at the Wilson Airport, the young female receptionist politely explained how to use the black rotary dial phone on the counter.

"Tell the operator what number you would like and then hang up. The operator will place the call and ring you back when the connection is made," she said. I did. I waited. No ring back. I tried again. No ring back.

The attendant took pity on me and graciously let me use her prepaid cell phone.

"I'm so sorry. There are only a few minutes of service left," she said. To thank her after I made my call, I gave her the Patricia Cornwell paperback book that I had just finished reading. She was so thrilled that she asked me to autograph it as if I had written it myself.

Geoff picked me up, but he stopped the car near the end of a runway.

"See those storks?" Geoff asked. Indeed, there were 5-foot-tall storks strutting about. "They like to hang out here for some reason. They cause a lot of problems with the planes and get themselves killed."

Geoff drove us into the gently rolling hills to Karen, an elite suburb approximately 20 miles from downtown. After lunch at the posh Karen Golf and Country Club, he declared he had a surprise for me.

"My home is being renovated so my mother-in-law can move in with us," he said. "So I have arranged for you to stay somewhere else." There was a happy twinkle in his eye.

When I tell people about my brief friendship with Geoff, they get concerned. Why did I trust him so easily? How did I know he was not leading me to harm? I cannot provide tangible reasons. The trust came from instinct, from a mysterious place where other ways of knowing things come from, a place I had lost touch with a long time ago. The connection started coming back when I started following Servane's advice. I gave less credence to my thoughts and more authority to my body's reaction to any given situation.

"Have you seen the movie *Out of Africa* with Meryl Streep and Robert Redford?" Geoff asked as we pulled up to a walled property and waited for the uniformed guard to open the wrought iron gate.

"Yes."

"This is the Swedo House. It was once part of the Blixen's estate," Geoff said, taking pleasure in my stunned expression. "I took the liberty of renting you a cottage here. I hope you like it."

He had rendered me speechless, something my friends had been trying to do for decades.

"Many strangers have done wonderful things for my wife and daughters when they traveled," he continued. "Now it is my turn to do something for a traveler."

Built around 1907, the Swedo House was the estate's original hunting lodge and farmhouse. Back then, it was surrounded by bush and grasslands that were eventually cleared for crops, particularly coffee. Aake Sorgren, the Swedish consul in British East Africa, and Sir Northrup MacMillan formed the Swedo African Coffee Company in this house and later commissioned a one-story stone farmhouse called Bogani to be built up the road in 1912. Swedish Baron Bror von Blixen-Finecke bought the coffee company in 1913 and his wife Karen (who used the pen name Isak Dinesen) lived in Bogani between 1914 and 1931. It was prominently featured in the movie.

The Swedo House was a classic example of colonial residential architecture. Raised above the ground on stilts, it had a railed veranda, an arched roof and corrugated iron walls lined with wood that was eventually replaced with plaster over chicken wire.

Fast forward in time. The original Blixen estate was broken into pieces. The 5.5-acre Swedo property, now with cottages surrounding the original building, was owned by a woman from Texas.

My cottage, named *Ndege* (bird), reflected the Swedo House style. Past the tiled front porch and French entry doors, the interior had pristine white plaster walls, hardwood floors, high ceilings with exposed wooden beams and subtle lighting. In the living room, two chairs faced a wood-burning fireplace and a TV. To the left was a queen-size bed with snowy white sheets and a fluffy down comforter. The canopy had side panels of unblemished mosquito netting. No Band-Aids covered any holes. The study area held a sleek modern desk and an Internet connection.

The pinnacle of the cabin's perfection, however, was the spacious bathroom. Its walls, floors and counters were covered with green-gray slate tile. The bathroom had a separate tiled shower stall, a collection of bath products, a blow dryer and a stack of fluffy white towels. The porcelain bathtub was deep enough and long enough to comfortably soak my 6-foot-long body.

The cottage was the poshest place I had ever stayed.

Geoff needed to put in a few hours of work before we had dinner together, so I lounged on the cabin porch, nibbling pieces of pineapple and mango that had been individually wrapped in cellophane before being arranged in my room's fruit basket. Tropical confetti—bougainvillea, hibiscus, geraniums, nasturtiums, poinsettia and phlox—sprinkled the courtyard garden. Three men quietly tended the grounds, hand clipping grass and picking up leaves knocked down by the last rain storm. One used a rake made from a stick and gnarly twigs held together by twine. Small birds with aqua blue bellies and crimson cheeks pecked around a feeder.

The tranquility of the moment made me think about how the unknown twists and turns in my trip had led me to Geoff. Who would have guessed that the problems flying out of Dar es Salaam would lead to something as incredible as this? It just reinforced my need for acceptance and patience when faced with obstacles, delays or changes.

Embracing this perspective was one of the hardest lessons travel forced upon me. I had been spoiled by American expectations—that if I paid for it, I would get it immediately; that schedules were meant to be followed; and that I should have 24-hour access to everything I wanted.

GEOFF GAVE ME A TOUR of his home in an upscale neighborhood. A two-story colonial house with a neatly appointed yard, it was similar to one I had lived in as a teenager, except there were bars on all the windows and doors, and there was a house staff of five that included a security guard.

The home's décor was clean and simple. The furniture and artwork reflected a lifestyle influenced by many cultures. The aesthetics were marred, however, by the barred door at the top of the stairs to the second floor.

"It gives us a safe place to go if someone breaks into the house," Geoff explained. "Everyone around here has them." Standard protocol or not, that level of protection gave me the creeps.

Afterwards, we went to a Chinese restaurant in an upscale shopping mall that was protected by high walls, barbed wire and armed guards. Dinner conversation slid from enlightening to disheartening. Geoff gave some insight as to why Tanzania and Kenya ranked in the top 10 most corrupt governments. International aid and various countries had sent billions of dollars to fund building projects that were never completed.

"Too many hands took too many pieces of the proverbial pie," he said between bites of General Tso's chicken. "That's why there are so many abandoned construction sites around town."

Geoff also explained that some tribal men do not want to marry a woman unless the woman can prove she can bear him children. As a result, a majority of first children are born out of wedlock. If the relationship does not work out, the new mother moves on to the next man and the next baby. I wondered if this explained some of the single moms at the YWCA.

"There's one tribal custom that requires a newly widowed woman to have sex with the village 'cleanser' to purify her soul before she can attend her husband's funeral," he said, shaking his head sadly. "They believe that condoms would prevent the bad spirits from passing between them. That's true if you consider HIV a bad spirit."

"I met an American woman in Dar es Salaam," I said. "She saw a roadside stand selling condoms, but each one of them was nailed to the display. They were useless."

When Geoff dropped me off at the Swedo house, a uniformed guard with a green-striped golf umbrella escorted me through the rain to my cottage. Inside, I giggled with happiness. The staff had started a fire in the fireplace, set a flashlight on the nightstand in case the power went out, lowered the mosquito nettings around the bed, turned down the corner of the bedding and laid out a plush bathrobe.

Even though I was tired, I could not resist a soak in the bathtub as rain drummed on the roof. Later, in the dark bedroom, snuggled in the bathrobe, I danced the flashlight beam around the room. For that one evening, I was a lottery winner, an heiress, a person of privilege.

THE NEXT MORNING, I WALKED along the worn footpath next to the paved road to the Bogani house. My walk drew polite yet curious looks from the only other people, black people, who walked or rode their bikes along the same path. The museum was not open yet, so I wandered about the grounds. Karen would be sad if she saw this land now, coffee trees gone and the views of the nearby Ngong Hills blocked by construction. I sat on the veranda until I noticed the footstool next to me. It had once been a real elephant's foot, complete with scalloped yellow toenails. The arrogance and lack of respect for life that it represented horrified me.

When I finally entered the house, I walked into a simpler time. Handcrafted furniture. Walls lined with bookcases. Oil paintings. A phonograph. A lion's pelt on the floor. Clothes worn by Streep and Redford in the movie *Out Of Africa* were laid out on one of the beds. The kitchen was in a separate building connected to the main house by a covered walkway. Its wood-burning stove, dry sinks and rudimentary cooking utensils seemed so primitive and labor-intensive compared to the conveniences of modern kitchens.

Afterward, Geoff and I visited Giraffe Manor. Built in 1932, the stone manor house was converted in 1979 to a wildlife sanctuary by Betty Leslie-Melville, an American living in Nairobi, and her British-born, Kenyan-citizen husband, Jock.

The couple had learned that there were only 130 Rothschild giraffes left in the world, and they were stranded on an 18,000-acre cattle ranch in Kenya that was scheduled to be subdivided into plots for local landless people. A reprieve came when a military threat from Uganda caused the Kenyan government to divide up only half the ranch and make the other half an army base. This gave the couple time to move four breeding giraffe groups to four national parks.

They also moved a young giraffe named Daisy to their manor in Nairobi to create awareness of the Rothschild giraffe crisis. The family's life with her was captured in the book *Raising Daisy Rothschild*, and the movie *The Last Giraffe*. As more giraffes were relocated to Giraffe Manor, the couple created an education center so that school children could see the giraffes and learn about conservation.

Even though the center became a success, Daisy's life did not end on a happy note. In 1989, she escaped to the nearby Nairobi National Park to mate and bear a baby girl named Pansy. Trying to find her way back to the Giraffe Manor, Daisy strayed into residential areas and followed anyone with a bag or basket, believing them full of familiar grain pellets. All attempts to capture her were unsuccessful, so she was tranquilized for transportation back to the center. During the transfer, she choked to death on her cud.

Daisy's grandchildren now wander the manor grounds and poke their heads through the French doors to inspect the breakfast table. From the second story of the manor's tree house, Geoff and I watched three adult giraffes nibble tree leaves. As the world's tallest mammal, growing up to 19 feet tall, they had the same number of neck bones (seven) as humans, but their bones could be 10 inches long and form an eight-foot-long neck that weighed up to 500 pounds. To keep blood circulating, a giraffe's 22.5-pound heart had to beat twice as fast as a human heart.

A Daisy descendant—a petite 14 feet tall at 16 months—ambled over to check us out. His dark black eyes peered into mine. I desperately wanted to pet the velvety knobs (horns called ossicones) that tilted back between his ears, but he had no patience for my adoration. He only wanted to snatch grain pellets from my palm with his raspy black tongue.

For lunch, Geoff and I went to Rangers, a restaurant at the entrance to the Nairobi National Park. Only 20 minutes from downtown, the park's 113 square kilometers (27,911 acres) contained plains, cliffs, rivers, dams and thousands of native animals. The parking lot was crowded and decorated with informative, sometimes humorous signs. One read, "Warthogs and children have the right of way."

The Langata Cemetery across from the park seemed as busy as the national park.

"So many people are dying of AIDS," Geoff explained.

Again I felt a great sense of frustration and helplessness.

When it was time for me to leave, Geoff arranged for his driver to take me to the Primetime Safaris office.

"Thank you so much for your kindness," I said to Geoff as I hugged him goodbye.

"My pleasure," he said. "I'm happy to help you step off your map and into the world."

Driving on half-baked brownies

Safari in Kenya

DOWNTOWN NAIROBI'S FRENZIED ENERGY was unnerving after the suburban calm of the Karen neighborhood. Yellow triangle-shaped traffic signs with black exclamation marks in the center appeared at regular intervals.

"What do those signs mean?" I asked Geoff's driver.

"Drive with caution," he replied.

"Do they know that's what they mean?" I asked as cars and trucks recklessly raced around .

He chuckled and shrugged. "This is the way we drive."

I was happy to escape into the Contrust Building. A sign next to its phone booth-sized elevator with a metal gate stated that the Primetime Safaris office was in the eighth floor penthouse. It turned out that the elevator only went to the seventh floor. As I climbed a flight of stairs to the penthouse, I startled the young Maasai man who guarded the door. While he did not speak, his eyes widened ever so slightly. I was tall enough to look at him eye to eye. I wondered if he found me as intriguing as I found him.

"*Jambo*," I said. He nodded slightly and stepped aside to let me pass through the open door.

The living room of the former apartment was now full of old metal office desks. The small bedrooms contained stacks of bunk beds. One bathroom served all.

After brief introductions with the three staff members, I claimed a bed, bummed that last night's nest of pampering had been replaced with a foam pad on a narrow bottom bunk. To rub in my demotion, a cockroach-looking bug scurried across the top bunk before I could kill it. Traffic noise from the street far below sounded like the horn section of a symphony endlessly warming up. Back to the joys of low-budget travel. At least I had the room to myself.

The view from the apartment balcony gave me three distinct impressions of the city. To the left was a modern face—glass-covered skyscrapers, well-kept high rises, satellite dishes and shiny new SUVs. Straight ahead were three-story, walk-up colonial buildings, a church steeple and rundown cars. To the right was an abandoned construction site. People pecked at garbage in an empty lot as *matatus*, white minivans that provide public transportation like *dallah-dallahs* in Dar es Salaam, drove by.

As I watched the tiny pedestrians below, I thought about the story I heard from Venke, the woman I met briefly in Dar es Salaam. An impatient Japanese tourist went for a walk here by himself and returned an hour later robbed of his camera, jacket and shoes. Urban myth or words to the wise? Even the *Lonely Planet* guidebook warned, "On the downside, Nairobi is becoming increasingly lawless, and you'll have to be on your guard."

A French couple and a German man soon arrived and joined me on the balcony. They were wired with excitement after completing a three-day safari. They had seen a cheetah kill a gazelle and feed it to her young, only to have a lioness steal the carcass and threaten the cheetah cubs. Nature at its fiercest.

The French woman, Louisa, added to my apprehension of the city.

"So I gave a couple coins to one of the boys begging in the street. Then he asked for more, saying it was for medicine," she said. "He pushed up his shirt sleeve, and his arm was covered by a runny infection, so I gave him some more money and went on my way."

"That's so sad," I said.

"What was really horrible is that later I met a lady who said that if I had not given him more money, he might have flung some of that infection at me."

I shivered. Humans at their fiercest.

With some apprehension, I walked with the threesome to the Pizza Inn around the block. When we returned with bacon-pineapple pizzas, we found the three Primetime staff members mesmerized by *The Young and the Restless* soap opera crackling on a black-and-white TV.

"You know that's not real, right?" I asked during a commercial break. "That's not how people live in America."

Everyone politely nodded, but I was not convinced they believed me.

After dinner I noticed a newspaper clipping on the bulletin board by the stairs. It was about a lioness in the Samburu Game Reserve, one of the scheduled stops on our safari. The lioness had adopted a newborn oryx calf after she frightened off its mother. Normally, the lioness would have eaten the antelope-like animal for a meal. It was a mystery how the lioness and calf communicated. Lions rely largely on sight while oryx survive by smell.

Wildlife experts had no explanation for the odd-couple friendship that lasted for 15 days before an older lion from another pride killed the calf while the lioness was drinking at a river. It was an unusual lapse of care on the lioness' part, considering she had previously warded off other dangers by walking defensively behind the calf as she would have done with her own cubs.

A second newspaper clipping continued the mystery. The lioness adopted a second newborn oryx until game wardens took it while the lioness was away hunting. These unexplainable situations deepened my awe of nature and raised my excitement about the safari. It would not be a choreographed experience. We might see anything.

I WOKE UP WITH A RUNNY NOSE and clogged sinuses. It was a frustrating way to start the seven-day safari. The French/German threesome had left, and my four safari companions had arrived. Their leader was an outgoing young Israeli woman named Gili. She had cropped black hair, honey-colored skin and a sturdy build. Think compact GI Jane with a heavy accent. She had been traveling around Kenya for many weeks and had been on this safari before. This time she was enjoying it with her father, Sami, and his two inseparable sisters who were always referred to as the Aunties.

We met our guide Isaac, a soft spoken man from the Kikuyu tribe. He had a pleasing full-moon round face and was dressed in a polo shirt and slacks.

When we settled into a white Toyota Land Cruiser, I sat up front with Isaac. The others were happy to sit in the back together. There was a hatch on the roof of the truck so they could stand on their seats and look out in every direction when it was time to watch wildlife.

I quickly grew fond of the foursome's passionate ways. They were constantly making noise—talking in English and Hebrew, singing, laughing, squabbling and enjoying everything to the fullest. And it did not hurt that the Aunties constantly whipped out snacks to share—dates, cookies, dried apricots and bread sticks.

Our safari began with a long but fascinating drive into the Great Rift Valley, a crack in the planet so large that astronauts can identify it from space. It cradles a plain 100 miles wide and about 3,700 miles long.

Wooden shacks perched on the brink of the valley. Behind them, the land sloped down and transitioned from tree canopies to scrub brush to grasslands to flat, arid soil. Like white tiddlywinks caught in mid spin, two giant satellite dishes tilted on the valley floor. It seemed like a weird place to put them. Later I learned that scientists used the Longonot Earth Satellite Station to search for extra-planetary telecommunications. I thought that kind of thing happened only in the movies.

We descended into the valley, past goats and people walking with donkey carts piled full of apples and corn for sale. Isaac laughed at how excited we got when a baboon loped across the road and disappeared into the overgrowth. Our first wild beast! Sadly, we also saw our first flamingo as pink-feathered roadkill.

The few towns we passed were reminiscent of the American Wild West, with wooden one-story buildings and benches on the narrow front porches. It was market day, so people crowded around goods displayed on blankets on the ground. Small herds of cattle—family fortunes on the hoof—grazed near the road under the watchful eyes of boy herders. Trucks hauled lumpy bags of mysterious goods. An industrial tractor rumbled by, fringed with men catching rides. Maasai men gathered near a Coca-Cola stand. The red of their blankets matched the red paint on the stand.

We rumbled and bumped through the morning and into the afternoon. The road slowly degraded from smooth pavement to dirt. Ruts yanked the truck from side to side. As a light rain began to fall, we crossed paths with a broken down Primetime Safaris truck. Isaac fixed the truck's problem with electrical tape, but nothing would fix the passengers' woes.

"They are going back to Nairobi early because it rained the whole time they were in the game reserve," Isaac said when we got back on the road. "They decided they were not seeing enough animals to make it worth staying."

That seemed like such a spoiled brat kind of attitude. Just being in the Maasai Mara had to be intriguing, and you cannot see wildlife if you are not where the wildlife lives.

By the time we reached the Oloolaimutia Gate of the Maasai Mara Game Reserve, the sun was back out. A good omen. Funny how the massive yellow stone and timber drive-through arch of the entrance was just for show. There were no fences on either side of it.

Two wildlife officers with camouflage jackets and rifles checked Isaac's paperwork and waved us on.

"Please stay inside the truck at all times," Isaac politely requested. Good call. Swept up in the moment, I would not put it past any one of us to bolt out of the truck to try to have a Dr. Doolittle moment with an unforgiving animal.

Isaac followed a dirt track that wove around rolling plains punctuated by sparse acacia trees. There were no road signs or signs of civilization in any direction. It was just nature and us. This could have been Kansas or Iowa if it were not for a zebra only a hundred feet away. The grazing animal ignored the frenzied clicks of our cameras as we caught every expression, every flick of its tail and twitch of its ears. Isaac drove a little closer, setting off yet another frenzied round of picture taking. I caught a pleasingly quirky image of a zebra, but kept taking photos in a vain attempt to possess the moment. How cool was this? I was on safari in Kenya.

We grumbled when Isaac slowly drove on.

"We will see more zebras," he patiently assured us. "I promise."

A few minutes later we parked near more zebras that grazed with a herd of springy, deer-like Thompson's gazelles. Black racing stripes separated their tan backs from their white underbellies.

After seeing these two species, we were pumped with anticipation. We fidgeted with our cameras, ready to shoot the next Kodak moment. It took its sweet time coming. Used to instant gratification, we had to adjust our expectations to the unpredictable viewing of animals in the wild. This was not a zoo.

While we hoped to see the famous Big Five safari animals (elephant, lion, leopard, rhino and African buffalo), Isaac kept us entertained by pointing out other animals and sharing facts about them. Kori Bustards were the world's heaviest flying birds. Males, weighing as much as 35 pounds, were nicknamed "Christmas turkeys" because they made a fine meal. A pair of crowned cranes, with golden mohawks on their heads, were famous for their synchronized mating dances.

"Ostrich eggs are so big that it takes about 33-44 days to hatch one," said Isaac, "and 90 minutes to hard boil one."

Lumpy termite mounds rose out of the grass, each with dried mud ventilation chimneys sticking up like chunky table legs.

I read that grasses prevailed in the Maasai Mara for several reasons. Shrubs and trees did not grow well in the calcium-rich, ashy soil. Elephants liked to uproot trees so they could eat the leaves on the high branches. Fires, started by lightning or Masai, made room for tender new grass to be eaten by wild animals and domestic cattle. Wildebeests favored young grass. Zebras were best at eating old grass. None of the grazers liked the tall grass, which could hide predators.

Isaac drove along a hillside until he slowly stopped the truck. We looked around but did not see anything.

"Keep looking," he said. Still nothing.

He pointed to a patch of grass, and then we saw what he saw. The straw-colored coats of a lion, a lioness and their cub seamlessly blended into the landscape. We were thrilled until we noticed that the cub's jaw dangled at an odd angle. His dull mangy coat rippled over his ribs. His walk was listless.

"A hyena may have broken his jaw," Isaac said softly. "The wildlife officers will not intervene. The cub will either adapt or become food for other animals. You can never tell what will happen. Just when you think an animal will die, it lives. Just when you think it will live, it dies."

We rode in silence for many miles, knowing this was the way it should be, but not liking the helplessness that came with the acceptance.

Eventually, we dropped the Aunties off at the upscale Mara Sopa Lodge that was built on a high ridge in the southeast corner of the game reserve. No roughing it in tents for them. They had a first-class room with a private veranda where they could sip cold drinks from a mini-bar. According to the lodge's website, "More formal attire might be advisable for cocktails and theme evenings, while swimwear is needed by the pool."

It was dark by the time Isaac, Gili, Sami and I made our way to Simba Camp. How Isaac found his way along the unmarked dirt tracks was beyond me. Kangaroo rats—balls of fur with long, tufted tails—bounced in and out of the truck's high beams.

"One of the not so famous Small Five," Isaac joked.

An impressive barricade of branches formed the perimeter around the camp. Inside, a fortified meeting hut with a thatched roof took center stage. Its walls were bark-free logs sunk into the ground about six inches apart. More logs were placed at its entrance to force people—or animals on attack—to slow down and zigzag to get inside. Even a suburban dweller like me noticed that our sleeping areas around the meeting hut were vulnerable, just green canvas tents shaded by thatched canopies. And I was not a fast runner.

A corrugated tin and cinderblock bathroom made up for the comfort that the tents lacked. A fire heated underground spring water for the showers. A staff member hung a lantern in one of the stalls with a Western toilet each night, so we could find our way in the dark.

The camp staff played checkers on a commercially produced game board, a gift from a previous guest. From their portable radio, Cher sang,

"Do you believe in life after love… ." When the game was over, they cooked our dinner over a fire. At wooden picnic tables in the meeting hut, we ate *chapati*, veggie soup and fried chicken. Jam came in a can with a plastic lid. The raw sugar looked like brown sand. The Blue Ban margarine was surely a lesser cousin to butter-flavored Crisco.

After Isaac used the two-way radio in the truck, he returned to the meeting hut and said quietly but proudly, "My wife had a baby girl today."

"Isaac, that's so wonderful!" We all shook his hand or gave him a hug.

"You shouldn't be here with us," Gili declared. "You should be home with her."

He waved our sentiments aside.

"We are grateful that I have this work," he said. "It helps me provide for my family."

Perspective was everything.

I KNEW THERE WERE WILD ANIMALS on safari that could rip the flesh from my bones, impale me with their horns or trample me to death with their hooves. But I had not given any thought to the region's stealthy insects. One wounded Gili the first night. As she slept, a poisonous caterpillar crawled over her face, leaving a trail of caustic slime.

"This will help it feel better," Isaac said as he handed Gili a piece of wild aloe to soothe the itchy, blistery welt that scored her cheek and neck.

The morning air was warm and sweet with the smell of drying grass as the sun floated across the sky. Isaac heard from another guide that a cheetah and her almost grown son were in the area. We finally found them resting under a tree. The pair struck typical housecat poses, assuming a false air of ambivalence to their surroundings. I made the same sip-sip noise I often used to get the attention of my cat Roxanne. The youngster did not turn his head, but his ears turned ever so slightly in my direction. I stopped when I realized I was as selfishly annoying as the people who tap on the sides of fish tanks.

Miles down the road we found a leopard perched on a tree limb, a dead impala dangling nearby. He was resting after the exertion of the hunt. We could hear him pant, see the rosette-shaped spots on his coat rise and fall with each breath. I wanted desperately to stroke his thick velvet tail as it curled back and forth.

More bumpy roads and chance sightings. Knobby heads stuck out above a cluster of bushy trees as Maasai giraffes ate their daily 75 pounds of leaves.

"See that one," Isaac said. "A lion tried to kill it."

There were healing claw marks on its flanks.

At a bluff leading to the Mara River, we ran into another Primetime Safaris tour group. Olen and Daniel were handsome, rambunctious Americans in their early 20s. They had just spent five weeks helping out at the Heri Adventist Hospital in Kigoma, Tanzania. Their experiences ranged from helping treat landmine wounds to racing around their dormitory room trying to kill a rat with a machete. I was not sure how well those two skills would serve them when they went to medical school in California in the fall.

Our guides let us out of the trucks to stretch our legs. We bounded down the dirt bank, past a few bushes and tilted palm trees. In a couple of months, more than a million wildebeests would trample down this same bank as part of their annual Great Migration. Each June, the wildebeests gather in the south Serengeti to calve and congregate into a vast single herd until the dry season withers the fresh grass. In July, the smell of rain draws the animals northward to the Maasai Mara where they spread out again to graze. In October, the herds backtrack south to the Serengeti, completing the annual cycle.

In addition to their role as roving manure spreaders, the wildebeests were food for predators. Lions dragged down stragglers. Packs of hyena feasted on the young and the weak. Only one out of three calves survived its first migration. As if those challenges were not enough, the wildebeests had to cross this river, which most likely would be a raging torrent from the spring rains. Many drowned in the powerful current or died in the jaws of crocodiles.

We stood on the shoreline, gazing at the muddy water as it flowed smoothly by, imagining the stampede of thousands of hooves, the shoving, the trampling, the bellowing against the struggle.

"Sirs, madams, please come back up here. Now." Isaac pointed to the far side of the river. "There are hippos over there."

"Over there is more than 50 feet away," we grumbled in childish rebellion as we walked back to him. "We weren't bothering them."

"Those hippos can kill you," Isaac said firmly. He went on to explain that hippos were one of Africa's more dangerous animals. The cranky tubbies killed about three hundred people a year. In spite of their giant-baked-potato-with-legs appearance, they could swim up to 20 miles per hour and gallop at speeds up to 30 miles an hour for short distances.

"You won't see them coming at you under the water," he said. "They could hurt you before you got to the truck."

We stopped whining, grateful that he was there to protect us from the hippos and our ignorance.

Our two trucks parted company, and we drove over to a Masai village where we donated 500 shillings ($6.50) each to take a tour of it.

Some of the tribe gathered outside the village barrier, a prickly wall of branches with narrow entrances that were sealed up every night. Most men wore red plaid blankets tied around their necks like a cape or across their chests and knotted at the shoulder like a toga. The women wore large, brightly colored squares of fabric called *kangas* as scarves, skirts or slings to carry babies. Primary colored beads dangled from their ears, necks, elbows, wrists and ankles. Some were barefoot. Others wore simple leather sandals.

Young children, no older than about five years old, ran around, playing make-believe games. They wore a mixture of clothes and drapes of fabric. All wore beaded jewelry. None were allowed to shake hands with adults or wear traditional red blankets until they passed through the initiation rites into man- or womanhood.

A group of men were branding a cow stretched out on the ground. Her legs were tied to stakes. With a red hot iron, they burned a unique family pattern into her hide as she groaned and rolled her eyes into the back of her head. There was no ignoring the cow's distress, the smell of burning skin, or my inability to change the situation.

Cows equal money, so cattle theft was a major problem in this area.

"If a man suspects someone of selling stolen meat," Isaac explained, "the accuser demands to see the hide."

I walked away as fast as I could.

The village barrier formed a muddy corral for the cattle each night where they milled around family huts. Each hut was about the size of a two-car garage, and was built with mud, ash, grass and cow manure over a frame of twine and sticks. Giant mud warts. We stooped over to enter a hut and baby-stepped down a narrow passage, past a tiny room where the family goats slept, to reach the central communal space. A metal pot of something murky bubbled on a wire rack over a fire pit. Smoke wafted away through fist-sized holes in the ceiling and outer walls. Tiny doorless sleeping rooms, each about the size of a double bed, opened into the communal area. One room each for the children, parents and grandparents.

"Do you want to drink some cow blood?" asked the interpreter, who held out a flask.

"Salty," Gili said after taking a swig.

Sami, the Aunties and I declined. Not only was I grossed out by the idea, but I also had not eaten beef in a couple decades, so this was out of the question.

To escape the hot smoky layer of air against the ceiling, I sat in a sleeping room doorway and marveled at the simplicity of everything I saw. There were no interior decorations. No furniture. No mirrors. No appliances. No entertainment. No privacy. There were only worn hides on the sleeping room floors. This was not about comfort and vanity. It was about shelter and security. I could certainly live with fewer things, but I was too spoiled to permanently give up electric lights and running water.

The Maasai world was so foreign and fascinating to me—the construction of their homes, their cattle-based economy, their clothing, their customs, their intimate relationship with weather and the environment. And based on the way they casually watched me—a six-foot tall, white-skinned, red-headed, green-eyed woman—I brought some foreign to them.

At the end of our village tour, locals presented things for us to buy—jewelry made from beads and seeds, woodcarvings, and red blankets with stripes or plaid patterns.

"Maasai tribes buy blankets in bulk from the factories and distribute them to families for a small price," Isaac explained. "The families resell them for higher prices and keep the proceeds. That's how they raise money."

I bought three red blankets with yellow, white and black pinstripe patterns, each packed in a clear plastic bag. Later, when I saw how much dirt came out of the blankets as I washed them, I realized I may have bought someone's dirty laundry.

On the way back to Simba Camp we lost a battle with nature and gravity. The dirt mound between ruts in the road had caught the undercarriage of our truck, and left the tires with no traction. We were stuck. Where were all the rocks we had been bouncing over all day when we needed them?

Isaac asked us to gather branches to put under the tires, so we dutifully headed toward the closest bushes. As our hands reached out to them, Isaac yelled, "Stop!" with an authority that spoke to the child in each of us. Everyone held still.

"Not from that bush, please," he said in a gentler tone, walking toward us. "That one is dangerous."

He pulled back some dense leaves to reveal finger-sized, poisonous caterpillars with white, neon green and black markings. We laughed when we all turned back to the truck to get our cameras to photograph them.

Alas, our collection of branches did not help. The only comfort came from knowing that Isaac had radioed the park rangers and help was on the way. The sun set behind a low hill. The orange glow along the horizon faded to black. The more stars that twinkled in the sky, the more hungry and restless we got. The Aunties smoked. I blew my congested nose and chomped gum. We all paced near the truck, mindful that we were no longer at the top of the food chain.

When we saw two bright dots bobbing and blinking in the darkness, we moved closer to the truck. Was it the reflective gaze of an animal in our truck headlights? Hardly. It was a white minivan full of Maasai men and two park rangers. They wore an eclectic mix of red blankets, T-shirts, khaki pants, flip-flops and rubber boots. Some had stretched their ear lobes out so far that they looped them over the tops of their ears. No capes or masks, but heroes nonetheless.

Despite of an hour of digging and pushing, their brute force did not succeed. Isaac sent us back to camp in the ranger minivan while he remained with the others to free the truck.

Later, as I settled down to sleep in my tent, I was proud to have lived another day. On the African plains, that seemed to be a measure of success.

WHEN IT IS LEAST CONVENIENT TO PEE, my bladder often demands relief. So, about 3 a.m. I woke up, put on my shoes and slowly unzipped the tent to head toward the lantern glow in the outhouse. These unexpected, unidentifiable noises, however, beckoned a crouching, growling, fang-bearing camp dog.

I about peed in the tent at the sight and sound of him bearing down on me. I had no clue what to do, but went with the desperate hope that the dog would respond to tone rather than words.

"Hello puppy, good puppy, nice puppy," I said in my warmest, friendliest voice.

Instantly, the dog turned into a tail-wagging, groveling beast of love.

THE NEXT DAY, WE HAD ANOTHER GAME drive and dinner at Simba Camp. Afterwards four Maasai men performed traditional dances associated with lion hunts, circumcision, cattle herding and weddings. Three wore traditional red blankets while the fourth wore a toga of bright pink cotton sheeting and a pointy hat made from the woolly mane of a lion. Each dance combined chanting, jumping and gesturing with sticks.

The interpreter explained that boys now killed African buffaloes, rather than lions, as part of their initiation rites into manhood because these animals breed more easily and frequently than lions. We saw an African buffalo on our game drive. Its horns draped down the sides of his head and curled up at the tips. It was a silly look for a muscle-bound beast that weighed almost a ton and had the reputation for being the region's most dangerous and ill-tempered animal.

Girls did not kill animals during their initiation ceremonies into womanhood, but they were circumcised at age 15. The girls must not scream during the procedure because it would dishonor their families. When I asked what girl parts were removed, the interpreter said, "Just the outer parts. We are not butchers like the Ethiopians."

Interesting point of view on a delicate subject I found horrifying.

Before the wedding dance, the interpreter approached me.

"Nkashu Mpai, that man over there, would like to know if you will be his bride."

"Sure," I said as I smiled at Nkashu. I was flattered. Perhaps he was wooed by my tall stature and wide, easy-to-bear-a-baby hips.

As I held his warm, calloused hand, he wordlessly gestured to me when to jump and when to step under the crossed sticks held by the other dancers. I briefly thought about my first wedding ceremony long ago in Estes Park, Colorado. A long white satin dress with lace and beads. A black tuxedo. The walk down the aisle. White flowers and a three-tiered cake. The telling way the organist played the uplifting *Jesu, Joy of Man's Desire* like a funeral dirge. The ceremony sealed with a kiss that had not endured.

The wedding ceremony did not include a kiss, but it did include a bride price. Through a camp interpreter, Nkashu offered 50 cows for my matrimonial hand. I do not think he was serious, but I promised to pass the generous offer on to my father for consideration.

When my parents, who lived in an upscale neighborhood in urban Ohio, heard the offer, they laughed and asked, "What would we do with all those cows?"

This fake bride price reminded me of the real bride price my cousin Todd wrote about in his book *Eating Goat Parts for the Glory of God.* It was a collection of stories about the experiences he and his family had while living with the Sukuma people in Bariadi, Tanzania. One recalled a local family that had received a bride price for the upcoming wedding of their 16-year-old daughter Minza. Todd wrote, "Finally, the negotiations were done—nine cows, two sheep (without runny noses), eight goats (size agreed upon), 2,000 shillings now, and 108,000 shillings later (about $140). Once the final agreement had been reached, the women of the family came over, made celebratory noises, and they brought out the bowl of cow fat to anoint the older men with a blessing, symbolizing peace after the negotiations and a beginning of a new relationship."

After the Maasai dances, I shared my photo album with the staff and my truck mates. My world was as strange to the Maasai men as theirs was to me. The photo they found most puzzling showed my friends wearing small bathing suits and lounging in a fizzy hot tub. After I explained how to use a hot tub, the men laughed and wished they had one.

I also laid out a small map of the world. It helped show how far Gili's family and I had traveled to be there. The Maasai men said most Maasai never leave their region and never learn any other language but their own. Sounded like many Americans I knew.

EARLY THE NEXT MORNING, we headed east to Lake Nakuru to see pink flamingos. It was only 217 miles away, but it took 10 jostling hours, mostly because of the dirt roads and stops to help safari minivans snared by mud pits. The tacky black mud caked the tire treads as if we all had been driving on half-baked brownies. After our fourth rescue, we stopped trying to help others. Isaac heard later that one mud pit was so big that it had caught 18 minivans at one time.

As the miles passed by, I thought about how the Maasai village differed from cities that I knew.

"Isaac, what do Maasai do with their dead?"

"They used to leave the bodies above ground for the hyenas and vultures to eat,"he said, "but now they are required by law to bury them and cover the plot with rocks."

I wondered how many other rituals they would be stripped of before their culture became so diluted that it could not survive.

Eventually we returned to the paved road that spanned the floor of the Rift Valley. Isaac was driving aggressively down the road, like all the other drivers, when a calf bolted away from its young herder toward the front of our truck. We heard a thump, but the calf was still standing when we looked back in concern. Perhaps we just hit a hoof or a tail. The boy yelled at us and waved his stick around in anger as we continued on.

"It would be very bad for the boy if one of the calves was hurt during his watch," Isaac said.

We stopped at the Transit House for lunch. Bougainvillea vines draped in thick magenta waves over the restaurant's front porch. The hundreds of leaves quivered as a sprinkling of rain fell. The menu was curried chicken cut into boney chunks, cooked cabbage, fried potato wedges and rice. So many carbohydrates, but we were hungry and grateful for the hot food.

In Narok, we drove past a group of teenage girls wearing kelly green dresses with short sleeves and modest hemlines. White headscarves covered their hair. They walked in pairs with regal posture and slow measured steps, ignoring the bustle of people, traffic and animals around them. Isaac could not explain who they were, but odds were good they belonged to a religious order.

Miles, miles and more miles passed as the landscape shifted from arid dirt to grasslands to lush rolling hills covered with crops. On the side of the road, two men herded a burly pig. It had escaped from the overcrowded bed of their truck as it slowly labored up a hill.

Dusk brought stunning vistas as mist and rain mixed in the fading light over crisp green fields of young wheat. The crops seemed tacked to the earth by randomly placed acacia trees.

The pastoral beauty gave way to Nakuru's urban sprawl, unlit congested streets and blinding rain inspired terror as Isaac swerved and slammed on the brakes to avoid hitting stray animals, people on foot or on bikes, and erratic *matatus*, trucks and cars. My final words to the world perched on my lips.

Tired, cranky and sore-tailed, we finally arrived at our hotel, only to learn that the manager had given our reserved rooms away. Isaac was livid. There was no mistaking his expressions and gestures as we watched him and the manager argue in front of the truck. We were shuffled to another hotel of lesser quality, where we could hear our neighbors as if we were sharing beds with them.

I chucked my sour-smelling socks and boots into the shower stall and shut the bathroom door. There was no point washing anything. Nothing would be dry by the time we left at 6 a.m. the next day.

We regrouped in the hotel's empty dining room. As we waited for our meal, it was obvious Isaac was coming down with a cold.

Isaac drank several cups of hot water to provide relief from his stuffy nose and scratchy throat. This familiar remedy thrilled the Aunties. Even though we all came from such different cultures, it was comforting to discover things we had in common.

Before my trip I had worried about catching the foreign illnesses listed on the few of the U.S. Department of State health info sheets that I had read. They made me think about wearing a biohazard suit as I traveled. Avoid swimming in lakes, streams and rivers because of parasites. Avoid crowded public places and public transportation due to people with contagious tuberculosis. Avoid exposure to mosquito bites, which could lead to yellow and dengue fevers. Avoid direct contact with the blood or body fluids of people ill with Ebola. And those were just the precautions for Kenya. Yet I was probably the one who infected Isaac with my cold.

We swore the cook sent a child out to kill an old warthog, the meal took so long to arrive and the meat was so tough to chew. And the waiter, who had been ready to go home when we arrived, was cranky about serving us. When we asked him to take our picture with my disposable camera, he pushed the button too soon on purpose so that the photograph featured the back of Isaac's head. We made him stay to take two more photos of us just to get back at him.

RAIN CAME WITH THE DAWN, but at least we were not driving over dirt roads. We were on our way to Lake Nakuru, the second stop in our seven-day safari. Between forested hills, we caught glimpses of its distinctive shores. Even from miles away, they shimmered with flamingo pinkness. A tree-lined street led to Lake Nakuru National Park's entry gate. Baboons ambled by in the shade. A baby clutching her back fur, the alpha female led the troop.

At the gate, Isaac gave the guard his national park SmartCard. It verified who he was and paid for our park entrance fees.

"We used to pay cash to the guards when we entered this park," Isaac explained when the guards were out of hearing range. "When all of the Kenyan parks switched over to the Smartcard system, millions of shillings magically appeared. It almost doubled the income for the parks."

Established in 1968, this park included 72 square miles of marsh, grasslands, rocky cliffs and forest. It was home to hundreds of bird and animal species. Some had oxymoronic names like spectacled elephant shrew or ant bear. Bats took the blue ribbon for diverse names like African mouse-eared, Angola free-tailed, epauletted fruit, false vampire, hollow-faced, Lander's horseshoe, lesser- and long-eared leaf nosed, yellow-bellied and yellow-winged.

At the heart of the park was the shallow lake, about three meters at its deepest. The lake had almost dried up several times in the past 50 years, and no one knew if the cause of this was natural or man-made. Called a soda lake, its alkaline water was the result of ancient volcanoes that had covered the area with ash. While a normal pH would be about 7.0, Lake Nakuru water measured a whopping 10.5, a level that nurtures a dense, blue-green algae bloom.

According to my guide book, more than a million flamingoes could be at Lake Nakuru at any given time. The overcast sky vibrated with clicking sounds as their beaks skimmed the water for the algae and shrimp that gave their feathers the cotton candy pink color. I laughed whenever the birds took flight. They looked like characters from a Dr. Seuss book, their stick legs dangling back beneath them. As I tucked a discarded pink feather into my journal, I remembered sadly that ancient Romans ate flamingo tongues as a delicacy.

At the top of the park's Baboon Cliff, Isaac warned us to close all the truck windows because baboons would search the truck for food. We walked over to the edge of the cliff. Below, dense forest gave way to emerald green grass crisscrossed by tire ruts filled with water. The metallic surface of the lake blushed with pink as if pollinated. Each flamingo added a fleck of color.

After I shot a roll of film, I went back to the truck to get another roll. One of the white-haired Aunties was rifling through a bag in the backseat. I was about to ask what she was looking for when she turned her head, bared her fangs and screeched at me.

"Isaac, it's in the truck!" I yelled, pointing to the baboon. The thief dashed out the open back window gripping two ripe mangoes and dropping a third. It was worth the loss of Gili's fruit to watch the baboon dodge our half-hearted attempts to get them back. The thief scrambled to the truck roof. He slid down the side of the hood. He darted under the truck. He ran across the parking lot and scrambled up to the stone pavilion's roof. He fought off others who wanted a share of the loot.

Once we got back in the truck, we headed down the cliff and circled around the lake, spying new animals like Verreaux's Eagle-Owls, warthogs, jackals, storks and hyenas. The rock hyrax resembled a cat-sized, brown guinea pig.

Isaac stopped the truck when we saw a small herd of black rhinos grazing to our right. These endangered animals, nature-made tanks, were unpredictable and easily irritated. According to Save the Rhino International, there were 100,000 black rhinos in Africa until the 1960s. By 1997 there were just 2,600. The hostile animals made for exciting hunting, and their horns were coveted for ornamental dagger handles and Asian medicines. A kilogram of horn could be worth more than 10 times what the average East African man made in a year. We quietly applauded ourselves. We had finally seen all of the famous Big Five game animals.

After we left the park, we headed to Thomson's Falls in Nyahururu, one of the highest towns in Kenya at 2,360 meters (7,740 feet). Along the paved road, the landscape became ever more lush and mountainous, the dirt becoming darker and richer. Soon neatly tended fields of coffee and tea appeared on the slopes.

"This region is known for being able to grow anything," Isaac said.

We passed a billboard that read "Itching For Success? Keep Scratching!" It was an ad for Sprite. What motivation and a soft drink had to do with each other was beyond me.

When we arrived at the falls, a swarm of polite but determined women approached us in the dirt parking lot.

"Please, madame, come visit with me. I have many things you will like."

"Perhaps later," we repeated over and over as we walked down the trail to the wooden viewing platform. In front of us, the frothy café-au-lait-colored water plummeted about 17 stories to explode on the black rocks below.

In 1883, 25-year-old Joseph Thomson was commissioned by the Royal Geographical Society of London to explore the uncharted land that later became Kenya. He was the first to chart the Nyahururu River, and the Thomson gazelles were also named after him.

WE HEADED EAST TOWARD THE SAMBURU National Reserve. Traffic came to a standstill where long metal spike strips crisscrossed the road. Police stopped every vehicle to check for illegal goods, mostly animal-related products.

When we turned off the paved road onto a dirt road, we passed a bunch of barefoot boys who shouted and waved at our truck. I had a peanut bar that no one wanted, so I tossed it out the window to them.

"What did that just teach the children about mzungas in safari trucks?" Isaac quietly asked.

It was a polite way of telling me that I was teaching them to beg, like when I gave money to the boys at the museum. I was ashamed that I had not given my well-intended actions enough thought.

Later, we passed another group of boys who cheered and waved at us. This time Isaac abruptly stopped the truck. His face was stern when he walked back to the boys.

"Oh, you're in trouble," we five whispered in unison, pressing our faces against the truck windows.

After a solemn conversation, the boys bowed their heads. Isaac returned to the truck and handed me a stick with a three-horned chameleon clinging to it. Its unblinking bulbous eyes stared at me.

"Many local people believe that chameleons are bad luck, so bad that to kill them would bring even worse luck," Isaac explained as he drove on. "Those boys threw that chameleon at our truck hoping we'd run it over and kill it for them. They do not understand that chameleons eat the insects that ruin their crops."

Before we set it free in some bushes down the road, I marveled at the intriguing curves of its body and tail, as if it was an ornate punctuation mark.

ARRIVING IN THE TOWN OF ISIOLO in the late afternoon, Isaac and I made a quick stop to buy food for dinner. Isaac and I would be staying at a public campsite in the Samburu National Reserve, while Gili, Sami and the Aunties had paid extra to stay at a swanky lodge. As we all got back into the truck, Gili got agitated about how much farther we had to go. She kept pushing Isaac to drive faster, to get to the border of the Northern Territory as soon as possible. Enough already.

"Isaac is not the problem, so there's no reason to get in his face," I snapped at her, surprising us both. "We're the ones who made us late. Every time he stopped the truck, we wasted time."

There was an uncommon silence in the truck for the next few miles.

What I did not know (though it would not have changed my opinion) was that we had to pass a guarded checkpoint at the edge of the Northern Territory by 6 p.m. The stretch of road beyond the checkpoint was a politically unstable area that was closed to traffic after dark. We arrived 15 minutes late.

In the opalescent dusk, Isaac walked over to a booth to talk with the uniformed, rifle-toting guards. As we waited in the truck, dark-skinned hands shoved handmade bracelets through the open windows.

"Sir? Madam? Please buy this bracelet," voices called to us.

The simple jewelry was made from twisted copper and silvery metal. Stunned by the aggressive sales approach, we rolled up the windows.

When Isaac returned to the truck, he waved them away, and we drove the truck past the guard booth.

"They steal metal from everywhere to make that jewelry," he said.

"That's why no telephone lines run through this area."

We all pondered the implications of that, until Sami asked why the guards let us pass.

"I blamed the Aunties," he explained. "I said 'They do not like to ride in the truck when it rains.'"

We all laughed. Our safari would be two weeks longer if that was true!

Isaac also tipped the guards 800 shillings ($10.40) for their patience and understanding. He had no choice. They knew that the Israeli family had rooms at the Samburu Serena Safari Lodge, which was located within the reserve and that the room charges were nonrefundable if we did not show up.

The landscape faded into complete darkness. We rumbled down the gravel road that rippled like corrugated metal. There were no houses, lights or passing trucks. Only stars and our high beams. Here tempers flared, violence erupted, lives ended and darkness cloaked it all. Isaac's eyes scanned back and forth for trouble. Both of his hands gripped the steering wheel. Like children sensing a troubled parent, the Israelis and I were nervous and alert.

At the border of the Samburu National Reserve, more armed guards greeted us.

"*Jambo*. Good to see that you arrived safely."

An alert would have been sounded if we had not arrived in a timely manner. Isaac relaxed in the driver's seat. One of his hands dropped from the steering wheel. We ate some of the Aunties' snacks as we drove on to the lodge. Driving at a more leisurely pace, we had another 12 miles to go.

"Snake!" I yelled, pointing to the right side of the road.

Isaac hit the brakes, backed up until we saw the last two feet of its body slithering into the tall grass. Its back was a mosaic of yellow and dark brown chevron shapes. It was a puff adder, Africa's most common and most poisonous snake and the second largest of all vipers.

When we finally arrived at the lodge gate, it was locked and unmanned. The staff assumed we were not coming. Even though Isaac had had a long day of driving on bad roads and suffered from a head cold, he shimmied on his belly under the electric fence and walked the quarter mile to get the staff to let us in. He would not let any of us do it for him.

The Samburu Serena Safari Lodge had made *Travel & Leisure* magazine's list of the 500 greatest hotels in the world for many reasons. This oasis of civilization offered 62 guest rooms (some were private cabins), a currency exchange, babysitters, lunch boxes, shoe shines, cakes and flowers for special occasions, a petrol station, and mechanical parts and services for safari vehicles. The lodge even had a 24-hour on-call nurse and Flying Doctors Service with emergency Medivac from the nearby airstrip. The buildings were constructed with natural yellow stone and decorated with the symbols and weapons of the Samburu tribe. The open-air reception and waiting area faced a small pool of lily pads centered in a manicured lawn.

As Gili, Sami and the Aunties checked in, I realized Isaac and I still had to get back in the truck, bounce down dirt roads to the camp, wait for the cook to prepare dinner and go to bed without a shower. Time to consider a better option. I slid my Visa card across the counter.

"May I please have a room for myself, a room for Isaac in the driver's quarters, and meals for both of us in the dining room," I said.

The black receptionist's eyebrows raised ever so slightly.

I could not tell if he objected to me paying for Isaac's room or Isaac eating in the main dining room or the validity of my credit card because I looked (and smelled) more youth hostel than premiere hotel. It did not matter. I was not going to change my mind.

"Is there a problem?" I said as I pushed the card another inch across the counter. After taking a long second to reconsider, he looked down as he picked up the card.

"No, madam."

I turned away before I grinned. I had always had a dysfunctional relationship with authority, rarely standing my ground and quick to give my authority away to others. This stance was a vast improvement, but the thrill of personal accomplishment was short lived. I realized I had not asked for Isaac's approval before making the new arrangement.

"I'm sorry, Isaac. Is this okay with you? I'm just so tired, and you're sick, and I thought we could use a break."

Isaac solemnly took my hands.

"Thank you so much for your kindness," he said.

Never in my life had I seen anyone gaze at me with such gratitude. That moment reminded me of the movie *Pay It Forward*, based on a book by Catherine Ryan Hyde. As a class assignment, young student Trevor McKinney was asked to "think of an idea to change the world and put it into action." Trevor's idea was that when one person benefits from someone's act of goodwill, he or she should "pay it forward" to three more people, who would do the same. Strangers paid it forward to Geoff's family. Geoff paid it forward to me. I paid it forward to Isaac.

A uniformed porter carried my backpack as he walked me to a cabin. Small electric lanterns lit the stone paved sidewalk between islands of foliage and other cabins. The darkness clicked with insect gossip. Inside my cabin, a queen-sized bed with dark green mosquito netting beckoned my tired body, but I was hungry, and there were chores to be done. It took three rounds of washing to get the water to run clear from my socks and pants.

The lodge's open-air dining room overlooked a swimming pool and terrace by the banks of the Ewaso Ng'iro river. We were too late to see the staff throw scraps down the embankment to expectant crocodiles. I had mixed feelings about wanting to see such a cheesy tourist stunt.

Dinner included the expected spread of prime meats and fish, vegetables and an iced salad bar. As we ate, uniformed staff members stood silently nearby to keep away marauding monkeys and birds. The brandy snaps—crisp molasses shells oozing with cream filling—gave me the sweet fix I needed like some people need an espresso or a cigarette after a meal.

Afterwards, green geckos cruised the reed-lined ceiling above my bed as I thought about this safari experience. I could easily see how traveling with friends, staying in upscale lodges and touring in hired trucks could insulate a person from the unpredictable details of travel. My trip so far had been so much richer due to chance meetings with new people and unplanned discoveries.

THE CLOUDLESS MORNING SKY was bright and crisp. With Isaac's approval I wore shorts, keeping my long pants in my backpack just in case. We would not be running into anyone who would be offended by seeing my bare legs, and the weather would be scorching by noon. At breakfast, we were all in better spirits after good food, deep sleep and some time away from each other. After pocketing croissants, our merry band hit the road for a game drive.

The arid rolling landscape bristled with scrub brush and had rocky outcroppings large enough to be called mesas. It reminded me of the western foothills of the Colorado Rockies where my father grew up.

"Kenyan snow," Isaac said, pointing out a red dust cloud when it appeared behind the truck.

Along one bend in the river, a doum palm fanned out into an airy canopy of fronds. Considered sacred by ancient Egyptians, these trees were still popular today. Its red-orange, apple-sized fruit added a gingerbread taste to many recipes. Its hard white nuts could be fashioned into buttons or ground into medicines for wounds.

Isaac continued to amaze us with his knowledge.

"See that bush there?" Isaac pointed out a plant that looked like most of the other plants. "It likes to grow in salty soil. You can use its leaves to add salt to food when you're cooking."

He picked small branches and showed us how to chewed the ends and rub them against our gums as natural toothbrushes. Another time he stopped the truck and walked out into the tall grass, only to lift up a yellow and brown leopard tortoise about the size of a 25-pound frozen turkey.

"It's a baby deer!" Gili yelled when a small animal froze for a moment in the grass before bolting away. Looking like a giant Chihuahua, Kirk's dik-dik was a reddish brown dwarf antelope, only 14 inches tall at the shoulder and 12 pounds when fully grown. My cat could beat up this antelope!

As we drove along the pleasantly hard dirt tracks, not a mud pit or trapped minivan in sight, we passed areas thick with the pungent smell of manure. The first elephant dung pile we saw could almost fill a bath tub. We all giggled when we actually saw an elephant pee and poop. It was a time-consuming and voluminous effort. Elephants ate 18 hours a day to consume about 550 pounds of green material—bark, leaves, roots and branches. It was no wonder they went through as many as six sets of teeth in their lifetimes.

"Female elephants have ducts behind their eyes to rub against trees to leave messages for other elephants," Isaac explained.

"Like 'Young fertile female elephant seeks dominant male'?" I suggested.

Messages like that had obviously been well received. The proof was in the two baby elephants we saw trunk wrestling.

After dropping Sami, Gili and the Aunties back at the lodge for lunch, Isaac and I relocated to a campsite. It was a grouping of green canvas tents in an area lightly shaded by acacia trees. Off to one side was a tarp-covered cooking area. With the help of a teenage boy, an old, wiry man cooked meals while another man guarded the camp. All three were quiet and overly polite around me, the only guest. It was awkward.

"They are used to being seen but not heard," Isaac said quietly.

"Not like the Israelis," I joked.

Isaac laughed and nodded in agreement. "Yes, they are like a flock of birds."

There was some down time before the next game drive, so I sat at a wooden picnic table to scribble in my journal, but nature foiled my plan. Birds—bright flashes of metallic blue, fire red, lemon yellow—darted about. A black bird with a brick red chest and white collar pecked at my journal until I shooed it away. Redheaded weavers tucked sticks into their nests, which dangled like twiggy grapefruits from the tree branches overhead. A red-billed hornbill (like Zazu in *The Lion King*) watched me from a nearby branch. A ground squirrel dug a shallow hole in the dirt by my feet, peed in it and ran away. A cream and pale brown vervet monkey raided the cooking area for food. No question that the monkey was male. I could not help but notice his robin egg-blue scrotum as he ran away from the camp guard.

WHILE THE AUNTIES LAPPED UP the luxury services at the lodge, Gili, Sami and I spent the afternoon at a Samburu village. We gathered at a hut outside the village barrier, about 20 feet from the river. The hut had a thatched roof and thinly woven stick walls that let sunlight and breezes waft through. Several bare-chested men sat on small wooden stools inside.

An English-speaking member of the tribe was our interpreter. In return for a donation of 500 shillings ($6.50), we were welcome to take as many pictures as we wanted.

"Excuse me. Would you please ask that man if I may take his picture?" I asked before we left the hut to tour the village. I nodded to a man with cropped hair, hooded eyes, a short beard and brilliantly white teeth. In spite of the heat, he wore a striped red blanket around his shoulders.

"He's quite handsome and reminds me of a friend back home," I said quietly to Isaac.

I did not have to understand the Samburu language to know that when the guide translated my request, he included my comment. All the men in the hut laughed. I was slightly embarrassed but received a flirtatious smile for my picture before we entered the village.

Like the Maasai, the Samburu built their huts with earthy materials, but also included curious bits of cardboard, plastic sheeting and metal baling straps. The huts were surrounded by tufts of green grass, a telltale sign that cattle were not grazing there at night.

"The men have taken all of the village's cattle far to the south to protect them from marauding cattle thieves that come from the north," Isaac explained.

The children were more curious about us than the Maasai children.

They followed us with wide eyes and shy smiles. One wore an oversized T-shirt with a Canadian Maple Leaf flag on it. Another wore baggy sport shorts.

A row of women in brightly colored *kangas* stood in the patchy shade of an acacia tree and performed traditional songs for us. Their rhythmic chanting sounded like a lullaby. A pointy-tailed gray kitten rubbed against their beaded ankles. It seemed so out of place, so vulnerable in this world of carnivores. A regal woman stepped forward to perform a solo. As if her shaved head were Saturn, rings of yellow, red, blue and black beads formed a band nearly a foot wide around her neck. It was a display of great wealth. As the woman sang, she closed her eyes and tilted her chin and palms toward the sun. I could not understand her words, but was swept into the grace and devotion of her performance.

The final part of the tour was a walk down a seller's gauntlet. On each side of the path leading out of the village, women displayed their wares on the dirt or on top of tattered squares of fabric. A majority of the merchandise was beaded bracelets and necklaces. The woodcarvings showed wear and tear, as if they were popular toys when not for sale.

"You like? You buy," the ladies chirped. "Very cheap."

Near the end of the gauntlet I caught sight of Handsome Man yet again. During the tour, we had been exchanging peeks at each other. I removed a simple metal ring from my finger and approached him. I held it in my fist, palm down, towards him to see if he understood this gesture, to see what he would do. He understood. He shyly stepped forward, away from his pack of male friends. He held out his hand, palm up, to see what I was offering. His eyes grew wide with delight when he saw my present.

"Hello. My. Name. Is. Kristine," I said slowly with a smile. The men rushed up to see what he got, and I returned to the market.

About 10 minutes later Handsome Man came up to me and slowly said, "Hello, my name is Leesh."

"*Jambo*," I said.

"*Jambo*!"

"*Habari*? [How are you?]"

"*Mzuri.* [Fine]" He quickly fell into a full-blown conversation and was lost to me.

I shrugged my shoulders and shook my head to indicate that I did not understand. I hoped my gesture was received as one of friendship and kindness from one person to another, that it was not just a pleasing windfall from a tourist.

After our village tour ended, we picked up the Aunties at the lodge and headed out for another game drive. We bumped along dirt roads in the reserve. The skies were overcast with steel gray clouds. A cool breeze shimmied the tops of the acacia trees.

As twilight arrived and we started to head back, we were pleasantly delayed by a pride of seven lionesses enjoying a social hour in the middle of the road. Some laid down for full-body stretches. Two gently chewed on each other's ears. One draped along the top of an old termite mound. Even their nonchalance seemed powerful.

NIGHT REDUCED THE CAMP SITE to pools of lantern light. Beetles and double-winged dragonflies buzzed about. After a fire-cooked meal of curried chicken and rice, Isaac told me about Kenyan cowboys—mostly British men—who came to Africa.

"They took credit when things were good," he said. "But they left and blamed other people when things went bad. They treated 'true' Africans as if they were an ignorant, lesser people."

"How do East Africans see Americans?" I asked. I hoped I conveyed a sense of inclusiveness, openness, curiosity and respect. "And don't fib because I'm an American."

"In general, they have a good reputation in Kenya," he said. "They ask hard questions when they see injustices, and they welcome all people into their worlds, not just as servants."

He recalled one American tour operator in Kenya who had a reputation for paying drivers and guides what they deserved (enough for a decent quality of life) rather than the pitiful national standard.

When Isaac and I moved over to the cooking area, the cook and the young helper were skeptical of this atypical move, despite Isaac's reassurance. Back in Isiolo, I had bought a packet of popcorn. I could not remember the last time I made popcorn over an open fire, but it was time to do it again. I hoped not to disappoint my audience.

After we sat on the ground around the fire pit, I poured a puddle of oil in a large metal pot, perched the pot on a rack over the glowing coals and tossed in a few kernels. Everyone watched me as I waited with anticipation. When the kernels exploded into the air, the cook and the young helper jumped back like startled cats. They started asking Isaac questions in Swahili. Could this amazing thing be done with any kind of corn? Where did this corn come from? What made it fly like that? With Isaac as an interpreter I answered their questions.

When I added a small handful of popcorn to the oil, they wanted to watch it explode, so we left the lid off the pot. I gestured for everyone to lean back. We laughed as white puffy rockets shot into the air until I finally put the lid on the pot. When the popcorn was ready to eat, the men ate modest nibbles until Isaac explained for me that we each got equal shares, and we must eat until the pot was empty.

So there I was under a starry African sky, sitting around a fire pit, sharing popcorn with new friends. This moment became one of the high points of my trip. It was life at its sweetest and most simple.

AS I WAITED IN MY TENT for sleep to come, I heard a rumbling growl. A leopard? A lion? A hyena? It was a good time to realize that this camp had no barrier or fortified meeting hut. I hastily bound the tent flap grommets together with my clothesline. At least I would get a warning if something tried to get in. I would experience my life-threatening mauling to the fullest. Even though the air in the tent got hot and stale, I still kept my long-sleeve shirt, nylon pants and socks on because there was no mosquito netting. I clutched my turtle sarong under my chin.

I slowly fell into a fitful sleep, which lasted until about 4 a.m. when, of course, I needed to go to the bathroom. Isaac had warned me not to wander into the overgrowth at night, so I dashed out to the big tree in the middle of the camp, peed at record speed and dashed back into the tent. I was like the ground squirrel I had seen that morning.

IN THE PALE LIGHT OF DAWN, the birds kicked off a deafening social hour. I could not count all the different whistles, warbles, calls, clicks and chirps. As the young helper washed our truck, Isaac and I searched the camp for signs of a predator but found nothing. I was embarrassed, but Isaac kindly pointed out how well sound travels and that I might have heard an animal from far away.

I had mixed feelings about this being the last day of the safari, of heading back to Nairobi today. I did not want the experience to end, yet it was hard to be sad because I had months of travel ahead of me.

In the stark daylight, the once scary road between the Samburu National Reserve and the Northern Territory border guard station was nothing more than a bleak dusty road. We stopped for a moment where the road ended in a T intersection. There were no road signs, only miles and miles of flat scrubland in all directions. Turn left to reach Ethiopia. Turn right to go back to the border.

We had careened around this same corner in the darkness days ago. Where were the demons of our imagination? The fierce animals? The violent men? The poisonous snake? We felt foolish, like children afraid of monsters under the bed at night, only to find dust bunnies in the morning.

"Do not be fooled," Isaac said solemnly. "The dangers are very real."

I would have been more afraid if I had read the U.S. Department of State information sheet that stated:

"There has been an increase in armed banditry in or near many of Kenya's national parks and game reserves, particularly the Samburu, Leshaba and Maasai Mara game reserves... The area near Kenya's border with Somalia has been the site of a number of incidents of violent criminal activity, including kidnappings. There are some indications of ties between Muslim extremist groups, including the Osama Bin Laden organization and the roving groups of Somali gunman."

HEADING SOUTH BACK TO NAIROBI, we stopped at a sign that marked the equator. Not to miss out on an economic opportunity, someone had built a little strip mall along the road next to the sign. Under its long tin roof, each sales stall had plank walls, concrete floors, and crude wooden shelves and tables. None had electricity.

Eager vendors rushed to our truck, encouraging us to visit their stalls first. Not everyone was happy when I decided to go from left to right, following the large red numbers painted above each stall.

One woman vendor had a map of the United States on the wall. I pointed out where I came from and where my relatives lived, in places that included Alaska, Wyoming, Colorado, Iowa, Ohio, Pennsylvania, Maryland and Georgia. She was perplexed.

"Why is your tribe so spread out?"

I had no answer.

"You are tall like the Maasai," she added.

"Yes, my tribe is very tall. My father is 6 feet, 7 inches."

This brought a wide-eyed look of astonishment to the woman who was barely 5-feet tall.

AT THE MAYFIELD GUEST HOUSE in Nairobi, I said my goodbyes to Gili and her family at the truck. I wished there had been more time to learn about each other and our traditions. The Israeli family was as interesting as the people in the villages we had visited. Sami and the Aunties were leaving town sooner than they had planned. Kenya had been more primitive and more fierce than they had expected.

Isaac walked me to the guest house door.

"I wish I could take you to America and give you a tour of my world," I said, wishing I also had clothing and books for his family. The best I could do was slip him some cash, get his address and give him a long, heartfelt hug.

I settled into a room and went to the dining hall for dinner. The evening's menu consisted of pepperoni pizza, salad and ice cream. It was delicious if for no other reason than it was so familiar.

THE NEXT DAY, ISAAC TOOK another tour group out, so another Primetime Safaris guide named David took me to the post office and then to the Sheldrick Elephant Orphanage. The post office was on the first floor of a modern skyscraper in the heart of downtown. From a kiosk in the center of the vast, marble-floored lobby, a postal clerk directed patrons to one of the 26 service windows. I wanted to ship to America a package of souvenirs I had bought.

I was directed to an office where a male postal clerk stood behind a metal office desk. Two female employees stood quietly behind him.

"I must inspect everything in your package before it is sealed," he said. "All boxes must be wrapped with brown paper. The post office does not sell the required tape or paper." He reached for my box. Uh oh.

I did not mind showing the clerk the Maasai blankets, *kangas* or hand-carved wooden bowl. It was that last-minute item I playfully tucked in the box that embarrassed me. It was a 12-pack of primary-colored, fruit-flavored condoms, a brand I had never seen before and thought a friend of mine would find amusing.

I blushed when the postal clerk held up the condom box and gave me a disapproving look. He had no interest in my juvenile explanation. The two ladies, however, laughed and nodded with approval.

Having passed inspection, I waited in the lobby with my box while David dashed to a store to buy tape and paper. It was odd that the postal clerk did not care that we repacked, sealed, wrapped and labeled the box in the lobby before returning to his office to pay for shipping. I could have slipped other things into the box without him knowing.

Picking one of the two shipping methods was simple. If I sent the box the cheap way, via ground service, I would mostly likely beat it home after traveling around the world. The package also might be lighter due to theft, if it arrived at all. So I paid for the 10-day air delivery.

I hit another snag when the postal clerk said that the post office did not take credit cards. Fortunately, the second ATM machine I found down the street worked.

Back at the post office yet again, one of the female postal clerks chastised me for using such narrow tape on the box. That same tape became insignificant when I pointed out that David bought it. The woman ever so slowly completed her paper work as I chewed on my unspoken derogatory comments.

"The postage machine is on loan to the other post office," she said, crossing her arms across her chest. "You must buy stamps."

I licked and stuck 51 stamps onto the box. This experience shipping one box gave me a much clearer appreciation of Geoff's tribulations as he tried to move cargo containers around Africa.

Postal mission complete, we headed to the Sheldrick Elephant Orphanage. It was the culmination of decades of work by Daphne Sheldrick, the widow of the late David Sheldrick. One of Kenya's best known game wardens, he played a key role in the 1970s ivory-poaching wars in Tsavo National Park, a park which he founded.

Daphne had perfected the formula and husbandry needed to hand-rear milk-dependent infant elephants. Before then, only weaned orphans could be saved.

The muddy orphanage parking lot was divided by narrow straw-covered trails for pedestrians. The walkways between the buildings and the animal barns were paved. All visitors stood behind a cordon next to a viewing area. Behind it was a stunning vista of savanna and acacia trees.

It was chilly and rainy, so the six baby elephants arrived wearing blue nylon tarps over magenta and navy blue striped blankets—gifts from British Airways, the company that generously transported their unique soy formula. In the wild, the babies would stand under their mothers for additional heat and protection from the rain.

These babies were orphaned through a variety of means. Two lost their mothers to poaching. One baby was rescued from a hunter's snare. Two others were rescued after getting perilously stuck in the mud by a watering hole. Another was abandoned when it could not keep up with its mother, who ran away from a noisy truck.

The baby elephants immediately demanded their liter-sized bottles with loud trumpeter cries. Normally each one had his or her own keeper, but today one keeper was missing, so another had double duty.

He held a bottle for one baby while lovingly stroking the trunk of another who was vocally indignant about waiting.

Baby elephants must be fed on demand, but gradually settle into feedings every three hours until they begin a yearlong weaning process when they are 1 year old. At that time they are also exposed to fresh elephant dung to help them establish the correct stomach flora needed to digest solid foods.

Once the baby elephants are weaned, they relocate to Tsavo National Park with their keepers, spending their days foraging in the bush and their nights sleeping in a stockade. By the time they reach puberty (between 12 and 15 years), they will have made the transition from a human-based family to part of a wild elephant herd.

Mothering a baby elephant is a full-time job. As a surrogate elephant mother, a keeper must be with the baby every minute of every day. Even a minute alone can cause distress. Yet, the keepers must rotate shifts so that the infant does not develop a deep attachment to a particular keeper whose absence at any time might prove stressful.

New arrivals at the orphanage need at least two keepers. One fetches items like milk, water and blankets. The other provides the essential constant physical contact. Baby elephants need to be washed down after each soiling, and their stools scrutinized for diarrhea before being buried. Babies also need to rest their trunks against something that feels a bit like mother before they will suckle, and endless patience is needed until the infant figures out how to use its trunk.

The keepers also teach proper elephant behavior, the way a mother teaches her child manners. Discipline is done very carefully, usually with tone of voice, but it must be followed with a big show of forgiveness so that the baby does not harbor a grudge.

After all the babies were fed, the keepers laid branches on the ground. The baby elephants brandished them about or picked leaves off of them to eat. One walked along the cordon, smelling visitors. As instructed, I gently held her muscled trunk in my hand and blew down the end of it. This baby would remember my smell for the rest of her life—possibly 100 years.

WHILE I WAS ON SAFARI, my cousin Tamara and her family had relocated to Nairobi with their missionary group. They still had not decided whether to stay in Africa or go back to the U.S.

Tamara and Todd took me to their new apartment, a fascinating glimpse into Nairobi housing. The apartment complex was on a dirt road off a main paved road. It resembled a typical middle income apartment complex—rectangular four-story buildings separated by paved parking lots, except it was surrounded by high walls topped with electrified wires. Armed security guards manned the entry gate.

"A great way to get your exercise," I said after walking up four flights of stairs. The family had the penthouse apartment with a private balcony, but there was no elevator.

The two-bedroom apartment came furnished with angular 1970s-looking furniture. The kitchen was designed for people at least a foot shorter than me.

The boys went to their rooms to read, and we settled onto the couch.

"It's convenient," noted Tamara. "Rent includes maid and laundry service, so every time we leave the complex, we have to leave our keys at the reception desk."

Todd added, "All telephone calls are routed through the switchboard receptionist. She also takes messages if we don't answer our phone."

When I first passed through Nairobi, I left two boxes of supplies for my cousins to pick up at the Mayfield Guest House. Their wish list included Dum Dum lollipops, M&M s (plain, peanut and almond), Hershey's miniature candy bars, Crystal Light drink mix and Nestlé's chocolate chips. We shared some of the coveted M&Ms as we chatted about my experiences in East Africa, which would come to an end the next day when I flew to Nepal.

"It was fun to see what was familiar to me but not to the Israelis and vice versa. One of the Aunties got beyond excited about a yellow, daisy-looking flower she saw in someone's yard. She made Isaac stop the truck so she could photograph it. She'd never seen it before," I smiled. "It looked just like a Black-Eyed Susan from my dad's garden."

I also confessed that I had kept an eye out for African violets. Because they were in almost every grocery store I had ever seen, I expected the plants to be everywhere. I never saw one.

SITTING AT THE JOMO KENYATTA International Airport, I marveled at how much I had experienced in the past 24 days. East Africa was surreal, perplexingly different and familiar at the same time. It was such a raw, energetic mass of extremes in poverty and wealth, pollution and natural landscape, agriculture and wildlife. And it ran on a distorted clock built by artist Salvador Dali.

I was glad I had given up trying to know everything about East Africa (an impossible goal) before I arrived. It would have overwhelmed me and filled me with fear. So many times, my ignorance empowered me and freed me from expectations.

Thirty-eight Snickers to a better attitude

Mumbai, India

IT WAS NOT A GOOD SIGN when the airport security guard, rifle swinging from his shoulder, asked me to step away from the departure gate turnstile I was trying to pass through. An even worse sign was when five serious men in business suits gathered to inspect my plane tickets and passport. I had just arrived in Mumbai, India, at 2:10 a.m. and was trying to catch a 7 a.m. flight to Delhi, where I would catch another flight to Kathmandu, Nepal.

Fifteen minutes later, one man finally explained the problem. I was trying to change from an international flight to a domestic flight, but did not have the required Indian visa. Visas were not issued at the airport. They did not know what to do with me.

It was my fault. When I abandoned the plan to travel to Lebanon, I bought plane tickets to go to Nepal. It never occurred to me that I would need a visa to change planes because I did not know the domestic flight departed from another airport across town.

A petite, young woman with short black hair and another security guard escorted me to a transit holding area. As we walked, she explained that immigration had the authority to send me back to Nairobi, Kenya, but first they would see if my ticket could be altered to fly me directly out of the country. I embraced this morsel of possibility.

The transit holding area was a vast room with a bar and a duty-free shop along one wall. In the glass-enclosed room by the entrance, two guards slept on pieces of cardboard on the floor, using seat cushions from nearby chairs as pillows. The rest of the holding area's floor space was filled with rows of white plastic chairs and blue upholstered lounge chairs where people were curled up asleep. Tiny women in colorful silk saris looked like wilted squash blossoms.

So I waited. And waited. And worried. Would I get to keep traveling forward or be sent back? If I went back to Nairobi, how long would it take to finally get to Kathmandu? Was my backpack on its way to Nepal without me? What if I never saw it again? If I was sent back, how would I contact my friend Kathi who was already in Nepal? How long would I be stuck here? To keep me from getting overwhelmed by the swirling eddy of anxiety, I triaged the situation.

Was I in any pain? No.

Was my life being threatened? No.

Did I have access to a bathroom? Yes, but it scared me. I could smell it before I saw it. At first I saw only a low privacy wall in front of a bunch of floor drains with faucets nearby. That took care of the men. I waited to see what a woman would do. When one arrived, she walked past the privacy wall and down a small hallway that led to two unmarked doors. When she disappeared through one, I eased open the other door. The tiled room contained a sink and a Western toilet. There was a faucet on the wall, a small bucket, a drain in the floor and water splashed everywhere. Had the previous woman taken a bird bath?

After using the bathroom, I paced the length of the holding area. The bar was closed. That was a good thing because this was no time to become a sloppy, giggly mess. The pay phones only accepted rupees. This was good, too. My call would have freaked out people who could do nothing to help. The duty-free shop was open, so I bought a bottle of water and a bag of 38 fun-size Snickers bars.

I searched but found no comfort in the Tibetan saying, "If the problem can be solved, there's no use worrying about it. If the problem can't be solved, there's no use worrying about it."

On the bright side, my surroundings offered a few short-lived amusements. Two men wearing white plastic gloves headed toward the bathrooms with a cart filled with chemical-smelling, sparkly white marbles. An old man arrived to sell hot tea from a large silver urn. Everyone drank from the same five china cups that he hand wiped after each use. There was an eerie fluttering noise at one end of the holding area, like roaches in tap shoes running across linoleum. I finally figured out that the sound came from the little placards on the flight departure board, spinning and clicking into place. A security sign stated that, among other things, catapults were not allowed on any flight.

THANKFULLY, SOMEONE ARRANGED for food to be brought to me at 7 a.m. Breakfast was a delicious sandwich of hard boiled egg, chicken salad, tomato, cucumber and cheese on toast with the crusts cut off. Then bad news arrived. Northwest Airlines, issuer of my round-the-world ticket, would not honor a ticket transfer to any of the available carriers with direct flights to Nepal.

A security guard escorted me to another holding area. As we walked down the long hallway, every passing airport employee stopped to talk to the guard and look me over. I did not need to speak their language to understand that they were asking, "What did she do?"

Not long after, a Kenya Airways stewardess in a crisp blue uniform and red scarf sat down next to me.

"The Indian authorities will allow you to buy an Air India plane ticket direct to Kathmandu that does not require a visa," she said. Sounded simple. Wrong.

"The ticket office does not open for another hour, so there is no way to tell if the next flight has any seats available," she continued. "You are not allowed to leave this area, but I can try to buy a ticket for you if you give me your credit card and passport."

Faced with the possibility of going back to Nairobi, I handed her my two most valuable possessions. She walked away, past the armed security guard, out of my reach and out of view. I sat down in a chair, fighting the need to panic over my desperate act of trust. I wanted someone to tell me that what I had just done was not incredibly stupid, but I was alone. I zipped and unzipped my jacket and watched the clock.

An hour and the last five Snickers bars later, the stewardess returned. She handed me my credit card, a charge slip to sign and my passport. Heavy sigh of relief. The flight was at 5 p.m. A security guard took me back to the first holding area. I settled into a lounge chair using my green North Face jacket as a blanket and felt like a weed among summer flowers.

BY THE TIME I GAVE TRYING to sleep and took up reading, an Indian man in a long-sleeve dress shirt and slacks came over to talk with me. He had noticed me coming and going, and shared, in clipped British English, that he was on his way to London after resolving a visa problem.

When meeting fellow travelers, there were common questions most people ask. Where are you from? Where are you going? How did you end up here? Got any travel tips? General questions. This man's questions soon became strange, too specific, like what was my flight number out of Nairobi. I asked him to leave me alone.

"I'm not comfortable talking with you any more. Please go sit somewhere else."

He gave me a pouty, confused look.

"I prefer to be alone now." I had to flick a look at the nearby guard before the man would go away.

I like the idea that when I die, I will have a long sit-down chat with God and get answers to all my questions. For example, those apple cores that I threw out of car windows when I was a child—did any of them become trees? Few boys or men had ever asked me out. I told myself that it was because I was almost 6-feet tall. Was that true or was there something humbling I needed to know? I would add this moment to my list of questions. Was I paranoid or was this man up to something devious?

Scribbling in my journal, I noted the ironies that fluttered around me. I was traveling around the world, but could not leave the airport. I had left my culture to explore others, only to find that this vantage point compelled me to examine my life in America. My body was the same, but I liked it better now because I was not constantly judging it based on the curveless twigs that American media hyped as the pinnacle of the female shape. In fact, two East African men strongly suggested that I gain weight.

AFTER I FINISHED A BOX LUNCH of chicken biryani sent by my benevolent captors, the ticket-buying stewardess and an armed guard escorted me to a departure terminal. It was like Disneyland compared to the two transit holding areas. There was a full-service restaurant, newsstands and even a jewelry store with a blinding amount of gold. Was it proper etiquette to bring your wife or girlfriend or lover jewelry when you came home from a trip?

The stewardess introduced me to the staff at the counter where my ticket had been purchased. Then she escorted me outside into the melting heat to the baggage handling area where I identified my backpack that had miraculously not gone on without me.

Starting to feel like a pinball, I was escorted back to the departure terminal again. I found my own way to the boarding area, only to be rejected by the attendant. He would not accept my ticket because there was no visa in my passport, so back to the ticket counter I went. The counter agents did not understand the problem. They called the stewardess back, who escorted me all the way to the door of the plane.

As I finally settled into my seat, I had to admit that the worst part of this experience was me—my discomfort at being out of control and my fear of the unknown. My mind hyped up far more drama than the situation deserved. If I separated these two weaknesses of mine from the real challenges, I would handle upsets better—now and for the rest of my life.

Yak cheese pizza and humble pie

Trekking in Nepal

BECAUSE I DID NOT HAVE MORE THAN "200 sticks of cigarette … 12 rolls of movie camera film … one set of fountain pen, one perambulator…," I was issued a visa at the Tribhuvan International Airport in Kathmandu and allowed to enter Nepal.

I walked out to the open-air arrival area, defined by steel pipe railings and scrutinized by security men with batons dangling by their sides. Airport workers passed by, pushing pallets of cardboard boxes with air holes on all sides. The distressed, staccato chorus of hundreds of chicks filled the air.

I had hoped my introduction to Nepal would include crisp spring air and bucolic landscapes framed by snow-capped mountains. What I got was bathwater-warm stillness and a dark starless sky. With a sigh, I sat with my backpack against a wall and waited. Kathi had arranged for trek organizer Raj to give me a ride from the airport to the Thamel neighborhood of Kathmandu. She would join me the next morning.

Raj found me about an hour after I arrived.

"We have been waiting for you in the parking lot," he said, obviously irritated. He gave my rumpled chambray shirt and khaki pants a dismissive look. He was dressed in a navy blazer and pressed jeans. He was handsome, and he knew it. I needed the ride, so I held my tongue from asking, "Why would you think I would recognize you or the car?"

Raj led the way through the crowded parking lot to a spotless Toyota Corolla. He sat next to his driver in the front seat. I sat in the back seat, wondering how Kathi wrangled him into doing this menial task.

We bumped along an unlined paved road, with no allegiance to the left or right side. The closer we got to downtown, the more frequent the police checks became. Each time, we showed our passports and explained who we were, where we came from and where we were going.

"Everything is fine," Raj nonchalantly said.

I wondered what it would take for him to say it was time to worry.

Thamel was Kathmandu's most popular tourist area. Its narrow streets were intimate and festive with tiny shops, daffodil yellow signs and strings of sparkly white lights. We inched around pedal carts, bicycle riders and pedestrians. The few white people, most wearing North Face or Patagonia jackets, towered over the dark-skinned locals. Nepali people, unlike their mountains, did not excel in height.

I checked into the Kathmandu Guest House where Kathi had made a reservation for me. Originally a 13-room private home, it had become a sprawling 115-room hotel compound with enough amenities to make it a city in itself—a restaurant, a communications center, an ATM, a travel agency, a barber shop, a beauty parlor, and shops that sold trekking provisions and mountain bike supplies.

It was too early to go to bed, so after a delightfully hot shower using the complimentary bar of greenish-black Niva Ayurvedic Herbal Amala soap, I went to the communications center to use a computer.

"The police are shutting the city down due to a Maoist incident," two new arrivals said. They had no other details.

In 1996, Maoists, who followed the doctrines of Chinese revolutionary Mao Zedong, surfaced in Nepal. Their leaders said they were fighting on behalf of the rural poor, who were trapped in a feudal system that only served the urban elite. The government called them terrorists. Our plan to visit Nepal instead of Lebanon to avoid political unrest had failed. I had to wait for Kathi to arrive the next day to learn if our plans had changed.

If I had an *I Dream of Jeannie* blink or Dorothy's red slippers, I would have gone home for a few days, recharge my mental batteries. I was excited about seeing Kathi and the country, but I wanted a break from constantly being alert in a new environment. Lacking a home, the talent and the footwear, I escaped into sleep in a twin bed.

MY MORNING STARTED WITH A HARSH REMINDER about traveling and tummies. I gripped the toilet seat, astonished by the sense of jet propulsion as the Mumbai airport food made a hasty exodus.

As a new sense of bodily lightness set in, I heard a familiar voice in the courtyard below my open window. Kathi had arrived. Seven years ago, I was the first employee at her gift basket company. It was my second job, working part-time during the holiday seasons to help pay bills and save money. As holiday seasons passed, other women joined the staff, and the work hours were flush with romantic gossip and late-night dashes in an old van over to the UPS office to ship boxes. Every January, we gathered like family at a restaurant to celebrate another successful year.

"Hey!" Kathi said as I opened the door. She swooped in for a warm hug. "You look great!"

"So do you! How was your trek?"

A strong-willed, powerhouse of a woman, Kathi had just completed a three-day trek around Mount Everest in two days. Nepal, home to eight of the 10 tallest mountains in the world, was her mecca.

"It was amazing. The trails were really challenging. You should see some of the bridges. I swear they're just made of sticks and twine," she said as she sat down on the bed with the bag she had brought. "So, I made arrangements for us to do the Annapurna Sanctuary Trek as far as the Annapurna Base Camp. It's called ABC for short."

"Cool."

"So we have a flight to Pokhara in an hour—that's where the trail starts."

My innards twisted painfully. The last thing I wanted to do was share my distress with fellow passengers.

"I brought you a present," Kathi as she presented me with a five-pound bag of shelled pecans. "They'll be a great snack while trekking."

"You so know me!" I adored pecans.

Neither of us mentioned yesterday's Maoist incident. Maybe she did not know about it. Maybe I wanted to forget about it.

I sorted out my belongings and took what I would leave behind to Kathmandu Guest House's stone-lined basement storage room. Guests had crammed it with an amazing collection of adventure gear—a veritable REI warehouse. We also retrieved the box Kathi had left there for me. I had packed packets of sugar-free cherry Kool-Aid, Cracklin' Oat Bran cereal, a black Patagonia fleece pullover, a baggie full of the pleasingly familiar-smelling Tide laundry detergent, rolls of film and an extra Nalgene water bottle.

The overcast morning blocked all views of the mountains as we took a taxi to Kathmandu's domestic airport. Previously its main airport, the facility was little more than a dingy concrete building with a dirt parking lot. Our luggage was not scanned or searched but weighed with great accuracy before being taken away. We were herded through a narrow curtained passageway—women to the left and men to the right—to be frisked by a security guard before entering the one cavernous waiting room that served all flights.

One wall of windows faced the landing field. Two walls were covered by giant Nepalese travel posters. Along the back wall, vendors sold Coca-

Cola, tubes of Pringles potato chips and local newspapers like *The Himalayan Times* in English and *Gorkhapatra* in Nepali.

My stomach churned so violently that I had no choice but to use the phone booth-sized bathroom. It was, by far, the foulest place I had ever known.Places where people touched the walls were black with skin oil. Holding my breath, I stepped inside. With Cirque de Soleil precision, I lowered my pants without letting them touch the ground, contorted over the trench-shaped toilet without touching the walls, and relieved my agony. Good thing I always traveled with toilet paper. None was provided. I used every square I had.

Yet another security guard frisked us before we exited the waiting room and walked across the tarmac to the Buddha Air plane. All 14 passengers, a full planeload, had to claim their luggage before the crew would load it into the cargo hold.

During the flight, the stewardess handed out hard mints, but they did nothing to soothe my stomach during the bumpy flight. It felt like we were bouncing on a trampoline. I was zombie green by the time we landed, but grateful not to have embarrassed myself.

BASED ON A FRIEND'S RECOMMENDATION, Kathi hired a man named Ram to be our guide during our trek. His daily fee included the services of a porter, lodging at guest houses each night and all of our meals except for sodas.

Ram met us when our plane landed at the Pokhara Airport. He was a swarthy man with a strong jaw line, a British accent, excruciatingly polite manners and a Barney purple T-shirt that advertised the company where he got free email for wearing the shirt. I grinned when he led us over to a 1978 black Toyota Corolla taxi. My introduction to teenage heavy petting happened in a similar vehicle, minus the colorful magazine pictures of flowers shellacked all over its interior walls.

Pokhara was the starting point for many treks and home to hippies for decades, so the small town seemed to have no shortage of hotels, restaurants and bars. The main road was wide and paved and edged with concrete sidewalks. The drab buildings were predominantly two-story concrete or brick boxes with yellow and red signs. Electric cables wove a complex web above it all.

Our first stop was the Fishtail Trekking Shop, owned by Ram's uncle. No bigger than a one-car garage, it was a pack-rat nest of clothes and equipment for sale or rent.

"I've got everything I need, but Kristine needs a sleeping bag," Kathi said.

Ram repacked our belongings into two large backpacks that he and Amrit, Ram's cousin and our porter, would carry. The fact that my few belongings were now divvyed up between the Kathmandu Guest House store room, the Fishtail Trekking Shop, and Amrit's back made me feel vulnerable. We would only carry our daypacks. I never saw Ram or Amrit pack anything for themselves. They must have kept stashes at the guest houses.

To give us a head start, Kathi and Ram decided we would take a taxi to the small village of Dhampus. From there, we would walk for the next six days. The scenic paved road turned to dirt as it zigzagged up the foothills, weaving through leafy woods and terraced fields, slowly rising above a river that was milky white with glacier runoff. About half way to Dhampus, in the middle of a hardwood forest, a mud pit spanned the width of the road. Visions of East Africa came to mind, though this situation was far more dangerous. A swerve in the wrong direction here could send the car careening down to the valley floor below.

The pit had snagged a little white Toyota, the only other car we saw on the road once we left Pokhara. Six women and children stood off to the side as the driver struggled to free the car. In spite of our advice and pushing, it remained stuck.

As for our taxi, Kathi, Amrit, Ram and I watched as our brazen driver revved the engine and raced his car across the pit. Deformed clumps of mud flew into the air. The rear of the car shimmied. The driver kept a firm grip on the steering wheel. We cheered as the car lurched onto hard dirt on the far side.

We piled back into the car, but the success was short lived. There was another long stretch of mud a few hundred yards down the road.

"I cannot go any further," the taxi driver declared.

We thanked him for his services, donned our packs and started walking. When we left the forest, the dirt road turned to terracotta orange clay and a mountain range came into view. I stopped in my tracks. My jaw dropped. I instantly felt small, insignificant, humble. The grandeur was stunning. Surely these must be the most impressive mountains in the world.

"Aren't they great?" Kathi said blissfully. "Annapurna I is the tallest at 8,091 meters. That's 26,545 feet. ABC is where people start out if they are going to summit Annapurna I."

I nodded as I started walking again, but still gazed at the mountains.

Slowly my attention shifted to the randomly spaced houses nearby. All were built with stacked yellow stones, topped with tin roofs and painted the same terracotta orange as the dirt road. The windows had no screens. Smooth columns made from tree trunks held up the front porch roofs.

It was so serene to be ambling along. The sun was out. My stomach had settled. There were no walls topped with broken bottles and barbed wire. No rifle-toting guards. No dangerous animals or insects (that I knew of). No one was trying to sell me something or take what was mine. I had not realized how drained I had gotten by the stresses in East Africa.

I was startled when Ram led us up the steps of one of the homes. It turned out to be his house, where his mother, his wife and his four children lived. It had been passed down through several generations to him. He only lived there during planting and harvesting season. Otherwise, he was guiding treks or sharing a tiny apartment with Amrit in Pokhara while drumming up business.

The front door opened into an entry room with a bare light bulb, a handmade wooden bench and rough-hewn plank staircase. The kitchen—no more than a wood-burning cook pit, pots, wooden utensils and two wooden benches—was off to the right. The plaster walls and timbered ceilings of both rooms were black with creosote. There was no chimney. Smoke wafted out of the house through the gaps at the tops of the walls. Ram said there were sleeping rooms upstairs.

"I had electrical service installed two years ago," he said proudly. I saw lights in the house but no electrical appliances of any kind.

Ram's tiny mother only smiled and cooked *dal bhat* for our lunch. A staple of the Nepali diet, the thick stew was made from lentils (*dal*) and spices, and served with steamed rice (*bhat*). We ate the delicious meal facing the mountains, our legs dangling off the edge of the front porch. It became my No. 1 place in the world to have lunch.

"Ram, what are those for?" I pointed to the strings of eggshells swinging from the porch rafters.

"They bring good luck. They help our chickens lay more eggs."

"I wonder if they will make us more fertile?" I whispered to Kathi. Neither of us wanted to have children. We giggled and moved away from the eggshells.

A water buffalo, used to plow fields and haul wood, was tethered up in a shed next to the house. It stretched its thick hind leg over the top of its head to scratch an itch as if it were a giant cloven-hoofed cat. We laughed at its gurgling, long-winded farts.

Before we left, Ram's children gave us each a bougainvillea lei, a bright magenta send-off to the adventures that lay ahead. We spent the rest of the afternoon walking at a moderate pace up gently slopping land. Kathi and I caught up with the details of each other's lives while Ram and Amrit listened with great interest.

THE SUN WAS SETTING when the dirt road gave way to a flagstone walkway. We had reached the tiny village of Dhampus. Groupings of low stone buildings perched on the mountain ridge. Narrow terraces staggered down from them to the summer-colored valley floor below.

"Ram, what happened to this tree?" The stunted tree had a strangely wide trunk, chubby branches and oddly spaced clumps of leaves.

"The villagers take its branches to feed water buffalo and to burn for firewood."

The tree reminded me of all the jobs I had ever had, how each had made demands that shaped me. Sometimes the change was subtle, like slowly making me tolerant of sitting behind a desk for 40-plus hours a week. Sometimes the change was harsh to the point of damaging my sense of self-worth. A few years after I graduated from college, I worked for a Chicago-based magazine with a staff of five employees.

Bill, the unhappy editor, was getting progressively more unprofessional, like illustrating an article with hand-drawn lopsided smiley faces on lined notebook paper.Short-sighted, naïve editorial assistant that I was, I brought this to the publisher's attention. The publisher talked with Bill, but he needed Bill to publish the magazine, so Bill was able to force the publisher to fire me.

At the time, I believed that good people were not fired, so shoving me into the unemployment line meant I was not a good person. It took me years to understand that I was a good person who would never be good at grasping the subtleties of office politics.

We stopped at Hotel Mountain View Restaurant (it was also a guest house) for the night. It had the same construction as Ram's house, but the front of the building was painted flamingo pink with black lettering that read "May Have Your Good Day!" A petite couple with black button eyes and shy smiles bowed to us in greeting.

Kathi and I shared one of the petite upstairs rooms. A bare light bulb illuminated the plastered walls and low rattan ceiling. There were two single beds of familiar construction—a fabric-wrapped, high-density foam pad on top of a wooden frame. The room was standard issue for all of the guest houses that we would stay in while trekking.

As bearers of good luck, swallows flew in and out of the guest house's unscreened windows and doors at will. They raised their young in the nests they built among the rafters. Cardboard egg cartons on the floor under the nests caught bird droppings.

The shower was a concrete outhouse downhill from the guest house. It had a couple of hooks on the interior wall for clothes, a small hole in the heavy wooden door for light, and a hole in the sloped floor so that water drained out to the cornfield below. When it was my turn to wash up, I received two metal bowls of water—one hot, one cold. With a bit of mixing, I made enough warm water for an efficient wash and rinse. It embarrassed me to think about how much water I had used in my life taking long hot showers and soaking in bath tubs.

The bathroom was a smaller outhouse downhill from the shower house. It contained a squat toilet and a tin box to hold used toilet paper that was later burned. We used the provided saucepan to ladle water from a bucket into the toilet to flush our waste downhill.

Curious children pranced about, listening to our foreign words. I told them my name. They giggled and repeated it over and over. When I told them Kathi's name, they rushed to the shower door and screamed it until she came out to greet them.

As sunlight gave way to starry skies and fall-like weather, even though it was June, I showed Ram and Amrit my photographs from home. They liked the men who wore *boke dari* [male goat beards], their name for goatees. Neither of them could grow such whiskers.

Because Dhampus had road access, Hotel Mountain View Restaurant offered what I would later call a substantial menu of vegetarian food. I selected cabbage soup, French fries and Tibetan fried bread—like a crispy pita bread—with homemade strawberry jam. Cooked over an open fire, all the food had a delicious smoky taste, though I was surprised that the owners had not converted to kerosene stoves to reduce smoke pollution and the demand for firewood.

Before bed, we poured boiled water—tomorrow's drinking water—into our Nalgene bottles to cool.

"Up ahead, bottled water is banned to reduce the amount of trash trekkers leave behind," Kathi noted. "That's why the guest houses sell boiled water, so they can still make money."

As the guest house keepers recommended, Kathi and I closed the blue wooden shutters on the windows before we settled into our sleeping bags. I swear I heard something fly into one of the shutters during the night. A swallow? A bat? A wandering spirit? There seemed to be a religious altar everywhere we turned.

AFTER EATING MORE TIBETAN BREAD and jam, Kathi initiated me into her water-drinking habits before we started the day's trekking.

"When you wake up, drink a liter of water," she said.

I gave her a skeptical look as she continued.

"Then you drink another three, four, maybe five during the day."

"I'm going to be squatting behind walls every hour!" I protested.

"Trust me. You'll sweat it out," she said.

We hit the trail and quickly got down to business. Kathi and Ram took the lead. I came in third with Amrit taking up the rear. Within minutes we were soaked with sweat. Trekking was like using a stair stepping machine for hours. The trail, sometimes packed dirt, sometimes paved with stepping stones, went in and out of valleys, across rivers, and around or over mountain ridges. Corn, potatoes, beans, garlic, mustard and onions grew on the surrounding terraces.

Soon enough we declared me Queen of Down Hills and Kathi Queen of Up Hills. Kathi was also Queen of Gravity Wells because if someone was going to fall down, it was her. For the most part we had to keep our eyes on the trail to avoid twisted roots, loose rocks and water buffalo piles shaped like round loaves of dark rye bread. We also kept a wary eye out for leeches on the person in front of us.

Nowhere on my round-the-world itinerary did I say that I wanted to experience these blood-sucking critters. When Kathi and I discussed going to Nepal, leeches were not part of the conversation. Yet, here they were, looking like red earthworms. One end stuck to the ground or a branch while the other end waved around until it touched the next meal, be it human or animal. We had seen water buffalo with dark trickles of blood running down their ears and legs where leeches had been.

If I had read a guidebook, I would have known that leeches thrived in Nepal at elevations between 4,950 to 11,550 feet during the rainy season. How delightful that we arrived when they were most plentiful.

To give us a defensive edge against the leeches, Ram built a "power wand." He placed a wad of ammoniated tobacco and salt in a patch of fabric, moistened it with water, and tied it to the end of a bamboo stick. When he touched the wand against leeches, they shriveled up and dropped to the ground. He smashed them with his shoe.

"Leech game over," he proclaimed. He was not Buddhist.

THE BUTTERFLY GUEST HOUSE was a stone motel strip with an impressive collection of battered paint cans overflowing with petunias and nasturtiums. We waited at a rickety picnic table as the cook made our dal bhat lunch from scratch. I took my hiking boots and socks off to dry in the sun. Trickles of blood oozed from the leech bites on my ankles. Sneaky buggers.

Uphill from the guest house was a U-shaped, one-story school with a tin roof and white plaster walls. Young children, wearing white shirts and blue skirts or pants, ran around the playground. When we met children along our trek, we repeated the mantra Ram taught us. "No sweets, no pens, only *namaste* [a customary greeting like hello]." Just like in East Africa, the goal was to stop teaching children to beg.

Squiggly red graffiti marred one of the school's exterior walls.

"What does it mean?" I asked.

Ram hesitated and then finally said, "The Maoists wrote it. It means 'We are No. 1.'"

"Will the school repaint the wall?"

"No," he said. "It might cause trouble."

An elderly man sat by the trail collecting donations for the school in a glass-sided box. We donated generously after Ram confirmed that he was legitimate.

AS THE SUN SAILED ACROSS THE SKY, it was apparent that yesterday was a fun walk. Today was serious business. I struggled to find a balance between keeping up with Kathi and Ram and taking pictures and appreciating my surroundings, like the rusty red hen and her clutch of puffy chicks, the young girls watching a mother goat and her leggy newborn, and the butterflies resting in a thicket of marijuana plants.

Before we passed through a foggy section of forest, Ram's body language changed. He kept our foursome close together and armed himself with a hefty stick and a big rock.

"Ram, what's up?" we asked.

"A couple was mugged here a few days ago, but do not worry. They did not have a guide and porter with them," he explained.

"Were they Maoist rebels or general bad guys?"

"We do not know," he said.

We took a break at Nice View Lodge even though fog blocked its nice view. We shared the terrace with a local woman and her bare-footed, pigtailed daughter. She wore a tattered blue gingham dress with a lace ruffle at the hemline and yellow- and gray-striped leggings. While Kathi sat on a stone wall and read her guidebook, the little girl peered intently at the upside down book as if she, too, found it more fascinating than her surroundings.

My body creaked when we got back on the trail. I had moved past the excitement and enthusiasm for the adventure, past the momentum of pride-fueled endurance and was fast approaching the wall of defeat. My body was giving out. And it did not help that the steps on the trail were built for people with size four feet. My hip and knee joints were turning to jelly.

I went from walking with purpose to just throwing each foot forward with the hope that it found a sure landing. Kathi and Amrit kept a measured pace as if they were mountain goats. They got farther and farther ahead of Ram and me.

"We are almost there," Ram said when he noticed my distress. He pointed toward our destination, the Hotel Evergreen Guest House in the village of Jhinnu. I fought the urge to fall down and cry. Not only was the guest house on the other side of the valley, but it was also the highest building on top of the ridge.

I stopped walking, closed my eyes, just stood there sweating, praying that I would sprout wings, that the land would become flat, that my legs would surge with superhuman strength.

When no miracles arrived, I sighed and said, "I will do this."

Ram happily waved me forward and said, "Yes. You will make it."

Followed by my personal cheerleader, I labored upward. A few steps up, rest. A few steps up, rest. I did not look up. My mind was willing, but my body was a dying battery. This was unquestionably the most physically demanding day of my life. My pride and body took a harsh beating.

"You can have anything you want for dinner," I told myself. "As much as you want."

When I finally saw it up close, Hotel Evergreen Guest House had obviously been built to house trekkers. Two-stories tall, one wing of the L-shaped building had guest rooms that opened onto a narrow railed porch. The other wing was dedicated to the kitchen, dining room and staff quarters. I dropped into the nearest white plastic chair on the terrace. Ram brought me a bottle of Fanta Orange soda. I downed it. He brought me a another one. As I finished it off, I gave the door of our second-floor room the evil eye. My sad state did not bode well for the next five days.

The only other trekker at the guest house was a lanky British man named Anthony. He had just come down from ABC.

"It rained the whole bloody time I was up there. Everything I have is wet," he complained, but then broke into a smile. "But for just a few seconds at sunrise, I got to see the top of Annapurna I."

Kathi beamed as if he had just told a heroic story, but I wanted details.

"How was the trail from here?" I asked.

"Steeper, muddier, colder, wetter," he said.

I turned to Kathi.

"I reserve the right to bail on this," I said. "I can take or leave reaching ABC, and I don't know if I can keep up this pace." I wanted to be engaged with my surroundings, not plowing through them.

"You'll do better tomorrow," she said as she patted my leg. "We covered extra ground today because we were supposed to trek past Dhampus yesterday. Tomorrow, the trail will be steeper, but the distance will be shorter."

I would have been more motivated if she had said there was a Dairy Queen up ahead.

My inertia came to an end when I needed to pee. The first-floor communal bathroom was a large white tiled room that contained a seatless Western toilet, a sink and a shower head but no shower walls or curtains. My quivering legs refused to let me squat, so I sat on the cold toilet bowl rim. Quarter-size welts swelled around the leech bites on my ankles.

Even though the cotton T-shirts and shorts we wore while trekking were wet with sweat, a cautious sniff revealed that they did not stink of body odor. Perhaps our copious amounts of sweat washed away the bacteria that caused the smell. We decided to wear the same clothes every day while trekking and wear our few clean clothes at night after washing up.

"If you lay your trekking clothes under your sleeping bag, your body heat will dry them out by morning," Kathi said. How resourceful.

For dinner, I rewarded my endurance with gluttony, ordering my first yak cheese pizza. The crispy crust was covered with gooey cheese that tasted like mozzarella. As we ate, Kathi, Anthony and I marveled at the amount of human and donkey labor it took to build and maintain the guest houses, to stock the kitchens, and to haul kerosene for the water heaters. When the guest houses were full, the demands would be tremendous.

When my calzone-sized apple turnover arrived, Anthony told us about his experience arranging a trek through a taxi driver.

"He promised me there would be other trekkers in the group, that there would be a knowledgeable guide who spoke English, porters to carry my gear and a luxury bus to take me from Kathmandu to Pokhara," he said. "Lies. All lies."

We did not ask why Anthony made such a poor decision. It was common knowledge that a vast majority of taxi drivers would say anything a prospective paying customer wanted to hear. They had no accountability. I privately gloated that Ram was a licensed professional who was doing an awesome job.

After our meal, we three sat on the terrace and looked out over the valley. When the stars appeared, flying ants swarmed out from under the guest house. Like a magical tornado, thousands of wings shimmered in the beam of a floodlight before disappearing into the night.

TYLENOL PM TO THE RESCUE. I took it before bed and felt surprisingly flexible in the morning. I was ready to give the day my best shot. Good thing, too, because the first 90 minutes of trekking were straight up as a gentle rain came down. Each of us hunkered into our own strides and thoughts. Even though I was taking each step at a slow pace, if I broke the measured rhythm, sped up even the tiniest bit, I started to lose my breath.

When the trail passed through Chomrung, it became a flagstone superhighway, wide enough to support two car lanes though it only served foot and hoof traffic. It reflected the town's strategic location where several main trails intersected. With the grace of a Southern plantation staircase, the impressive trail rippled around white-washed guest houses and small businesses perched at sharp angles on the mountain ridge. Sadly, it was a short-lived glory. It changed back into a dirt footpath as it sloped downhill along a swift creek and water buffalo paddocks until it reached a river.

The river's milky waters boiled around white boulders and under a modern metal suspension walking bridge, complete with wire railings and pyramids of stone anchoring each end. Kathi and I were startled to see it. The bridges we had crossed so far looked like primitive combinations of wooden slats, logs and flat stones. Only a meager amount of rope and gravity seemed to hold them together. Each crossing was like a game of chicken.

Ram and Amrit stopped to perform a small ritual. After they placed a sprig of greenery on a bridge anchor, they touched their fingertips to their foreheads and then their hearts.

"We are asking for forgiveness for walking over the dead," Ram explained. "We spread the cremated remains of our people into this sacred river so that they will flow out to the ocean and join our ancestors."

The sun blazed during the rest of our morning trek. Kathi and Ram took the lead, with me about a quarter mile behind and Amrit patiently taking up the rear. During one scorching piece of trail, however, Kathi and I walked together, torturing ourselves with talk of food. Watermelon. Frozen margaritas. Dairy Queen Heath Bar Crunch Blizzards with extra fudge sauce.

SINUWA LODGE HAD A GRAND NAME, BUT it was nothing more than a quaint guest house where we stopped for a *dal bhat* lunch. An old man sat at the edge of the terrace, using his hands and feet to break bamboo poles into long narrow strips that he would eventually weave into a durable carrying basket to haul goods through the mountains.

Like most guest houses, Sinuwa Lodge sold sundries from a box made of scrap wood and chicken wire. Goods included bottled sodas, canned fruit juice, Snickers bars, cookies, ketchup, instant oatmeal, San Miguel beer, toilet paper and spaghetti noodles. I bought some Wow's Milk Magic and Lacto Fun candies. Ram said Europeans bought most of the Marlboro cigarettes. Smoking trekkers seemed like an oxymoronic combination.

With full bellies, we hit the trail again as the landscape grew more lush. The terraced fields gave way to ferns, moss-covered rocks and glossy rhododendron trees. Warm rains swept by like low-flying birds.

"Hey, stop there. I'll take your picture," I yelled to Kathi, who was on the far side of a bend in the trail ahead of me. She scowled. I should have known that she was all business when I learned that she brought only one point-and-shoot camera for her whole Nepal visit. I could go through more than a roll of film in less than a day.

More hours of trekking. In some places, the trail was covered with dicey slivers of shale that kept sliding out from under my boots. This was definitely a "fend for yourself" kind of adventure. No guard rails. No warning signs. No public safety measures.

Just when I started to gain a little confidence in my trekking abilities, an old Nepalese man wearing flip-flops raced by me on the trail. A fully loaded basket hung against his back from a strap wrapped around his forehead. He was followed by a boy, maybe 12 years old, carrying a case of ceramic tiles. I carried only a bottle of water, pecans and toilet paper.

"YOU WANT TO LEAVE ALREADY?" I asked Kathi when I arrived at a rest stop. Always in the lead, she had been there long enough to drink water, eat a snack, check for leeches and put her daypack back on.

"No, I'm fine."

"So why'd you put your pack back on?" I asked dropping mine to the ground.

She only shrugged. Her focus was aimed at ABC, and it was clear that I was just along for the ride. This was not about us sharing an experience together. I found this disappointing but, having been her friend for many years, not unexpected. One of Kathi's most enviable, success-producing traits was her dogged ability to pursue her goals.

CLOUDS FILLED THE SKY as we approached our stop for the night, Dovan Guest House. My body had performed well, though I was not sure if I wanted to continue on to ABC at this militant pace. There was no time to stop, explore and enjoy. I focused every ounce of my attention on the trail. A bad step could lead to harm. If I was seriously hurt, the only way to get medical care was to walk or be carried out. The nearest telephone was back in Chomrung. No one heard me laugh at the thought of Nepalese men trying to carry me back downhill.

Dinner was another delightful yak cheese pizza, plus a *rosti*—a patty made of mashed potato, onion, garlic, spinach, fried egg, cheese, tomato, curry powder and soybean sauce.

Ram had grown more comfortable with us, so our conversations had become more personal.

"When I was 12, my arm went limp," he recalled. "I could not move it at all. My mother got a bowl of uncooked rice and raised it over my head so spirits could rise into it."

I fought back a smile. What was normal to him sounded absurd to me.

"She took the rice to the local medicine man so he could tell what bad spirit was in my arm. In a week, he forced it out with prayer. I was cured," he said as he raised his right arm and wiggled his fingers.

Western medicine did not hold all the answers, but it was hard for me to embrace many of the spiritual nuances of Eastern medicine.

For dessert, the cook wrapped a crepe around a Snickers bar and deep-fried it until the outside was crisp and the inside was a hot, gooey mess. At 8,550 feet, he served a taste of heaven.

Just as I finished off a second Snickers dessert, a bearded, stocky man walked into the dining area.

"Hello, I'm Philip, from that guest house over there," he said. "Thought I'd come have a chat."

"Hello," said Kathi, pulling out a chair for him. "Where are you from?"

"New Zealand."

After we swapped pleasantries, he shared the latest trail news.

"There's a group of young trekkers from Israel at ABC causing problems—getting drunk, smoking dope, keeping everyone awake at night."

We shook our heads at their disrespectful behavior.

"And they keep haggling with guest house managers over the cost of their rooms."

Another mark of shame. It was general knowledge that all guest houses charged the same price, no exceptions, so that all could earn reasonable incomes.

"Did you hear about the guide who fell to his death?"

We waited for Philip to provide details.

"He was climbing with a Brit, but they called it off due to bad weather. The guide belayed the man down a sheer cliff, but didn't use ropes for his own descent. He fell and died. A helicopter has retrieved the body. The authorities are still holding the Brit while they conduct an investigation."

Kathi and I were stunned. Ram and Amrit seemed sad, but not surprised.

DUE TO THE COLD MORNING RAIN, KATHI put on a pair of black nylon gaiters and a clear plastic poncho that draped over her body and her daypack. I had gear envy, but my North Face jacket and hood would have to do.

The challenging trail was even more arduous due to mud puddles and slick paving stones, yet the brutal pace continued. As the trail curled around bends and dipped into valleys, my thoughts ambled along as well. What was the best way to use the squat toilets? I had been having trouble with splash back, so I tried facing the wall when squatting and had better results. Had I been using the toilets backwards all along? (Kathi later confessed she had similar issues.) And leeches? What if we dried our socks after rinsing them in salty water? Would that keep them away or just irritate our skin? And what other candy bars would be good deep-fried inside a crepe?

In a dense forest we stopped at a stone Hindu shrine built on an outside bend of the trail.

"It honors the god of water," said Ram. To show respect, we placed fern fronds on its tabletop, said *namaste* and rang a bell to announce that a prayer was being sent. It had been a busy day for the god. It had rained so much since breakfast that run off had formed seven narrow waterfalls on the slope across the narrow valley. The view was dramatic until it was blocked by fog.

Yet another hour of trekking in the rain before we reached the Himalaya Guest House where I made a hard decision. I could force my body to finish the trek to ABC, but what was the point? My interest in reaching ABC was dissolving. ABC was not the same gold medal of accomplishment for me as it was for Kathi.

I sat on a wet bench next to her, wiping rain from my face.

"I'm done," I said.

"What do you mean?" she asked, dumbfounded.

"I don't want to go any further."

"You can't be serious!"

"I'm done. I've had enough."

"But we can't quit now. We're so close!"

"I'm not saying you can't go on without me. You take Ram and go on. I'll take Amrit and go back down."

"But I have this dream of us getting there together, seeing the peak together."

"It will be okay."

Kathi pouted.

"We'll meet up at the Bamboo tomorrow afternoon. It's all good. You go on with Ram."

Kathi left with Ram, and, with each step I took downhill toward a grouping of guest houses called Bamboo, the more I knew I had made the right decision. The sun came out. In spite of his limited English, Amrit bloomed into a curious chatterbox. We dinked along at a leisurely pace, noting strawberries, fiddler heads on ferns, different textures of moss and massive rhododendron trees.

With Amrit's encouragement, I started teaching him English words for things around us, like pebble, stone, rock, boulder, fence, hedge and wall. The tricky part came when I had to explain how these words were different from each other. We also worked on his pronunciation. He struggled with "p" and "sh" sounds. He also wanted to learn polite ways to say things a porter would say. For example, if he wanted to make sure he was the last in a group on a trail, he learned he could say, "After you, please."

On a steep river bank, Amrit and I lay like marmots on a warm boulder, soggy footwear and smashed leeches cast to the side. He was thrilled to try my munchies—Twix candy bars, pecans, peanuts and dates—all new to him.

I tried to describe one of my favorite foods.

"So to make deviled eggs, you boil chicken eggs, then peel the shells off of them and cut them in half."

Amrit nodded.

"Then you put all the yolks—the yellow parts—on a separate plate and mash them up."

He nodded.

"Then you add sweet pickle juice to them."

He nodded.

"Then you add Miracle Whip. It's like mayonnaise."

He frowned.

"Um, it's a creamy white stuff made of oil, egg yolks and vinegar."

He looked skeptical.

"You mix all that together with a little mustard."

"The seeds?"

"No, it's a creamy yellow stuff made from mustard seeds."

He nodded.

"Add a little salt and mash it up some more. You put the mashed stuff back inside the egg whites where the yolks used to be and then you eat them. Good stuff."

"Sweet, oily, mustardy eggs?" he asked.

"That doesn't sound so good, does it?" I laughed.

Amrit tried to describe sekuwas, quantees and achars to me, but his English failed him.

"I am not a porter," he confessed. "I am a cook, but when business is slow, I help Ram."

"Do you have a family?"

"A wife and a son."

"When do you see them?"

"Once a week."

Amrit's dedication to his family reminded me of Isaac in Kenya.

When we finally arrived in Bamboo, I was the only trekker there. At the door of one guest room, a woman was scolding something. When I approached, she pointed at two gray-green striped cats who had curled up on a porter's bed. I grinned. I knew from experience that if she wanted the cats to leave, she would have to physically move them herself.

Using a pink bar of Puja soap, Amrit and I washed clothes at the spigot sticking out of a concrete block. In the bright sunlight they would have dried quickly, but a rainstorm arrived about a half hour later. It was a good excuse for five idle workers to sit around and play an unfamiliar game that involved slapping cards down on a table. Before long, I was teaching them how to play blackjack, using rocks as money. After a bit of discussion, they taught me the words they thought best translated into "hold" [bow-cee-o], "hit me" [dee-nus] and "busted" [goy-yo].

We played until Hombard the cook lost all of his rocks.

"To pay your debt, please make me a pizza," I joked.

And he did, the most perfect pizza from scratch without using measuring cups or spoons. He placed herbed tomato sauce and an artful arrangement of tomato slivers on top of the dimple-edged buttery crust. He topped it off with finely grated yak cheese before he baked it.

"It's beautiful!" I gushed as he beamed with pride. "Let me take a picture of you with it."

Afterward, I was still hungry, so I joined Amrit and the men at a plywood table in the dining room for *dal bhat*. Trying to eat it the same way they did, I used the fingertips of my right hand to mix the lentils and rice into a small clump, and then tried to flick the clump into my mouth with my thumb. I caused a lot of laughter and quite a mess on my shirt before I got the hang of the flick technique.

I could have stayed at the Buddha Guest House for days. These were the kinds of interactions I was craving. It was so much more my style than doggedly marching along a muddy trail. I hoped Kathi was having as good a time as I was.

BEFORE BED, I STARTED READING Kathi's copy of the *Lonely Planet Trekking in the Nepal Himalaya* guidebook. Nepal had five vegetation zones. Depending on the altitude, the landscape included familiar trees like chestnut, maple, walnut, birch and hemlock. There was even a variety of acacia, the tree so common in East Africa.

The country was home to more kinds of birds than the United States and Canada combined. The animal roster included Bengal tiger, one-horned rhinoceros, Gaur bison, red panda, Indian flying fox, muntjac (barking deer) and leopard. Sadly, loss of habitat and poaching was taking its toll on Nepal's wildlife.

The book noted that the distance between two points on a trekking map were relatively meaningless due to twists, turns and changes in altitude on the trail. Most people averaged 10 to 20 kilometers a day. The Annapurna Sanctuary trail had been designated medium difficulty and involved "steep climbs and often crossed exposed cliffs and bridges of dubious construction." True enough. My jaw dropped when it stated, "You can make the trek from Pokhara in as few as 10 days, but it is best to allow two weeks to fully appreciate the high altitude scenery." Kathi's schedule had seven days.

The book also warned trekkers about ascending too fast. If they ascended faster than their bodies could adjust to the increased altitude, fluid might fill their lungs or gather in their brains. Either could be lethal. Some people were more prone to altitude sickness than others, but most trekkers could safely and rapidly ascend to around 9,184 feet without getting ill. The trick from there was moderating the pace. If symptoms of altitude sickness (headache, loss of appetite, nausea, vomiting, fatigue or dry cough) started to appear, descend immediately.

Kathi was pushing it by going from about 8,000 feet to the Annapurna Base Camp at 13,546 feet before descending back down to the Bamboo, all within about 24 hours.

WHAT A GLORIOUS MORNING. The sun was out. I had slept well. My body felt rejuvenated. Amrit and I took a walk along the river, discussing the plants and insects. I made a cheat sheet of English words for him, and he wrote Nepalese translations next to each one so he could memorize the list.

We had *dal bhat* for lunch (good thing I really liked it), followed by card-playing and a running commentary about the determined trekkers who gave me curious looks as they trudged by. By late afternoon, Kathi triumphantly returned.

"It was so amazing. I wish you had been there," she said, giving me a jolly hug. "We saw the peak. It was just like Anthony said. At sunrise the clouds parted, and there it was."

By evening, our guest house was packed with hungry trekkers, and the kitchen was slammed with orders. Staff members from other guest houses came over to help cook and serve food. Eric Clapton music played from an old pair of speakers. It was sad to see the guides and porters eat inside, while Kathi and the trekkers mingled on the outside patio.

Meanwhile, I sat between baskets of onions and garlic in the kitchen, an 8-by-8-foot room with wooden counters, four kerosene burners and an industrial metal sink. I flipped my journal open to a new page, eager to write down Hombard's recipes. He pried the lid off a metal box and poured seeds into an old blender.

"What kind of seeds are those?" I asked.

He poured some in my hand. Marijuana seeds. No point in writing that recipe down.

"It goes with the *dal bhat* for the porters and guides," he explained. The seeds were a logical choice for the Nepali diet. Marijuana was grown for hemp and medicinal purposes, so the seeds were plentiful, and they were a good source of fiber and protein.

After the dinner rush was over, Hombard and I ate Snickers rolls packed with some of my pecans. Best. Dessert. Ever.

When I wandered out to the patio, I overheard a woman complain about the chocolate pudding she ordered.

"It's warm, and there's not enough cocoa and sugar," she whined.

It was like Club Sun and Sand food. Looked right. Tasted wrong. I just smiled at the memory of my dessert. It paid to be friends with the cook.

"Anyone know how Thomas is?" one man asked the group.

"I heard he was okay," said another trekker. "He only remembers bits and pieces of what happened."

"Who's Thomas?" I asked Kathi.

"He got altitude sickness last night," she said. "He just happened to tell some people that he felt dizzy and had a headache, so they had porters carry him down to a lower altitude in the dark. If he'd gone to bed, he might have died in his sleep."

AFTER BREAKFAST THE RAIN STARTED to fall as Kathi, Ram, Amrit and I got back on the trail. Sharp pains in my right knee on downhill steps took the thrill out of being back on the move. After trekking only three hours, mostly downhill, Kathi announced that we were done for the day. I was furious.

"Seriously? We're stopping now? Why did I have to do a two-day death march when now we have all this extra time? What was the big damn hurry to reach ABC? If we had trekked at a reasonable pace, I would have gone on to ABC."

I flailed my arms, refusing to enter our room at a guest house. Kathi was speechless. Amrit and Ram watched from the balcony. They were stunned by my sudden outburst and did not know how to deal with it.

"I'm leaving," I said as I grabbed my day pack. "I'm going on, whether you go or not."

I marched off, and for once they all followed me.

Nothing like anger to fuel physical activity, but the trekking eventually calmed me down. And with each step, I measured the facts. Kathi had arranged for rides, hotel reservations, plane tickets, trekking permits, and the help of Ram and Amrit. What had I contributed? Nothing. Had I taken an active role in planning the trip or reviewing the itinerary before we started? No. Did I have a right to complain? Absolutely not.

I did have the right to be angry at myself. Growing up I had little practice making decisions, and I carried a passive approach into my adulthood, as if others could make better decisions for me than I could. I floated along for years thinking life was supposed to be that way until Blair, my boyfriend at the time, made a curious proposal.

"We have a good relationship, but would you like to learn how to make it even better?" he asked. That was how he got me to start seeing a therapist. Six years later, Blair was no longer in my life, but I had started to take more responsibility for my actions.

I was ashamed to admit that I had given Kathi all the authority when it came to this trek. Crap. I could travel the world, but I could not escape myself.

Kathi and I never talked about what happened. We just silently let the disagreement fade into the past. She loved me enough as a friend to not call me out. No doubt Ram and Amrit were relieved when the tension passed like a thunderstorm.

At the top of the last God-awful switchback up a steep mountainside, we caught up with Jeff, who was from California. Kathi and this lone trekker quickly bonded when they discovered they had both gone to the Georgia Institute of Technology. Both of my brothers had graduated from there as well.

He, too, was going to stop for the night at the Trekkers Inn and Restaurant. Compared to other guest houses, it was a five-star establishment. The grounds included a rooftop terrace and a petite grass lawn. Geraniums bloomed along the balcony railings. Our room came with two beds, a private bathroom, and loaner flip flops. We three were the only guests there that night.

Ram and Amrit disappeared somewhere, while Kathi, Jeff and I had an impromptu happy hour on the terrace. The snow-capped Annapurna South view was sublime.

"These gaiters are great for keeping the leeches out," he said as he peeled them off. We laughed when he then found three of them stuck to his ankles.

This was not Jeff's first theory to go wrong.

"I hid $50 bills under the sole inserts in each of my hiking boots. That way I'd have money if someone stole my pack," he explained. "Sounded like a good idea at the time, but the sweat from my feet and the friction from trekking ground the bills into pulp."

We tried not to laugh too hard at his $200 learning experience.

We three continued our conversations in the dining room, where the tables were draped in white tablecloths. For dinner I ate an enchilada, an apple spring roll, veggie samosas and fried potatoes.

"It's going to be tough to cut back on eating when I stop trekking," I thought as I pushed back from the table, rubbed my full belly and sank into a dreamy food coma.

WE TREKKED DOWNHILL into our last valley as the day grew hot and humid. The nearby terraces became wider and the crops more mature. Orange cannas bloomed along the side of the trail. The surface of the nearby river was smooth, but its jagged shoreline suggested a temperamental flow.

When we stopped to drink water, we heard a growing clatter of hooves and bells. Everyone stepped aside as a donkey caravan clip-clopped by. Each animal wore a colorful belled harness and a decorative wool saddle pad as plush as an Oriental rug. At the end of the caravan, a man whistled or yelled commands to the lead beast at trail intersections.

Animals were not the only ones hauling goods along this route. A line of 10 equally spaced young women diligently trooped up the trail. One long metal cable, divided into bundles, spanned the baskets they carried.

There was no glory at the end of our Annapurna Sanctuary Trek, just Nayapul, a squalor of wooden stalls and a paved road where motorcycles, taxis and buses jostled for business. We all took a taxi ride back to Pokhara.

It was hard to say goodbye to Ram and Amrit. There was so much more to share with them, a mountain of details to learn about their lives. I hoped I could return their hospitality by sending clients their way.

Kathi settled into our hotel room while I dropped off a roll of film for developing. If the quality was good, I planned to develop all my film because prices were so low. Unfortunately, the photos had dull colors and most had a bluish tint. The owner, his wife and his mother were hand trimming my prints with scissors when I went to pick up my order.

AFTER THE FLIGHT TO KATHMANDU, Kathi and I checked back into the Kathmandu Guest House and spent the day exploring the neighborhood. Tiny shops sold something for everyone—adventure gear, jewelry, wool and cashmere clothing, gauzy hippie shirts, and musical instruments. A tiny Barnes & Noble bookstore sold new and used books.

Armed with an incredible exchange rate and Kathi's generous offer to carry back home what I bought, I went on a shopping spree: a North Face back pack, $14.38; Gore-Tex pants, $14.38; a hand-embroidered leather purse and matching wallet for $6.41; a 180 milliliter bottle of Mount Everest Whisky (a combination of malt whisky from Scotland and Nepalese alcohol) for $1.11; and a heavy duty black duffle bag to hold it all for $3.92.

The people-watching was as entertaining as the shopping. It was not uncommon to see two men holding hands while facing each other, fingers entwined during their conversation. On the flipside, it was considered offensive for romantic couples to kiss in public.

Declining offers to buy hashish, we stopped at a local bakery. None of its paste-colored goodies looked familiar. I bought a sugar-sprinkled twist that tasted like lightly spiced shortbread. The shopkeeper gave it to me wrapped in a piece of unbleached, unlined paper that had once been a child's homework assignment. Not sanitary, but it was thought provoking. The student, Dhiraj, wrote in chunky letters five questions and answers. "Who discovered the structure of atom? Rutherford and Bohr." "The explanation of fission was first suggested by whom? Meitner and Frisch." "Who constructed the first telescope? Galileo." "Who discovered radium? Madam Curie." "Who discovered the laws of motion? Newton."

The child knew more than I did.

I HAD MIXED FEELINGS about Kathi leaving Nepal the next day. I liked her familiar company, sharp wit, aspirations and tenacious nature. I was always learning new things about her and myself when we were together. I saw more of Nepal due to her planning and hard work than I probably would have on my own and for that I was eternally grateful. I hoped we would return to Nepal some day with a jointly created plan.

That being said, I was ready to get back to a slower, more interactive, detail-oriented pace. It was time to get back on my own trail.

Wavy chain of events

Kathmandu, Nepal

THE WAVY CHAIN OF EVENTS UNFOLDED like this: I moved into a single-bed room at the Kathmandu Guest House, where, on a snapdragon in the vase next to the bed, I found a plump caterpillar that I relocated to the garden, where I met a young English traveler named Julia, who asked me to go with her to Boudhanath, which was one of the largest domed Buddhist *stupas* in the world. These structures, which contain Buddhist relics, were used as places for meditation.

A taxi driver dropped us off at the end of a crowded side street. We walked into a giant ring of buildings that surrounded the mountainous dome. It perched on a series of plateaus, white as the snow on the Himalayas behind them. Black-rimmed blue eyes were painted on the sides of the stupa's peak. Strings of blue, white, red, green and yellow prayer flags (representing the sky, air, fire, water and earth respectively) fluttered down to the street. We fell in step with the sea of people walking clockwise around its base. Under the cloudless blue sky, the reverence and serenity of the place rivaled the inside of the Notre Dame Cathedral in Paris.

"We're supposed to walk around the stupa three times, twice a day, to improve our fortune and luck," Julia said quietly.

Some people performed pranama to remove the burden of their sins. After each step they made forward, they lay facedown on the ground with their hands clasped on outstretched arms. This caused foot traffic jams where the circling crowd narrowed to pass a tarp-covered funeral shrine filled with flowers and pictures of the deceased. Mourners gathered by tables covered with hundreds of candles in little metal dishes.

"The story goes that centuries ago, the country suffered a horrible drought," Julia said. "Nepalese astrologers said it would end if the people sacrificed someone endowed with 32 divine qualities, which would be the king or his son."

As we finished our first lap, I wondered how many divine qualities I had.

"So the king told his son to cut up the white fabric bundle he would find the next day. The obedient son did, only to realize the bundle was, of course, his father," Julia continued. "So the son prayed to a goddess to pardon his sin, and she told him that as the new king he should build this stupa. It took 2,555 days to do it."

At the end of our second lap, we talked about trekking.

"I trekked most of the ABC trail with a friend," I said.

"I tried to do it with a porter and guide, but I quit," Julia said, reaching into an alcove to spin a *mani* [a prayer wheel]. With the motion, the thousand "Om mani padme hum" prayers—a potent phrase that contained all 84,000 teachings of Buddha—inside the wheel floated up to Chenrezig, the embodiment of compassion. "It was too violent."

My eyes jerked from the life-size statues of royalty riding white elephants to her sad face.

"I met a nice British couple on the trail," she said. "They trekked with us for a while, but when we stopped near Pothana, they decided to go on by themselves. They came back a couple hours later. A gang had attacked them."

I stopped walking.

"That was you? We heard about that. What happened?"

"The gang got away with the wife's pack," Julia said. "But the husband gashed one of them in the face. They didn't count on him being a cop back home."

"Good for him," I said.

"The locals couldn't find the thieves, so I decided it was safer to stop trekking and find something else to do, like this," she said with a shrug.

We stepped to the side as five monks in tangerine orange-colored robes silently strolled past.

"I heard that Maoists caught three teenagers who were involved," she continued. "They shot one dead in front of some locals to make a point, and the other two were taken away. They haven't been seen since."

I wanted to believe that I had left the harshness of East Africa behind, but that was naïve. Conflict was a part of life. It was everywhere, even if I could not see it or understand why it existed.

We finished our third lap in silence and then veered down a side street. The reverence of the stupa evaporated, replaced with the weight of daily life. The paved road turned to dirt. Vendors sold vegetables and bundles of herbs. A man without legs gave pleading looks. Some of the children wore navy blue private school uniforms. Others wore street clothes, too poor to attend school or needed as workers by their families.

Julia led the way to a *gompa*, a Buddhist monastery, for an evening service. In front of the large white building, ancient magnolia trees stood sentry on each side of its two-story-tall entrance doors. Leaving our shoes and all leather items outside, we quietly stepped inside the building. Primary colored murals of mythological scenes and mandalas—diagrams that represented the forces of the universe—decorated the walls of the cavernous main room.

At the front of the room, wicks burned in umbrella-sized metal basins full of *ghee*, the golden oil that remains after water and milk solids are removed from melted butter. Rice offerings, *khata* [ceremonial scarves] and stacks of red prayer books surrounded golden statues of Buddha. We slid an odd, and therefore auspicious, number of coins into an offering bowl and then sat quietly on the floor toward the back of the building.

A procession of monks quietly filed into the center of the room. Most sat on small cushions on the floor along two low wooden tables. A few, perhaps novices, sat in a raised tiered section to the right side. An older monk with a portly physique, perhaps their teacher, sat on a cushioned dais several feet above them all.

As they flipped through unbound pages of books in front of them, the monks chanted, blew horns, crashed symbols, beat drums and held moments of silence as if they had stems. Sometimes the sounds were melodic. Other times they were jarringly discordant.

Throughout the service, another monk entered the room with a chalice. He filled it with a clear liquid from a pitcher next to a statue, chanted and walked slowly outside, only to return minutes later with the chalice to repeat the cycle again and again. I wished there had been a guide to explain the significance of his efforts.

As the monks prayed, sparrow-like birds flew in and out of the building. A blob of bird poop splattered next to me. Perhaps the near miss portended good luck, because when I got back to the Kathmandu Guest House, the laundry service had washed, pressed and crisply folded my khaki pants and five shirts for only 180 rupees ($2.35). The clothes had not looked so good since I left home.

I also reaped rewards from Kathi's departure. She gave me her rain poncho, a clean shirt, a bag of corn chips, a pen and two heavy duty plastic bags. I had grown to appreciate the value of such simple items. I also bought all of her single dollar bills. No matter where I went, I could always spend them.

THE NEXT DAY JULIA INTRODUCED ME to Allen, a fellow Kathmandu Guest House resident. He looked like Mark Twain with a better haircut. He was a sociology professor in Kentucky. He had just finished traveling throughout the Kathmandu Valley "conducting research on the perceptions of deviant behavior and mental illness in a developing society." This often required that he walk to remote schools to interview teachers. One of the schools Allen visited was a regular Maoist target.

"A large part of the Maoist strategy is to attack the schools in the areas where they operate," he explained. "They do this for at least three reasons. They raise money by 'taxing' the only people who can afford to send their children to school, they control what is taught in the school, and they force teachers and teens to join them."

It was such an ugly situation for such a beautiful place.

That afternoon, Allen and I went to Bhaktapur [the City of Devotees], the third largest town in the Kathmandu Valley. According to my guidebook, it was a processing center for crops and a production center for textiles and pottery. At the heart of the city's congestion was an ancient four-square-mile district surrounded by massive brick fortifications that had protected it from centuries of invaders, including much of modern civilization.

For 750 rupees ($9.80), we passed through a gate and back in time. It would have been easy to focus on Bhaktapur's quirky facts or legends. I read that the sculptor of the Ugrachandi and Bhairav statues in Durbar Square had his hands chopped off to prevent him from duplicating his masterpieces. Legend had it that the Dattatreya Temple was built in 1427 A.D. from the wood of a single tree. The Golden Gate, often considered the most magnificent piece of metalwork in all of Nepal, included a statue of Goddess Taleju, a four-headed figure with 10 arms. The struts under the roof of a temple built in 1482 had erotic carvings. They were said to keep away the virginal Goddess of Lightning.

I quickly put away the guidebook because it diverted my attention away from the impact of the old city's visual feast. It was astounding to consider how many old-growth trees were cut down to build the massive multi-tiered pagodas. There were monuments and carvings of wood, stone and metal everywhere, be they gods, goddesses, griffins, rhinos or legendary wrestlers. A magnificent doorway surrounded by intricate gilded statues led to the royal palace. In one of its secretive courtyards, a bronze cobra kept a watchful eye on an abandoned bathing pool.

Shopkeepers touted fruits and vegetables from hole-in-the-wall shops.

Chickens strutted along balconies draped with strands of dried garlic and onions. A woman rhythmically tossed threshed wheat into the air from a rattan screen. A hazy cloud of chaff wafted off to the side. An old man balanced piles of straw on a wooden yoke over his shoulders as he walked down the street. Long black braids swished behind women in pastel colored saris. Young boys in white shirts and navy blue pants harassed each other until one approached me to ask, “Do you know Steven Spielberg?”

Each turn brought glimpses of a life draped with spiritual reflection. Doorways were marked with symbols of protection and well-being. Shrines were layered with generations of melted candle wax, flowers, burnt incense and rice offerings. People rang temple bells to notify the gods of their presence and to perform a brief puja (an expression of worship and devotion).

When we walked back through the historic gate, we sat for a while on the platform around the trunk of a massive tree with a broad canopy. It looked to be a close cousin to a live oak.

“It’s actually two trees that grew together over the years,” Allen explained. “They represent Lord Vishnu and his wife Laxmi. The trees were planted together during a Hindu marriage ceremony and are protected for life. Tree couples like this have been planted all along the Kathmandu Valley as rest stops for travelers.”

Our taxi ride back to the guesthouse took us through rush hour traffic. Grit from air pollution sandblasted our skin. Most motorcycle drivers wore air masks with their helmets. I was afraid for the women who rode sidesaddle on the backs of the motorcycles. The hems of their saris flapped precariously close to the whirling back tires.

We passed a massive stockyard piled deep with thousands of red bricks. The manufacturing company had to make enough bricks during the dry season to cover all the demands during the rainy season (June through September) when it was too wet to bake the bricks dry.

If contending with reckless traffic was not challenging enough, the taxi driver had to avoid scrawny, dark-eyed cows as well. The cows were protected as sacred animals by the Hindus, so they could fearlessly wander the streets as vehicles raced by within inches. One even curled up asleep in a gutter.

“It’s very bad—karmically and legally—to hurt a cow,” Allen said. “Your prison sentence may be twice as long for hitting a cow than for killing a person.”

Back at the Kathmandu Guest House, Allen asked the bartender if he would store the small round watermelon we had bought in the restaurant refrigerator. The man looked at us as if we had asked him to chill our hiking boots, but he fulfilled our request.

For dinner, Allen, Julia and I went to the famous Rum Doodle Restaurant and Bar. It was named after Mt. Rum Doodle, the fictitious world's highest peak at 40,000.5 feet, from the 1956 novel *The Ascent of Rum Doodle* by W.E. Bowman. Established in 1980, the restaurant was famous to climbers and backpackers from all over the world. Its walls and ceilings were covered with autographs, advice and memorabilia from Himalayan expedition members, including Sir Edmund Hillary and Sherpa guide Tensing Norgay, who are credited as the first people to reach the summit of Mount Everest on May 29, 1953.

After dinner, Julia returned to her room and Allen and I spread newspaper on the guest house porch floor where we ate watermelon and spit seeds.

"I sometimes tell people I'm Canadian, depending on who I'm with," I confessed.

The Nepali prime minister had recently secured $20 million in U.S. military aid from U.S. President Bush to suppress the Maoists.

"I figured some people might not appreciate that and get mad at me instead," I said.

Allen laughed. "Me, too."

BEFORE I CAUGHT A MID-DAY FLIGHT to Thailand, Allen and I spent the morning wandering around Pashupatinath area, home to many shrines and one of the most important Hindu temples. Because we were not Hindu, we were not permitted to enter any buildings, only walk along the streets.

Normally cows roamed freely about, but one was chained up by a temple.

"Someone believes that this animal is a reincarnation of their deceased loved one," Allen explained.

We passed a withered *sadhu*, a Hindu wandering monk who had renounced worldy pleasures. He wore only a loincloth, dreadlocks and ashes. I could not relate to his level of devotion. I did not have allegiances like most people—even to colleges or sports teams. Perhaps my untethered nature allowed me to let go of my life in Charlotte and take this global trip.

We stopped at the top of a stone walking bridge over the sacred—but heavily polluted—Bagmati River.

"Most of the water that should be here has been diverted for city drinking water," Allen said. "That water down there is mostly drain water from houses."

Allen pointed to *ghats* along the shoreline. Attendants were stoking a funeral pyre on one of these concrete platforms. When the cremation was completed, they would brush the ashes into the river. People not allowed to use the *ghats* built funeral pyres on the sandy banks downriver.

Later that afternoon, I waited at the Tribhuvan International Airport for a 1:40 p.m. flight to Bangkok, hoping a new wavy chain of events would bring me back to Nepal again.

Flours along the trail

Bangkok, Thailand

MY THAI AIRWAYS FLIGHT arrived in Bangkok at 6 p.m. The in-flight dinner included a ball of purplish bean paste, a sweet indication that I was leaping into yet another culture.

The airport was cavernous and bustling with people. I hung around the arrival area for thirty minutes, waiting to meet Keith, a friend of my friend Dawn from Charlotte. He and his family were generously giving me a place to crash when my itinerary took my through Bangkok three times. I chastised myself for not having his phone number, though I was confident that I—a 6-foot tall, red-headed, white woman—could be easily found in a crowd where a vast majority of the people were a head shorter than me and had black hair.

An hour later, I finally heard my name paged. I met up with a man fidgeting at the information desk. He was tall and lanky, with a rumpled suit and mussed dirty blonde hair. I introduced myself.

"Oh, good, you're still here. Bloody traffic!" he said, giving me a clumsy hug. "Well, it's nice to meet you. Come on. Car's waiting."

Not only was the immaculate silver SUV waiting but also the family chauffeur, Khun Daeng, a young Thai man with fashionable clothes and curiously long fingernails. I knew that Keith worked for a telecommunications company, but I had not known that his lifestyle included such impressive perks.

As Khun Daeng merged the SUV into traffic, reality lurched into the fast lane. From rural villages to an urban city with millions of residents. From square, hand-painted signs to monumental, organically shaped screens with moving images. From terraced crops and towering mountains to terraced buildings and towering skyscrapers. The eight-lane, elevated superhighway probably had more cars on it than were in the whole country of Nepal. Even though it was past sunset, the highway was daylight-bright under evenly spaced streetlights. It was dazzling.

Eventually we turned into the entrance of a gated community, where uniformed guards checked our credentials. From there, we passed homes that dwarfed their quarter-acre lots. All were separated by fences or *klongs*, murky canals that collected rainwater.

Keith's house was a rented, split-level, three-bedroom house with a side garage. A tree heavy with green, football-sized jackfruit grew in the front yard. I was startled by the heat of the night when we walked to the front door.

"Welcome," said Keith's wife Maggie as she ushered me into the house. She was a petite woman with blonde hair and a gracious English accent. "It's so nice to meet you."

"Thank you for having me as your guest," I said.

The house's main hallway had a cathedral ceiling. To the left was a sunken living room with a side porch. To the right was a guest bathroom. Straight ahead was a sunken dining room that led to a kitchenette for the family to use. Behind it was the main kitchen and the living quarters for the Thai woman who cooked and cleaned for the family. All the rooms had hardwood floors, white walls and sparse but comfortable furniture. The few decorations reflected an international lifestyle.

"Here, let's get you settled," Maggie said, heading up the stairs, briefly pointing out the master bedroom and their preteen son Giles bedroom. She opened the door to the guest bedroom that had a double bed, a dresser and a private bathroom.

"All the bedrooms have their own air conditioners," she explained, pointing to the unit built high into the wall. "You adjust it with this." She pointed to a remote control tucked into a bracket next to the light switch.

When we settled into the living room to drink green tea and get acquainted, the conversation included a warning.

"Do not go outside for a walk at night. There might be rats or poisonous snakes in the yard," she said. "And there might be stray dogs, rabid ones, just outside the fence."

THE NEXT DAY, Khun Daeng took Maggie and me to Wat Traimit. There we made our bare-footed acquaintance with the world's largest solid-gold Buddha. Five tons of gold had been shaped into a 15-foot-9-inch-tall statue. Its reflective surface was mesmerizing, as if it was cast from honey and sunlight.

Its history was not so bright. Some time after the statue was cast in the 13th century, it was covered with thick plaster, most likely to hide it from invading Burmese armies. It was a secret the community took to their deaths. The plastered statue was eventually moved to a temple in Bangkok during the reign of Rama III (1824-1851). When that temple was deserted around 1931, it was moved yet again to a temporary storeroom in Wat Traimit. The true nature of the Golden Buddha was rediscovered when a crane operator dropped it in 1957.

After the visit, Khun Daeng dropped Maggie at home and took me to the Au Bon Pain restaurant to meet Keith and his friend, Clive, a physics teacher at a local private school. From there, we headed to a rural-looking part of town along the Chao Phraya River.

Along the way we passed a man casually riding an elephant along the six-lane road. We also saw several of the red-vested motorcycle taxis Maggie had warned me about.

"Only people short on time, long on bravery and heavy on insurance would use their services, the crazy way they zip through traffic," I said just moments before a car knocked one of the motorcycle taxis to the ground. The passengerless driver slowly picked himself off the ground and inspected his motorcycle. Traffic, including us, flowed around the scene without stopping. I wondered how much bloodshed it would take for someone to stop and offer assistance.

Keith and Clive were going to preset a trail for the Bangkok Hash House Harriers, a "drinking club with a running problem." This group was a local branch of an international organization with historical roots dating back to the old English school game of Hares and Hounds. Think fox hunt using people instead of animals. In 1938, Albert Stephen Ignatius Gispert and friends modified the game with a strong emphasis on camaraderie and alcohol. They added "Hash House" to the name of their game as a nod to the derogatory nickname for the local Selangor Club Chambers due to its lackluster food. The players were called hashers. The ones designated as "hounds" chased the player designated as the "hare," who set a trail of flour and chalk marks. The more challenging the terrain, the better.

Over the years, the game caught on and spread to other countries. There are now more than 1,600 hashing groups (known as kennels) around the world. They welcome people of all ages and athletic abilities. The only prerequisite is a strong sense of humor and deep-rooted tolerance.

I had learned about hashing from my North Carolina friend, Roger.

"Pretty much you run or walk a few miles total, but there are stops along the way where you hang out and drink beers," he had explained.

One trail, two beers and four new friends later, I was hooked. It was like adult daycare with a brand logo. I was seduced by everyone's friendliness, their sense of acceptance, the humorous rituals and the bawdy songs. Hashing was also a great way to meet guys.

After I hashed three times in Charlotte using the name "Just Kristine," it was time to christen me with a formal hash name. The naughtier the better. Double entendres encouraged. They hoped I would hate it. It was a quick process, one they explained to me later.

"So Kristine started hashing because she broke her arm while learning to play ice hockey," said Uranus.

"We can call her Zam-Bone-me!" suggested Swamp Pussy.

"Can we do anything with hockey puck or pucker?" asked Retread.

"Mother Pucker!" They cried in unison, and thus I was named. After months of pointing out that the name was "with a P as in pucker, not an F," the nickname mo"pee slowly caught on.

A few months after I started hashing, I went to "Hedon," a camping event for a few hundred hashers at a farm in Newnan, Georgia. There were trails to run, but the focus was more on partying, beer pong, wooing a one-weekend soul mate, dancing in the barn in front of industrial fans, and skits that included men wearing bikinis and blown-up condoms as hats. Some of the men with military training ate the bugs that flittered around the beer truck lights.

I stayed on the front porch of the farm house for most of the weekend, intimidated by the swirling sea of nonconformity. I felt like Laura Ingalls at a Madonna party. The person I remember the most looked like Bill Gates. He only wore sensible brown leather shoes, brown socks and a tuft of peacock feather that bobbed at the end of his penis ring. By the end of the weekend I saw more naked men than I had seen in my whole life. One terrifying penis I can only describe as an angry sea cucumber.

Yet, it did not scare me away. In fact, over the years, the hashers helped me find some peace with myself. I was accepted. I belonged. I could be or do anything I wanted. I could explore my boundaries knowing that nothing I could dream of would freak these people out. I could kiss a girl named Handjob for Humanity or let a man eat a Jell-O shot off my backside in return for his tank top from Borneo.

By the time I began my round-the-world trip, I had hashed for about seven years along the East Coast, discovering that each kennel had its own personality. One hash in Raleigh, North Carolina, was family-oriented with stroller-friendly trails, PG-rated songs and fruit juice stops. Near Fort Bragg in North Carolina, the Carolina Trash Hash House Harriers set boot camp-style trails, where I got muddy and bloody and proud. In Mobile,

Alabama, one trail ran through a field full of cotton, handy when I needed an on-trail pit stop.

The Bangkok Hash House Harrier's personality turned out to be long and hot. Keith and Clive started their trail by a Liberace-esque temple covered with colorful tiles and bits of mirror. I followed the two men as they paced along, dropping handfuls of flour that hashers would follow a few hours later. Instead of including beer checks on trail (where hares hide a cache of beer for the hounds to stop and drink before continuing on), they saved the beer for the after party.

The trail wove through dense undergrowth, along boardwalks by shanty homes on stilts, over algae-choked *klongs*, and between fallow fields and water buffalo pastures. Every so often we used chalk to place a "check mark"—a circle with an X inside it—that meant the trail could change in any direction from that point. The hounds had to figure out which trail set from the check mark ended with the letters YBF (You've Been Fucked) and which was the "true trail" marked with an arrow that had three parallel lines along its tail. The locals noted our curious behavior, but only one man asked what we were doing.

After two hours in the scorching sun, I short-cut back to the temple for shade, water and rest. Not long after, Clive conceded defeat and joined me at a roadside stand for cold sodas. The shop owner poured the Cokes into small plastic bags of ice and knotted the tops around straws before handing them to us. I sucked the bag dry before I thought about the safety of the ice, but Clive showed no concern.

By 5:30 p.m., two dozen hashers gathered to run the trail. Most were older ex-pats from England. I was too worn out to run the trail a second time, so when they took off, I sat in the shade eating mangosteens that hashers had brought from trees in their yards. The dark purple fruits had thick fibrous hulls and delicious, white segments inside. I will always remember them, if for no other reason than when I wiped mangosteen juice off my hands with my chambray shirt, it left permanent red stains.

When all of the sweaty hashers came back, we gathered at the open-air restaurant on a river barge. We had the place to ourselves, which was best, because hashers like to party.

Liter bottles of Carlsberg beer helped wash down spicy Thai dishes. There was flirting and bad jokes, news and rumors of the day, reenactments of bad behavior and attempts at new debauchery. No one was hungry or sober by the end of the night, when Keith and I staggered to the SUV.

"Take us home, Khun Daeng."

Thank you very big

Phuket, Thailand

WHOPPING HANGOVER. SORE THROAT. Churning stomach. Mad dash around the airport. Bumpy near-dawn flight from Bangkok to Patong, a town on Phuket (pronounced Pooh-KET), an island of tropical lushness south of mainland Thailand. At The Expat Hotel, I checked into a deluxe room (king-size bed, a color TV and private bath) for the off-season rate of 940 baht (about $21).

I spent the rest of the day in bed, too wiped out to explore. Snot filled my head as I napped and channel surfed. I missed my cat Roxanne. I longed to drape her across my chest as a healing poultice.

By the next morning, I decided there was a snake in my room. I could hear it hissing and spitting. Whatever. Perhaps I should hang my wrist off the bed. I wished it would put me out of my misery after a night of sinus pain, coughing, sweaty sheets and fitful sleep. It was frustrating. Exotic Thailand was just past the door, but the best I could do was drag myself to the bathroom and back.

I had exhausted myself to the point of a major crash and burn into sickness. When a coughing fit almost suffocated me to death, I smirked at the thought that my body would be found next to a mini fridge pre-stocked with Heineken beer, Snickers bars and neon-colored condoms.

When signs of recovery slowly appeared two days later, I realized that the "snake" was just an aerosol dispenser mounted high on the wall. I had never seen a gizmo like that before. It automatically spit air freshener into the room, but I was too congested to smell it.

I took a slow morning walk around the neighborhood, grateful that the streets were so flat. Cinderblock businesses—beachwear shops, an Internet café, a massage parlor, a tattoo parlor, a 7-Eleven convenience store, a book shop that catered to English readers—were spaced like a small village with more foot traffic than cars. A man sold grilled nibbles from the sidecar of his motorcycle. The KFC promised instant comfort food.

Cradling a precious red and white KFC box, I headed back to my room, passing a disheveled Thai woman in a skin-tight black party outfit. Her tangled hair, smudged lipstick and shaky walk insinuated a long night of pleasure or profit or both.

Belly full of chicken strips and a biscuit, I traveled via a documentary on TV about a rare Tibetan culture. It still embraced polyandry, the world's rarest form of marriage, even though a 1982 Tibetan law banned the age-old practice. Not only do the women have more than one husband, but they also marry two, three, four or more brothers within the same family.

Morality issues aside, these marriages preserved family assets like jewelry, rugs, saddles and land. They also acted as a natural form of family planning by maintaining a steady ratio of people per acre of land.

During one interview, a Tibetan wife said her husbands had a lot of pettiness concerning children and jealousy over the other husbands.

"They [the husbands] make more money and share it," she mused through an interpreter. "They also make more sadness and share it."

I hoped my future included one husband with some money and much happiness.

MY MORNING WALK PASSED through Patong's party central. It was an intimate maze of sidewalks lined with hole-in-the-wall bars. Strings of colorful party lights and lively dance music created a festive atmosphere. Petite bar touts, hired to lure guests into bars, wore come-hither outfits and swarmed unescorted men who walked by. Their tiny smiles, oddly robust boobies and spiked heels advertised a good time. They only glanced at me. My relationship with my surrounding culture had changed yet again.

For a different kind of thrill, some partiers paid to be shot into the air inside a ball-shaped cage, only to have bungee cords yank it back to the ground. A live video feed gave spectators like me a close-up of panic-filled expressions during the flight. It was fun to watch the riders scream. Not as much fun to watch them throw up.

Blocks away, the beach offered a calmer alternative. Palm trees fringed the vast curve of white sand. Gentle waves lapped the shore. Here, productivity withered and died and tumbled away on a breeze. From a rented lounge chair under a canvas beach umbrella, I blew my nose, ate spicy tomato-flavored pretzels and watched tourists parasail across the deep blue water. This was all very pleasant, but I did not come to Patong for the party thrills or the beach. I came to kayak.

On my way back to my room, I stopped at an Internet café. It was just a spacious white room with a dozen monitors set on banquet tables. Travel posters with ornate Thai script, coy Asian ladies and picturesque scenes decorated the walls. An email from a former co-worker said my old job had been filled. I was surprised that the news bothered me.

I realized that I did not want to go back to my old job, but I did not like having that option taken away. It was like not wanting to have children, but wanting the option to have children. I had to admit it was a control issue.

THE LOCAL HASHING GROUP gave me some instant friends. That afternoon I caught a slat-sided bus to a hashing event (Run #843) at Nai Fon Beach. Overcast skies alternated with rain as about 50 people attended the event. Most were retired English expatriates with Thai wives who were about a third of their age. I noticed that Heath, an American hasher whom I had met at the Bangkok Hash, was also there.

I skipped running the trail, but attended the ceremonial circle afterward. As the leader of the hash, the grand master led raunchy songs, made announcements, and, most importantly, called hashers into the center of the circle to drink beer for any real or whimsical offenses they could name.

"Mother Pucker!" the grand master called me out to everyone's joy. "You did not run trail, you are a visitor, and you are an American!"

The crowd roared with laughter.

"And when one American drinks, all Americans drink!" a man yelled. They pushed Heath and a retired man from Kentucky into the circle with me.

It was enough fun to send me back to bed as soon as the bus returned to Patong.

THE SUN GLARED ON SEA CANOE Thailand's cinderblock headquarters. According to the itinerary of its one-day kayak trip, the staff was "trained to Western standards." I was not sure what that meant exactly, but it sounded like it would dilute the experience, make it less authentic.

Our impressively tanned guide Somchai gave an introductory talk to me and six other adults.

"The islands in the bay used to be part of the largest coral reef in the world, but over time, rainwater, tidal erosion and changes in sea level created the limestone islands that we call hongs," he explained, holding up enlarged photos of the intriguing formations. "Sometimes the rainwater makes caves inside the hong like the ones we will visit today. Please help preserve these islands. Do not litter. Do not smoke. Do not make loud noises—it scares the wildlife. Do not take anything but photographs."

Somchai herded us down the paved street to the rickety looking Ao Por Pier. Narrow wooden long-tail boats feathered its sides. The name "long tail" came from the long drive shaft that spanned the distance between the boat's motor and its propeller in the water. Alas, we boarded a Plexiglas boat with banana-yellow kayaks stacked on the roof.

A pleasantly warm rain prickled the steely green surface of the Phang Nga Bay as we motored along. I marveled that this experience was inspired by an article that I had read in the *Denver Post* years before. It featured John Gray, the man who started Sea Canoe Thailand.

The first kayaking business in the area, Gray's company reaped international recognition for its innovative practices. It generated income for the local people while setting traffic restrictions to preserve the natural state of the hongs. Unfortunately, less scrupulous people started kayak businesses and started overwhelming the hongs with rowdy tourists. The battle between the two business approaches had yet to be resolved.

I had clipped that article and filed it away. I wanted to see the hongs. And here I was. That I could dream of something, like this global trip or this kayaking experience, and then to make it real was magical, empowering, intoxicating.

When we arrived at the first hong, the rain had stopped. I was too weak from being sick to paddle, so a guide named Niram and I shared a kayak. The other six adults followed us in double kayaks. We slowly paddled along, soaking in the sunlight.

Minerals formed rust-colored abstract murals on the hong's limestone walls. Delicate tufts of greenery grew out of tiny cracks. Sprightly lizards defied gravity as they darted about. Dolphins glided by, pausing long enough to play peekaboo with us. Sadly, we also collected floating bits of trash, mostly plastic drink bottles. They stuck out like dog turds in a museum.

Niram eventually turned into a jagged opening in the side of the hong. Sunlight bounced off the water and gave soft bluish glow to the rippled walls and spiked ceilings. Our whispers mingled with the sounds of dripping water. It was the kind of the place where pirates would hide treasure.

"Please don't touch," Niram said as we glided around a stalactite. "The oil from your fingertips will change the way waters flows down it and the way it grows."

At one point, we had to lay down on our backs to get past a part of the ceiling that was within two feet of the water. Moments later we popped out into the sunshine-filled center of the hong where time seemed to have stopped. Shaped like an upside-down cone, the interior of the hong was lined with lush vegetation.

"This area was once a giant cave, but the roof collapsed," Niram explained.

The warm humid air buzzed with the sounds of insects and the twitter of birds. A yellow snake hung from the arthritic roots of a mangrove tree. Crabs darted in the murky water underneath our kayaks. It would have been no surprise to me if a pterodactyl flew by or a brontosaurus raised its head above the tree canopy. There were no signs of human presence, not even a cigarette butt.

We floated around for a while, just taking in the ambiance, then returned to the boat for a lunch of coconut milk soup, spicy fish, tempura shrimp, steamed veggies, cashew chicken and watermelon.

That afternoon we paddled through the passages of another cave.

"This is the Bat Cave," Niram whispered.

No surprise there. The air reeked of ammonia. Hundreds of bats hung from the ceiling like a carpet of quivering brown kiwis. Using sonar navigation and high-pitched squeaks, they could detect objects as small as a human hair even in total darkness. Endearing tidbit: Thailand is home to the bumblebee bat, the world's smallest mammal. It weighs less than a penny.

Our one-day tour ended at the Mangrove Hong, named after its watery forest of mangrove trees that looked like a collection of sprouting sticks. According to Sea Canoe Thailand's booklet, destructive tour groups had killed off 75 percent of the original forest. They broke trees by trying to climb them and killed seedling by running them over with their kayaks.

We floated in the calmness of the Mangrove Hong until a dozen kayaks full of young Asian women arrived. I was amused by their trendy pompom-fringed plaid sweaters and neon-colored miniskirts, as if they were at an amusement park. The birds flew away from their loud chatter and shrill giggles. Time to leave.

ONE AFTERNOON I BRAVED A VISIT to a massage parlor. Somehow the name parlor, rather than spa, made the business seem a touch sketchy. I did not see any provocative pictures or dolled up women in the lobby, so I figured I picked an appropriate place. It offered an hour-long massage for 250 baht ($5.77). How could I not try it?

"I would like a massage please," I said slouching down as if that would shorten the 12 inches between the bottom of my chin and the top of proprietor's elderly head. She nodded and led me upstairs to a sunlight-filled, warehouse-looking space divided into bays by white cotton curtains. Each bay had a futon mattress on the floor. The place smelled like clean laundry. No one else was around, but it was the middle of the afternoon on an offseason weekday.

The proprietress gestured for me to lie down on a mattress, keeping my clothes on. Back home, when I got a massage, I took off all my clothes and covered myself with the proffered sheet in a cozy private room with background nature sounds made by a machine. Here, there was no sheet, no music, no soothing intimacy.

A bare-footed young woman with a pageboy haircut arrived.

"Hello," I said.

She bowed slightly and then got down to business. Silly me naively expected the long, flowing strokes of a Swedish massage, so I was shocked when she started bending my limbs and using the weight of her pixie-sized frame to grind into my flesh with her knuckles, elbows and feet. Sometimes she crawled on top of my body so she could press on a specific spot. It was awkward and painful. I did not like it, but was too proud to make her stop.

Odd little questions for her flittered through my mind as I clenched my teeth and endured. "How are you finding all these painful spots that I didn't know I had? What do you think about while you do this? Have you ever worked on such a big woman? Are you glad I shaved my legs?"

When she was finally done, she gestured for me to stand up. When I did, my body flushed with a delightful tingling sensation. I was miraculously lighter, taller, more flexible. She had released a load of stress that I did not even know I had been carrying.

"*Khob-kun-ka* [thank you]," I said to the woman as I tipped her heavily for my happy finish.

MY NEXT KAYAK TRIP was a two-day experience that paired me up with a rambunctious family from Texas—parents Betsy and Greg and their pre-teen children Chelsea and David. After a morning ride across the Phang Nga Bay in a long-tail boat, we leisurely paddled around hongs.

Our midday stop was Tha Khao Bungalows, our accommodations for the night. The bungalows formed a line where the jungle gave way to a crescent-shaped beach. The water just offshore was so shallow that the captain stopped the boat and encouraged us to jump overboard and splash our way to the shoreline.

Each picturesque bungalow was a wooden box on stilts with the expected thatched roof, a tiny front porch and a pair of Adirondack chairs. We were giddy with the tropical perfection of it all.

Part of our afternoon kayak outing included learning about the swiftlet conflict. Men climb rickety bamboo ladders up steep hong walls to collect the nests of these sparrow-like birds. The nests are made from spaghetti-like strands of hardened bird spit.

"People use the nests to make bird's nest soup. They can sell it for about $58 a bowl," Betsy explained to Chelsea. The demand for the soup, with dubious aphrodisiac and medicinal qualities, was so high that tons of nests (equaling millions of dollars) were harvested each year.

"Is that killing off the birds?" Chelsea asked.

"They don't know."

I had heard rumors about workers dumping out eggs and young birds to harvest a nest.

We visited the base camp of some people who monitored and defended several unharvested hongs as bird sanctuaries. Their bamboo and thatch huts perched above the tide line of a tiny lagoon beach. Huge seashells and Bob Marley posters decorated their open-air bar. Rope swings hung from the boughs of a massive tree. Our timing was off. No one was home.

Chelsea, David and I tried snorkeling in the shallow lagoon, but quickly abandoned the effort. Each time the waves swelled up and down, we feared being pierced by the spines of the black sea urchins on the rocky sea bottom.

We moved on to a less treacherous beach, where we bobbed over striking coral formations shaped like brains, plates, moose horns and long-fingered hands.

Starfish grazed across rocks and corals. Sand dollars shimmied into the sand. Sea cucumbers turned into gelatinous blobs when we gently lifted them out of the water. A victim of robbery, half an oyster shell shimmered like an iridescent saucer.

After a stop at the Tha Khao Bungalows, we gathered at the dining hut. I shared a table with Lawrence, a lanky man who had just dropped by for a meal.

"You must try this," he said as he ordered the first of many Sang Som rum and Cokes. As a result, all I remember about our evening was that he was a French-schooled man from Venezuela who fantasized about starting a swanky resort nearby. Hours later, I happily tottered along the sandy path to my hut, sun burned, crab stuffed and rum soaked.

A BIZARRE LARIAM DREAM ended my blissful slumber at sunrise, so I wrapped my turtle sarong around my shoulders and sat on the porch to watch the new day arrive. The smooth waters of the bay mirrored the opalescent pinks, blues and grays of the sky.

After our "wholesome Western-style breakfast" (Translation: sliced tropical fruit and pita-sized pancakes served with honey), we waited at a pier to board our boat.

When we got to our kayaking spot, I shared a double kayak with Peter the guide. We gently paddled through the twists and turns of a dense mangrove forest to where a hong split in half.

"No need to paddle now," Peter said.

Like magic, the incoming tide pushed us into a forested canyon of dappled light. The air smelled earthy, like rich black dirt. Tiny yellow leaves fluttered down from above and joined our flotilla. I leaned back in the kayak and draped my legs over the sides, trailing my toes in the water.

At one point, we realized we were not alone. A macaque, a small tan monkey, had spied the butter cookies we were passing around. He strategically perched on a mangrove branch just above the water. We had to float within arm's reach of him to get by. The proximity was unnerving. His black eyes showed no fear.

"Do not let him get a cookie," Peter said quietly. "It will encourage this bad behavior."

"So many places to travel," I laughed to myself. "So many ways to teach bad behavior."

The canyon ended in a large cul-de-sac. Steep, jagged limestone walls surrounded us. A dead puffer fish the size of a soccer ball floated belly up in the water.

"He did not wear sunscreen," Peter joked.

Nearby, several fishermen smoked cigarettes as they floated in a wooden boat in the shade of a cliff. They let us see their catch. They would eat the whole cuttlefish, a squid-like beast with ten arms. They would only cut the fins off the small shark for soup before chucking it back into the water to die. Another soup I vowed never to eat.

Our final stop was a small cove in a national park. Lunch was served at two picnic benches where dirt trails disappeared into the jungle. Each round bamboo container contained a delight: sweet and sour shrimp, a chicken and sweet potato dish, spicy veggies and wedges of fresh pineapple. Afterward, we fed the leftover rice to the neon-colored fish, even though it was a bad behavior.

SATURDAY WAS A HASHING DAY, so I met up with two hashers to go to the event: Heath from the Bangkok hash and Phil, an older Englishman who became my casual hangout buddy. Phil took me under his proverbial wing for my last five days in Phuket. As a result, the other English expat men could be around me without getting in trouble with their territorial young Thai wives.

Later we three joined an American named Tony at a bar the size of a carnival booth in a strip of similar bars.

"I like this one because the owners used to be prostitutes," said Heath, taking a seat on a bar stool. I was surprised by his comment because he contributed heavily to that line of work.

Dozens of dolled up Thai women watched as I sat with the men. No sooner had we gotten our first round of drinks when the waitress returned with a second rum and orange juice for me.

"Did you order this?" I asked the guys. They laughed and waited to see if I could figure out what was going on. I looked around for a drink special sign but found none.

"Odds are that if you get drunk, you'll only take one of us home with you," Phil finally explained. "They want you to hurry up and make a decision."

"I'm not sure yet," I joked, then turned to Heath. "So how do you pick a woman out of this eager crowd?"

"Doesn't matter," he said bluntly as the others nodded in agreement. "When their clothes are off, they all look pretty much the same—black hair, dark eyes, little bodies, no boobs or bought boobs, no hips and flat feet from working in the rice fields until they can work in the bars."

I found Heath arrogant, yet he seemed to have the experience to back up his opinion.

"The girls are eager to do anything and everything you want. Sometimes that's perfect," he continued. "On the other hand, there's something to be said for most American women. It can be hard to get them into bed, you never know what you'll find under their clothes, and you never know what they will or won't do."

I was proud to fit into that category.

About 2 a.m., after graciously declining their flattering, half-serious offers of physical affection, I started walking back toward my room. Women gathered around the men before I got to the sidewalk.

At my hotel, like many others, there were no doors or front walls to separate the lobby from the street. As a result, staff members watched TV or slept on mats on the floor when not greeting or serving guests. I had trouble understanding what the floor attendant said when I asked for my room key. I was tipsy, and his words made no sense. When he started making hand gestures, I finally got the message and politely declined his offer to give me a massage.

MY LAST ADVENTURE with Sea Canoe Thailand was a one-day sampler of Phuket highlights. It was a touristy but easy way to see a variety of things. My tour companions were Peter and Martina from Germany. Our guide William, an expatriate of retirement age from Holland, had, of course, a Thai wife and four young children. I envied his ability to speak English, Thai, Dutch and German.

We started off with a leisurely stroll along a footpath through a rolling tropical forest. William described local beetles and insects, an angular conversation about barbs, fangs and pincers. We were content not to see them in person.

"See how this fern frond looks blue from one angle and green from another," rambled William's informative commentary.

He pointed to a tree with wooden slats nailed along a towering tree trunk. "Men climb up there to harvest honey." Indeed, there was a rippled, yellowish comb draped over a high branch.

"This is a rubber tree," he said as he patted a tree trunk. Elmer's glue-looking sap oozed down a diagonal slash on its trunk and along a twig stuck in the tree so the flow would eventually drip into a coconut shell cup below. Many of Phuket's roads passed through miles of evenly planted rubber trees.

William explained that Brazil once had the monopoly on rubber production, and the export of seeds was strictly forbidden. In 1877, however, some 70,000 seeds were smuggled to Britain and grown in the Kew Botanical Gardens in London. In 1901 the governor of the Tran Province introduced some of the plants to his homeland in Thailand. The country now ranked as one of the world's top rubber producers.

"But most farmers can't survive on the money they make from collecting rubber," William noted. "It's very time consuming, and they only get about 25 baht [about $.63] for each sheet of raw rubber, about the size of a placemat."

Our next tour stop was a visit to the Gibbon Rehabilitation Project (GRP) headquarters, a division of the Wild Animal Rescue Foundation of Thailand. It had been illegal to have gibbons as pets in Thailand since

1992, yet people were still breaking the law.

Gibbons in their infancy were easy-to-handle, cuddly tan bundles of plush fur with endearing faces. But when they reached puberty, around six to seven years old, the once-loveable pets grew large canine teeth and became aggressive and unpredictable. The GRP tried to rehabilitate rescued gibbons from doomed lives as bar amusements, tourist lures and abused pets.

In the public area of the GRP headquarters, bulletin boards displayed information about rescued animals and the rehabilitation process. It was painful to see the restraints, chains and inhumanely small cages that had been used on the animals. Since the point of the GRP center was to break the gibbon/human tie and set them free in a dedicated nature reserve, we watched rescued gibbons in tree-filled enclosures from a distance. The staff even installed long-distance watering and feeding systems to reduce contact.

After lunch, we spent a leisurely afternoon watching a woman grind spices to make curry; a man hull a coconut and cook its flesh to make oil; and another man demonstrate how to process raw rubber tree sap with formic acid until he could form it into a mat that would be shipped to a processing plant. The tour ended with an elephant ride.

"They only keep females here," explained William. "If there's a male in the group, the females will fight for his attention." Sounded like last night's bar.

My trusty steed was the older lead female, with telltale pink age spots on her gray face. The guide straddled her neck and guided her movements with his feet. I gently climbed into the padded bench strapped to her back. Her warm leathery skin rubbed against my bare feet.

Peter and Martina mounted a second elephant, and we were off. All went well as we slowly swayed back and forth along a dirt path through a hardwood forest for about 10 minutes. Then Peter and Martina's elephant stopped to take a pee. This inspired my elephant to do the same. Being that elephants can drink about 40 gallons of water a day, these were time-consuming efforts.

Just when we thought the elephants would start walking again, the Germans' elephant pitched a fit. She stomped her feet, made trumpeting noises and flailed her trunk. Peter and Martina kept white knuckled grips on the metal railing around their bench seat. Their elephant pushed ahead of my elephant on the trail, only to falter and go back to second position and became docile again.

"She wants to be the dominant elephant," chuckled my guide, "But she needs more confidence."

I knew exactly how that young elephant felt.

I MOVED OUT OF THE EXPAT HOTEL and into a new room at the Arena Guest House, one block over on Soi Sansabai. My room was larger, brighter, quieter (no daily renovation noises or nightly rock music) and about $10 a night, half the cost I had been paying.

The new room had a vintage Floridian art deco feeling to it. The top half of the street-facing wall was all glass window panes. Two turquoise artificial leather chairs sat next to the bed. A green gecko lizard darted about as a mobile decorative touch. Again, the mini fridge contained beer, candy bars and condoms.

I washed clothes and watched the movie *Cast Away*. In the dramatic film, fictional character Chuck Noland is stranded on an uninhabited island after a plane crash. To play Nolan, actor Tom Hanks gained 50 pounds before filming began to give his character a pudgy look for the initial scenes. Filming then took a hiatus for a year while Hanks grew his beard and hair and lost a staggering amount of weight to reflect the four years that his character struggled to survive before being rescued.

Seeing Hanks' weathered, emaciated body made me think about my body. I had never been this suntanned before. There were stripes across my feet from the Teva straps. I also had been slowly losing weight. My belt hooked two holes tighter. I now ate when I was hungry, not when bored or frustrated from sitting at a desk for too long. I now walked more miles in a day than I previously did in a week. All my life I had struggled with weight issues, when all I needed to do was travel.

In the sweltering afternoon heat, I went to the bus stop to catch a ride to the island's big shopping mall. The old school bus with a wooden floor only departed on the half hour, so it was parked next to the curb. Three riders and the bus driver squatted nearby as they waited. I never got the hang of squatting. My legs would just cramp up until I fell over.

The driver kept looking at me. Finally he came over and squatted down next to where I was sitting. He furrowed his brow as he gathered his few English words.

"I sad for America," he said.

I waited for him to continue, to explain, but there were no more words.

He drew a long rectangle in the dirt. After crossing his thumbs and grouping his fingers into wing spans, he slammed them into the rectangle as he made a buzzing noise. The move destroyed his rectangle drawing. The man was referring to the Sept. 11, 2001, terrorist attack.

"*Khob-kun-ka*," I said, touched by his sentiment.

As we waited in silence, I thought about that day. It was the first time our hospital's marketing department had decided to meet in a downtown building rather than the usual hospital conference room. The change of place was supposed to help spark our creativity.

In the middle of the meeting, a receptionist had gently knocked on the door.

"Excuse me for interrupting. I just wanted to let you know that an airplane has crashed into one of the Twin Towers in New York City … in case anyone here needed to know."

We were startled and saddened by the news. No one was directly affected, so the director resumed the meeting. During a break, we were gathered around a television when the second plane slammed into the second tower. It was no accident. What did that mean?

"Charlotte is the second largest financial hub after New York," our director said. "We must be prepared for … something to happen here. Let's get back to the hospital."

I ran to the parking deck and got into my car. News on the radio sounded like the alien invasion from *The War of the Worlds*. The parking garage attendant raised the parking gate and fled. Construction workers scrambled down half-built skyscrapers and sped off in their trucks.

Charlotte was not attacked, but like everyone in America, we were permanently wounded by the terrorists.

The bus driver finally stood up and waved everyone onto the bus. We rumbled along paved roads until I got off at the stop by the mall.

I was surprised to see a store called Super C, similar to a Super Walmart. Its produce section was a botanical bonanza of unfamiliar fruits, like red ones with spiky green hairs. Some looked like cherries with psoriasis or immature pinecones. The meat section was heavy on seafood and sparse on red meat. I browsed photos on labels like an illiterate person. I laughed at the familiar products in the Foreign Food section like Campbell's soup and Heinz ketchup.

TO ESCAPE THE SOGGY HEAT one afternoon, I joined about 40 hashers at the pool in what looked like a typical American clubhouse in a townhouse development. Much of the development was in disrepair or abandoned before construction was complete.

"So, how was your date?" a hasher yelled across the group to another hasher, who blushed slightly and tried to ignore the question.

"What's the joke?" I quietly asked Phil.

"He took a friend home last night for a good time but didn't know she was a *katoey*."

Several hashers around us admitted to having made the same mistake at one time or another.

"What's a *katoey*?" I asked.

"A ladyboy. A man imitating a woman."

After the laughter died down, a man named Rosie asked about my trip around the world.

"So what's it like being a solo woman traveler?"

I laughed at the grand-sounding label.

"I go. I see. I move on," I said, not able to describe the experience. "When I was planning this trip, I didn't know anyone who had done anything like this. I felt like such an oddball. I'd rather spend money on travel than buying stuff."

"I'll drink to that!" someone said, raising his beer in a toast.

"You'll drink to anything," said a number of people in unison.

I talked a little about my adventures in Tanzania, Kenya and Nepal, and the unpredictable zigzags along the way.

"It's 'oppor-chance-ity,'" Phil said, perfectly naming the phenomenon.

After the hash, Phil and I ended up at Faulty Towers, a bar owned by an English expatriate. Another expat named David joined us.

"You should stop taking Lariam immediately," David announced after he learned that Phil and I were taking the medicine. "I've had all kinds of problems with depression and panic attacks. I bet that stuff's damaged my liver."

We thought David's problems were more likely due to too much beer, but later we reread the medicine's pharmaceutical info sheet. True, it listed numerous scary possible side effects, but it also stated not to take the medicine for more than a year. David had taken it for about two years. Besides the vivid dreams, Phil and I had no discernible side effects, so we stuck with our prophylactic regimens.

A ROOM FOR ONLY $2.31 A NIGHT? That was cause to move yet again to a clean and crazy-scheap room located above Sheila's restaurant before I had dinner with Phil.

"The hashers, they think we're having an affair," Phil said after we ordered a proper English meal of chicken and mushroom pot pie served with mashed potatoes, cauliflower and carrots on the side.

We both laughed. One of Phil's favorite sayings was, "Once you go brown, you can't go back."

"Well, I could be two Thai women in a long white wrapper," I joked back. "You just wouldn't know how to handle it."

Wrong. Phil had been a major player in his younger days.

"Back then, if you had three girls in bed with you at one time you were considered greedy. If you were too tired to go out and find a girl, you could order one from room service," he reminisced. "She might live at the hotel for just such requests."

My jaw dropped when he said the unofficial record for male prowess that he knew of was 45 different women during one 30-day visit.

As we walked away from the restaurant, Phil realized he was still holding his cloth napkin. Instead of taking it back to the restaurant, he tucked it into the collar of Sheila's mostly beagle dog who trotted alongside us. The dog liked to escort patrons to the end of the soi [street] and then trot back to the restaurant. We later confirmed Phil's canine delivery plan had worked.

For the next three hours, Phil and I hung out with other hashers at Faulty Towers. A flower seller wandered in from the street and draped a lei of fragrant jasmine blossoms around my neck.

"Which one of you drunken sots bought this for me?" I asked, but no one fessed up. The touching gesture meant more to me than I would confess. I had been feeling unattractively gigantic in the sea of petite Thai ladies.

As the night progressed and the beer flowed, our group became obsessed with creating a sentence that reflected our eclectic mix of legal, business and military expertise; bathroom and British comedy; the Southeast Asia habit of throwing in as many officious words as possible; and the fact that the Thai language does not have a word that means "much," thus the amusing phrase "Thank you very big." We proudly ended up with this weighty bit of text:

Begging the favor of your esteemed perusal, the frantically unraveled at the edges certifiable uncertified clinical microbiologist disgruntles mishandling the unsanitized unguntling machine that goes ping!, which happens to be the most expensive machine in the hospital, which has the proverbial psychobabble also known as eschatological significance of the fulfillment of the Masonic prophesy, which as we all know is called the terminological inexactitude, however we need a verb which can be purchased for half the cost of the aforementioned machine that goes ping! as listed on the first page of said document, paragraph 1, Section B, which appears in the fucking main head office executive loo (key not provided) but if you get stoned you will miss it or the beef bayonet, pork sword or ham dagger with foreskin fromage.

Thank you very big!

Spreading farang cooties

Bangkok, Thailand, to Vientiane, Laos

I FLEW BACK TO BANGKOK the next morning and bought a ticket for an 11-hour overnight train ride to Nong Khai, a town on the border between Thailand and Laos. From Nong Khai, I planned to cross the 1,000-meter long Thai-Laos Friendship Bridge that spanned the Mekong River to get to Vientiane, the capital of Laos.

The cavernous waiting area of the Hualamphong Train Station was surrounded with ticket counters, trinket shops and, surprisingly, a KFC, Dunkin Donuts and Dairy Queen. Above the entrance to the train platforms was a billboard-sized portrait of King Phumiphon Adunyadet in a white military uniform with a plumed pith helmet under his arm.

As I sat on a wooden bench and waited to board the train, a river of humanity flowed by. One man defied the majority with hair down to his waist. Another had tattoos that started on the back of his hands and disappeared under his shirt only to reappear above his collar. Each of his fingernails was neatly filed to about a half inch long. The uniform of a sailor practically glowed, it was so pure white. Long blue ribbons hung from the back of his matching cap. A stray dog chewed on the end of an unplugged electric cord. An old woman at the bathroom door collected two baht ($.05) to use one of the three not-so-clean squat toilets. The fee did not include any toilet paper.

There were few *farangs* [foreigners] at the station, but it was not long before one sat down next to me. The young man had a stocky build, dark hair, a wispy mustache and goatee, and wore a green T-shirt and baggie shorts. There was a slightly bloody cotton-gauze bandage wrapped around his thumb.

"Hello," I said.

"Hello, how are you?" His accent implied an English background.

"Fine. What brings you here?"

"My girlfriend's off exploring India with a friend, so I'm going to Laos for a bit of vacation and to renew my visa. You?"

Bummer about the girlfriend. He was handsome. I replied, "I'm visiting a friend and his wife in Vientiane."

"I'm a grade school teacher here. What do you do?"

"I'm not working right now, just traveling around." I was proud of how nonchalant I sounded about living out a dream.

"Where'd you come from?"

"Just did some time in Phuket. Before that I was in Nepal."

Tom and I swapped travel histories and advice. At 6 p.m. exactly—right when Tom admitted he was a hasher—everyone in the train station stood up, got quiet and faced the king's portrait. The national anthem played over the speaker system.

"This happens every day," whispered Tom.

When we sat back down, Tom picked at his thumb.

"What happened?" I asked.

"This American bloke was hitting a Thai woman to keep her from getting in a cab. I had to stop it, so we got into a fight. I got some good punches in, but the asshole bit me. Down to the bone."

"I'm so sorry," I said. "It was the right thing to do."

"Yeah, but the woman got mad and started hitting me too."

"No good deed goes unpunished."

He grinned and nodded.

Before we boarded the train and went to our separate seats, Tom asked, "Once we get to Nong Khai, do you want to cross the border together?"

"That would be great," I answered.

The impeccably clean sleeper cars were divided into compartments of two seats facing each other. Considering to my long legs, I was pleased the seat across from me was empty. A little after 9 p.m., the steward came by, pulled down an upper bunk above the seats and made it into a bed. He then pulled out an extension between the two seats for a lower bunk, where I slept. Each came with a plush terrycloth blanket the size of a beach towel.

What cleanliness and coziness the beds offered, the toilets lacked. When I walked down the aisle to use the toilet before bed, a tiny, dour old woman glared at me. I was not sure if it was my sleepwear (a black tank top and baggy shorts), a bad experience with an American or my possible status as a cootie-infested foreigner. Whatever the offense, she would not use the toilet after me. She waited until the other one was available.

Ladyboys of the night

Vientiane, Laos

IN THE MILKY MORNING LIGHT, the flat countryside outside my train window was a quilt of watery fields stitched together with low dirt walls. A scattering of trees and wooden huts on stilts poked out of the smoothness of the land. Men with conical, woven bamboo hats walked behind tethered water buffalos or washed them with wooden buckets of field water.

After arriving in Nong Khai, Tom and I hired a *tuk tuk* [a motorized pedicab] to take us to the border.

"My friend. He travel agent," the driver repeated as we got underway. "He help you get visa."

"No, thank you," we said for the third time. We had both been warned about such "friends," who charged more than double the $30 fee we would pay at the border.

I smiled as we rode a bus across the bridge, an area known as the "neutral zone" between Thailand and Laos. That phrase made me think of *Star Trek* and Romulans. The river flowed broad, smooth and brown. Even though it was the 12th longest river in the world and the 10th largest in terms of volume, it was not navigable year-round. No doubt some entrepreneur would figure out how to change that some day.

Once we got visa stamps in our passports at the Lao border, we hired another *tuk tuk* to take us to downtown Vientiane. The countryside transitioned from verdant fields to one-story cinderblock buildings separated by patches of tropical plants and garden plots. There were no sidewalks or traffic lines on the paved road.

Even though it was the capital of Laos, Vientiane felt vacant. It was mute in sound and color and oddly still for a Friday morning. No hustle, no bustle. Few cars. No people in business suits striding on a mission. No mothers pushing strollers around the landmark water fountain shaped like a giant bird bath. I only saw two ladies wearing bamboo hats and cotton aprons. They walked around barefoot as they tried to sell cigarettes, sunglasses, and hair clips from briefcases strapped to their chests, the way ladies used to sell cigarettes at night clubs.

As Tom and I walked into the lobby of the Phonepaseuth Guest House, I marveled how my arrival was due to a friendship with a man named Graeme that started in Charlotte, North Carolina, years ago. Since then Graeme, a native New Zealander, had moved to Laos and married a local woman.

Tom got a standard room. I splurged on one the finest rooms for $15 a night. Imagine a yuppie urban loft bedroom with a Thai décor: lime green walls, tangerine orange curtains, polished hardwood floors and a metal-railed balcony that overlooked the street. Fresh orchid blossoms and clean towels appeared on the bed each day. The one time I turned on the TV, there were three channels—MTV and two French stations. One showed American President George W. Bush Jr. with a French-dubbed voice.

The private bath gave new meaning to compact. I could sit on the toilet while washing my hands in the sink as the water from the overhead shower rained on my head. This arrangement turned out to be convenient when I wanted to shave my legs. A couple of the cinderblocks high on the wall behind the toilet had been placed sideways so that steam from the bathroom naturally vented outside, along with the air conditioning.

The room also came with a mystery. I had one of three guest rooms on the second floor, and there were no guest rooms on the first floor. So why was the room number 821?

After settling into our rooms, I walked with Tom to the Lao National Museum. For much of Laos' history, it had been pinned down under some other country's political thumb. The museum contained artifacts from the waves of political upheaval and military occupation, particularly during the 1960s and 1970s. What I knew about the America-Laos connection was not a thing of pride.

Heavy gauge wire tied down guns and firearms to display boards. Metal-barred cages surrounded the few gold statues and silver jewelry in the one room that had the museum's only security camera. Only glass and time separated me from the heart-ripping, black-and-white pictures of wounded soldiers, maimed children and dead civilians.

There were clever words for the ugly components of war. An herbicide called Agent Orange defoliated land to reduce the number of enemy hiding places. Yellow rain, an oily poison sprayed by low-flying planes, could cause blindness, tremors, seizures and death before it lost all of its toxic effects within 24 hours after being exposed to oxygen. Lima sites were simple labels given to locations with various or difficult-to-pronounce names, like Lima Site 20A, the headquarters of the Central Intelligence Agency. Combat aircraft mission flights called sorties dropped enough bombs during a nine-year period to equal about a half-ton of munitions for every local man, woman and child.

Tom and I were both quiet as we walked back to the guest house to meet Graeme, who still sported a cloud of white hair and a short beard. His passion for bicycling around the countryside kept his body trim.

"Hello," he said giving me a big hug and shaking Tom's hand. "Glad you made it. Let's go over to Khawp Jai Restaurant."

The restaurant was housed in a renovated two-story French colonial mansion with high ceilings, and door-sized windows. Tables filled the house and the brick patio that wrapped around it. It appeared to be a popular watering hole for travelers and expats.

We met Graeme's wife, Ott, who was almost half his size. Her beauty gave her an alluring doll-like quality.

When Graeme learned that Tom was a fellow hasher, he asked, "I'm setting a trail tomorrow. Want to coming hashing?"

"Yes," Tom and I said in unison.

While we ate pad Thai and yellow chicken curry, dinner conversation ranged far and wide after I updated Graeme on the lives of our mutual friends.

"So what's new with you?" I asked.

"Well, I've gotten quite busy. I'm not going to be able to show you around as much as I had hoped," Graeme fumed as the waiter cleared away the plates. "And my landlord hired some guys to replace the ceilings in our house. They only work a few hours each day—just long enough to make a mess—and then they leave. And the landlord wants all the wires on the outside of the walls. Looks so damn ugly."

"Did he say why?" I asked.

"That is way we do it," Graeme retorted in a bad imitation of the landlord's accented English. Ott giggled.

As we finished our beers, Tom asked me, "Do you want to go to Vang Vieng with me for a few days? It's off season, but it should be fun."

"Sure!" I said.

As we were leaving the restaurant, Graeme said, "So, we're moving back to New Zealand in a couple of months, and Ott would like to go to Luang Prabang to buy handmade paper."

He turned to Ott expectantly.

"Would you like to go with me? I would enjoy your company," she asked me.

"Seriously?" I was excited about seeing the historic city, but she was so quiet. I sometimes talked too much when around quiet people, as if the space had to be filled. I wondered if she would end up gritting her tiny white teeth with forced politeness.

"Yes, please. That would be very nice."

"Then it's a plan," I said. Within minutes I had an itinerary for my time in Laos. "What do you do with the paper?"

"I make decorative items like gift bags and lampshades."

"She's very talented." Graeme noted with pride.

We paired off to ride motor scooters for a short ride to a disco called the Chess Club. With my arms around Ott's tiny waist, I refused to look at the oncoming traffic. Even though the unmarked road was two lanes wide, everyone—including Ott—drove as close to the center of the road as they could.

The Chess Club—with its private booths and disco lights—reminded me of Club Bilicanas in Dar es Salaam. Cardboard egg cartons had been stapled to the ceiling as sound dampeners. Patrons, mostly pretty young women, moved through shadows and pools of light. We drank Beerlao and wicked pina coladas made with fresh pineapple and coconut.

"Careful which lady you flirt with," Graeme yelled to Tom over the music, casting a glance at the women who were eyeing him. "You might get more than you bargained for."

"No thanks," Tom laughed. "Ladyboys aren't my cup of tea."

We boogied on the small linoleum dance floor. We tried to guess who had been born as what.

Hours later, I left Tom, Ott and Graeme to walk back to the guesthouse. I turned down Graeme's offer to walk with me because I was sure I knew the way back. I was wrong. After wandering around for about thirty minutes in a dark neighborhood, I chanced upon some uniformed guards on sentry in front of a stately, government-looking building lit up by floodlights.

"Which way is Fountain Circle?" I asked slowly, knowing I could see the guesthouse from there.

They looked at each other and politely shook their heads. They did not understand.

Regretting I did not have a business card from the guesthouse to show them, I tried a second tactic. I had been told that Laotians often understood the Thai language, and I knew the Thai word for water.

"*Nam? Nam?*" I put my wrists together and wiggled my fingers. They broke out into smiles and pointed to the left.

"*Khawp jai!* [thank you]" I said as I continued on my way.

When I reached the fountain, the view was breathtaking. Hundreds of moths swirled around the vintage street lamps, like stars in the Vincent Van Gogh painting *Starry Night*.

ONE OF THE JOYS OF TRAVEL was finding delightfully familiar things in unexpected places. That was the way I felt about the sweet, moist banana bread at the Scandinavian Bakery. Tom laughed when I went back and bought a second mini loaf. It was the perfect way to start any day.

At a travel agency, Tom and I booked a two-day trip to Vang Vieng for some trekking, caving and kayaking. The off-season price of 306,000 kip ($31.67) per person included guides, kayaks, meals and one night of accommodation. No wonder Laos was popular with backpackers.

We searched local shops for a waterproof disposable camera for me to use while kayaking. There were no handy Walmart or Circle K convenience stores. One shop we visited was only half full of products, and they were unpredictably arranged on random shelves. While most items had a thick layer of dust on them, the pint bottles of Wall Street Whisky were sparkling clean.

Our next stop was the north end of Lane Xang Avenue, a traffic circle surrounding a gray concrete monument called Patuxai (Victory Monument). Built in 1958, it resembled the Arc de Triomphe in Paris. It was a giant squared arch topped with ornate cupolas. A small plaque at its base gave tribute to America. America had donated cement for a new airport runway, but the Lao government built this monument to commemorate those who died in revolutionary struggles instead. A rare case of art trumping commerce.

A steady downpour of rain began as we reached the gold brilliance of Pha That Luang [Great Sacred Reliquary or Great Stupa]. The monument—which over the centuries had been built, destroyed by the Siamese army and rebuilt by the French—was a dazzling collection of ornate walls and gilded spires. A pointy stupa rose symbolically like a lotus plant from the center.

By the entrance, monks with shaved heads and tangerine orange robes sat at a table under a tent. It was a strategic spot to collect donations from visitors to fund a new wat (monastery temple). A monk handed Tom a thin, mass-produced, red-inked certificate of appreciation for his donation. When I made a donation, the monk slid a certificate across the table toward me and then quickly tucked his hands in his lap.

Tom laughed as we walked away. "You have girl cooties."

The monk was not permitted to touch a woman, even through second-hand contact. I was not sure what to think about that. Were women too dirty or too powerful?

We explored the inside of Pha That Luang, passing prayer gates, ordination stones, statues and stone tablets. I have always marveled at the profound architecture mankind has produced in the name of religious devotion.

The rain stopped as we walked back to the guesthouse, passing through a street lined with wats and temples. In one section, performing a traditional cremation, men stoked the fire that burned on a concrete platform. Flames licked at a charred human foot.

The men noticed our wide-eyed expressions but said nothing.

"You know what bothers me the most about this?" I whispered to Tom.

"What?"

"I can smell the smoke and that means in some small way I am inhaling that person." I nodded toward the body. "He or she is becoming part of me."

TOM AND I CAUGHT A RIDE with Graeme to run the hash trail. For more than two hours, about a dozen expats and their Laotian sweethearts dashed through the countryside. Fireflies twinkled near the bushes. We passed families and their livestock. Though grueling, it was an intimate way to see rural Laotian life.

Afterward, all the hashers carpooled to an open air restaurant full of wooden picnic tables. At the center of each table was an electric cooking device. Imagine a boiling pot of water surrounded by what looked like a George Foreman grill plate. While drinking vast amounts of Beerlao, we became do-it-yourself chefs. Some people added ingredients to the pot to make a soup. Others, like Tom, grilled small pieces of chicken, shrimp, pork, octopus and beef.

"Here, try this," he passed me some grilled pork and pickled cucumbers on a plate. "So do they know you robbed a bank here?"

"I did not!"

"She walked out of the bank with a bloody paper bag full of money!" he explained to the hashers. "Looked like Santa Claus, she did!"

"How much money did you exchange?" asked the man seated next to him.

"$150."

They roared with laughter. That converted to about 1.4 million kip. The largest bank note was 5,000 kip, and banks liked to dump smaller bills on *farangs*. My paper bag contained more than two dozen bundles of money.

Chicken of the dark

Vang Vieng, Laos

AFTER WAKING UP AT MY LEISURE for weeks, crawling out of bed at 5 a.m. was painful. I shuffled over to the Scandanavian Bakery vainly hoping they were open, but my hopes were crushed. I stood forlorn on the street corner, backpack at my feet, waiting for Tom. I wanted to go back to bed, not ride in the back of a truck north to Vang Vieng. Even though the town was only 160 km (99 miles) away, there would be something—because there always was something—to drag the ride out beyond reason. We were scheduled to meet our guide there by 9 a.m.

As I moped about the plan, monks stole the limelight from my pity party. From around the corner they came, barefoot, a single-file line forming an undulating curtain of orange robes. Each carried a dull metal lunch pail and a quiet sense of purpose. As silently as they came, they disappeared back out of sight.

"Morning," Tom said when he arrived minutes later. He had the disheveled, post-party-without-a-shower, got-home-late look. Off we went to the travel agency to catch our pre-arranged ride to the truck market. Let the frustrations begin.

When our ride came, it was a man on a motorcycle who was not expecting two passengers.

"Remain flexible," I told myself. "This is only the beginning."

We spent the next half hour finding a *tuk tuk* for hire to take us to the truck market.

When we finally got to the market, it turned out to be a muddy commercial maze built of plywood, cinderblocks and sagging blue tarps. For the most part, the trucks were battered pick-ups with thinly padded benches, plastic canopies and metal tailgate platforms on the back. They came and went on no discernable schedule as locals tried to sell their produce.

Tom and I bought a loaf of freshly baked French bread for pennies. The bread was one of the delicious influences left by the former French occupation. Then we waited. And waited. The driver needed to collect as many passengers (thus more money) as he could before leaving. A half hour later, the truck finally left the market.

For 10,000 kip ($1.04), we experienced the joy and abuse of a stereotypical Third World truck ride. It randomly stopped to pick up more passengers until the head count peaked at 20 adults and one blessedly quiet baby. Commerce ruled over personal comfort and safety. One passenger tied a plastic bag around the feet of his two hysterical chickens before he shoved them under a bench. They calmed down immediately. A passenger boarded with six pineapples, their spikey tops lopped off and their long stalks tied together into a practical bundle. One woman sat on what looked like bales of collard greens. An elderly man kept a firm grip on a truck rail. There was a swastika, hopefully a religious rather than political symbol, tattooed on his hand.

We passed thatched houses on stilts, cultivated fields, grassy pastures, jagged hills and rivers swollen with rusty milk-colored water. The driver dodged pigs, cows, chickens, ducks (I think we hit one) and children. In spite of the thick plastic panels that rolled down from the overhead canopy, we were soaked by intermittent waves of rain.

While this experience was all new and exciting for the first hour, it was old and irritating three hours later when we crawled with stiff limbs and tender butts out of the back of the truck in Vang Vieng. Time for a quick pick-me-up of Oreos and Pringles from a roadside stand before walking about a half mile to the outfitter's office on the main street.

Vang Vieng had two paved, unmarked roads that formed a "T" in the center of town. The rest of the roads were packed dirt. A majority of the businesses were tourist oriented, though one was just a frontless wooden shed with an antique barber chair inside. While we did not see many farangs because this was the unpopular rainy season, the few we did see sported a curious blend of high-tech-meets-hippie-style clothing—Patagonia meets Haight Ashbury.

We met our guide, Muan, a chatty, vertically challenged young man who wore a faded red baseball hat. A Canadian woman with pinched features stood next to him. She had signed up for his two-day trip as well, but she must have taken a quick disliking to Tom and me. She had waited two hours for us to arrive, spent five minutes with us in the office, and then bailed on the trip. Tom and I were both relieved. She had that noxious yellow aura of a high-maintenance person.

With kayaks strapped to the roof of the truck, Tom, Muan, his assistant (a slight but attentive young man who never spoke a word) and I hit the road. Thirty minutes later, the driver dropped us off at a trail that meandered off between rice paddies before he drove on to where we would later spend the night.

We walked along the trail that followed a hand-tied bamboo fence tangled with vines. The path ended at the shoreline of a river and resumed on the far side about thirty feet away. Obviously, we needed to cross the swift-flowing waters that swelled past the banks and up into the grass. And to think that the big rains of July were still weeks away.

"They take the bridge away when the rains come each year," Muan said.

"So, how do we get across?" Tom asked.

"Please don't say swim," I thought.

Muan pointed to a skinny boat poking out of the tall grass. It was carved out of a single tree trunk.

"Ladies first," Tom said with a mischieveous grin.

Muan and the Silent One held the boat steady as I gingerly stepped in. Balance was never my strong point. (For example, check out the metal plate and seven screws in my left ankle from a skateboard accident.)

As they pushed off and paddled fiercely, I tried to sit still with my eyes focused on the far shore. Not an easy task when riding in a giant toothpick across choppy waters. When we successfully landed downshore, I bowed to Tom's applause. Muan and the Silent One paddled back across to retrieve him. Adventure for us. Routine for them.

Back on the trail once again, we headed to Tham Xang [Elephant Cave], a shallow, sunshine-filled cave.

"It is named after that," Muan said, pointing to a formation that looked like the head and trunk of an elephant. The cave's main attraction, however, was a reclining Buddha statue the size of two couches set end-to-end. Dressed in a golden robe, he lay unnaturally straight on his side, feet perpendicular to his body. His head rested on a wedge, a happy-go-lucky smile on his face. Life-sized statues of monks sat in prayer at his head and feet. Farther back in the cave was a large gong and a collection of sitting and standing Buddhas surrounded by flowers and incense offerings.

Tom and I drew numbered sticks out of a prayer box. Each represented a karmic prediction. Twelve was a very bad omen, and seven was good fortune. I picked a four, and Tom picked a three.

"Together, you have good luck," Muan said.

From the Tham Xang, we walked through a village of wooden huts on stilts shaded by a canopy of trees. No electricity. No plumbing. No pavement. Just boards laid across the muddiest parts of the path. Pigs were penned into four-foot-tall crawl spaces under houses. It took a while to explain why I started to sing the theme song of the television show *Green Acres*, about how I wanted to trade city life for farm living.

The sun came out blazing as we passed through hand-sown fields. Young corn sprouted around blackened stumps where the land had been cleared with fire. Thinking it was a burnt stick, I almost stepped on a poisonous snake.

At the base of a jagged range of hills was a forest of trees with leaves as big and round as tea saucers. Muan said these fast-growing trees were harvested to build huts. On the far side of the forest, a steep muddy trail led to the damp entrance of a cave. With snakes already on my mind, I was not surprised to see a banana yellow one disappearing into the cave's dark depths. Upon closer inspection, it turned out to be an industrial-grade electric cord.

"It is for the generator to light the cave," Muan explained. "We celebrate New Year's Eve in there."

Our spelunking goal was to reach the golden Buddha deep in the bowels of this cave, but 10 minutes into the darkness, I started to freak out. I paused long enough for Tom to snap a photo of me next to a delicate spider the size of my hand before I made a hasty retreat along the electric cord back to daylight.

The darkness, moist air and pitter-patter of dripping water had triggered intense memories from a spelunking trip gone bad. There were four of us on that fateful trip, all University of Georgia students. Brad was our experienced leader. I had known him for a while, but it was the first time I had met the two other guys who were from Germany.

We were exploring a North Georgia cave system, and our destination was a vast cavern known for dramatic formations. It was my first full-day trip underground.

As dawn broke, we crawled into a muddy hole in the middle of a field. The darkness within was absolute. I felt confident about the challenge and secure following the glow of Brad's carbide head lamp as two more bobbed behind me. For hours, we crawled over and around boulders, slid down muddy banks and squeezed through tight passageways. With the humidity of about 95 percent, everything was damp or slick or tacky.

I liked the physical challenge. Every movement forward had to be customized. Every crouch or bend or step had to conform to the organically shaped world of rock, mud and water. And the longer we adapted and persevered, the more dazzling the destination grew in my mind. I had visions of stalactites and stalgamites like teeth in a dragon's mouth.

I had trouble, however, with the mental challenge. Concerns floated into my mind. What if there was an earthquake? In a small passage, would we be squeezed flat like the cream in an Oreo cookie? Our lights were our Achilles' heel. Without them we would never find our way out. Exactly how long would our lights last if we got stuck for some reason?

After a few hours, the novelty of the experience started to wear off, and I started to think about what to do when I got home.

When we stopped for a break in a large room a short way from our goal, I asked if anyone else was shivering. I chalked it up to being sweaty for hours in the 54-degree air.

"Are you bumping into things more than when you started?" Brad asked seriously.

"Yeah, but I'm tired. This is a lot of work."

"Or you may be getting hypothermia." Brad furrowed his brow.

The two Germans exchanged a few sentences in their native language, then one said in English, "I will stay with her. You two go on."

"I don't feel bad or anything, just cold." I countered.

"It's not good," Brad said. "If you get hypothermia and can't get yourself back out, we'll be screwed. It's not worth the risk. We need to be safe."

One of the Germans took off his dirty outer shirt for me to put over my wool sweater and said, "Let's get your core body temperature up."

As I was doing jumping jacks, Brad and the other German disappeared into a narrow tunnel.

I had spent about 20 minutes vigorously moving around (and running my mouth with idle chitchat) when the duo returned, gushing with excitement. I pouted. No dragon's teeth for me. I would not make this trip again.

"Okay, time to go home," Brad said as he took the lead, and we fell in behind him. All went well for hours. Then there was a sharp bang like a gun shot. It reverberated off the walls. Rocks rained down on us. They thumped into my helmet. They bashed my shoulders and back. Gusts of air blew out our carbide lights. In the total darkness, I tried to scramble to the far wall, where I last saw Brad, as the ground beneath my boots slid downhill. Then everything stopped moving.

All went silent. I was too petrified to ask if everyone was okay. What if they didn't answer?

"Talk to me," Brad finally said with a shaky voice.

The Germans started swearing, and one finally said, "We are okay."

"I'm banged up but nothing major. What the hell was that?" I demanded with false bravado.

There was a flash as Brad relit his carbide light and looked upward. The ceiling was oddly bright colored and flat where giant pieces had cracked apart into rocks that had fallen on us and tumbled down the embankment we were climbing.

"A layer of the ceiling collapsed."

"Oh, I am so done," I said lighting my lamp. My legs were shin deep in rubble. "Get me out of here."

An hour later, tears came to my eyes when we finally crawled out of the ground and saw the darkening sky. I splayed out in the soft green grass, delighted to have so much freedom to move. I vowed never to go underground again.

The cuts and bruises healed and we four lost touch with each other. Over the years, I convinced myself that there was no permanent damage, and the experience became a good story. Yet in the Laotian cave—my first since the accident—I knew the fear was not behind me but right beside me.

That experience seemed so long ago as Muan, Tom, the Silent One and I stopped for lunch at an empty one-room hut. Black- and teal-striped butterflies the size of playing cards rested on its sun-warmed, woven bamboo walls. A nearby pomelo tree sagged under the weight of softball-sized fruit. The green orbs were edible but not as sweet as their pink grapefruit relatives.

Muan started a fire and prepared a meal of French bread, fresh mangoes, beef kabobs, stuffed fish and fried rice bundled in bamboo leaves. Tom and I laid our socks and boots in the sunshine to dry. Dozens of marigold-colored butterflies feasted on the salt in Tom's sweaty socks.

"Your socks are too stinky," Tom joked because my socks only drew two butterflies.

LATER THAT AFTERNOON, we trekked across a serene landscape of rice paddies. Water gurgled as it sought lower ground. The warm overcast sky was thick with the lazy murmur of insects and spiked with the shouts of little boys.

"They catch small fish," Muan explained. The boys waved to us, then returned to their hunt.

The Silent One startled us by catching one of the sardine-looking fish with his hands.

In one place, water swelled under the grass. The ground visibly undulated as we walked on it, as if we were walking across a waterbed. Tom poked the ground with a sharp stick, and a mini geyser shot up.

When we passed by a verdant field of young rice plants, I asked Tom, "Should we make rice angels?"

"That would be cool," he said.

"What are rice angels?" Muan asked.

"Normally, we do it in the snow, but it could work in the sprouts. We lay down and swing our arms and legs back and forth until it leaves an imprint shaped like an angel."

Muan was amused by the idea, but we decided not to out of respect for the farmer.

Minutes later, Muan pointed out an impressive pile left by a water buffalo and politely said, "Watch out for the shit."

Tom and I burst out laughing.

"That is not right?" Muan asked as he furrowed his brow with confusion and concern.

This led to a conversation about which English words for manure were polite and which were not. Muan shook his head, overwhelmed. We confused matters by pointing out the difference between British English and American English.

"To me a fag is a cigarette, but for her, it's a mean name for a gay bloke," Tom noted.

"And Americans don't use the word bloke," I added. "It means a man or a guy."

"Is the low dirt wall between rice paddies a dam or a dike?" I asked Tom, who was quick to point out that these were different from damn and dyke.

After we waded across a creek that fed into the Nam Song River, Muan stopped to pluck a deep green, ping pong ball-shaped fruit off a thorny tree branch.

"Kaffir limes," he said as he showed it to us.

"Excellent. We might need those for happy hour," Tom said, so we filled our pockets with them.

Our destination, the Tree House Guesthouse, was on the far shore of the Nam Song River. Muan and the Silent One nonchalantly stripped down to their boxer shorts, jumped from a tree branch into the river, swam across and retrieved a couple kayaks to shuttle us across.

The Tree House Guesthouse was a complex of buildings. One building was an open-air dining room with the kitchen and staff quarters off to the side. Ropes of plastic Beerlao flags fluttered along the roof eaves. Another building, with an outside sink and mirror, housed showers and western-style toilets.

Down from the dining building was a recreation hall. Stacks of amps and speakers sat unused until tourist season started in October. Next to the recreation hall two motel-looking buildings, with private rooms had beds with linen-covered mattresses. We opted to stay in the rustic, one-room, three-walled bamboo hut topped with a thatched roof. Its fourth side was a balcony that hung over the river. Our "beds" were fabric-covered foam pads paired up on the wooden plank floor under tents of mosquito netting. The guides shared one net. Tom and I shared the other one. We were getting more comfortable with each other.

Two charismatic dogs patrolled the guest house grounds. CeLo had the build of a Great Dane, the vanity of a princess and the protective disposition of a Rottweiler. YoYo, a rust-colored Chihauhau, was her entourage. He pranced around, happy to follow her every lead.

Happy hour at the recreation hall was quiet as we four were the only ones there. It was also a painful affair due to local Tiger whiskey. The clear liquid bore a remarkable resemblance to paint thinner. The kaffir limes did not reduce the afterburn of the shots. We soon switched to beer.

"Damn things," Tom said as he casually lit a cigarette. He wanted to quit smoking, but cigarettes in Laos were wickedly cheap. It was a good thing he smoked because it was a major turnoff for me. I was growing fond of him and his light sense of humor.

"You are weak. You are a weak English man," I teased. "With men like you, no wonder the British Empire collapsed."

It was like the pot calling the kettle black. I was addicted to sugar and enjoyed sweets every day, I thought as I popped my last Oreo in my mouth.

The sun had set by the time dinner was served in the dining room balcony. We ate bamboo shoot soup, cooked leafy greens, roast chicken and salad greens. The meal was delightful, with one exception. Things scratched and thumped across the tin roof above our heads.

"Rats," Muan muttered nonchalantly. I imagined a Chicago street rat as big as a cat. The kind that gnawed delicate bits off unattended babies in the night.

"I'll protect you," Tom said half seriously as I kept a wary eye on the ceiling.

When the sweet sticky rice was served, my apprehension ended as a rat scurried down the outside wall of the kitchen. It leapt onto a dangling bird cage to scavenge for seeds. I was gratefully disappointed by it. It looked more like a large mouse with a dark, silky coat and teddy bear ears. It was, dare I say, cute. If they kept their distance from me, I could tolerate them easily enough.

After dinner, I peeked into the screenless window of the staff quarters. More than a dozen people were crammed into the living room, some sitting in chairs, some laying on the floor, all watching a black-and-white TV program marred by grainy reception.

Before bed, Muan placed a kerosene lamp on the floor in the center of our hut and let it burn all night. I did not ask if it was a night light or rat deterrent.

IT WAS STRANGE TO WAKE UP, look over and see a man just a couple feet away. Tom looked so sweet, like a little boy curled up on his side, hands tucked under his chin. It was fun traveling with him, sharing the experience. Was he attractive in his own right, or was I just delighted to have a man around? Probably some of both.

Unable to go back to sleep, I sat by the balcony railing, feet dangling over the edge, sarong draped around my shoulders, and scribbled in my journal. The sky was overcast, and the river was visibly higher than it was the day before. The itsy bitsy spider would not be crawling up the waterspout any time soon.

A little after 9 a.m., after a hearty breakfast, we got down to business. Muan and the Silent One each paddled in sporty Dagger kayaks. Tom and I shared a bright orange, double sit-on-top kayak. The river swept us downstream at a heady pace. The surface of the café-au-lait-colored water was beguilingly smooth. We only paddled to steer the kayak. Pleasantly warm bouts of rain came and went. We passed embankments, rice paddies, small hills and stony cliffs. Turkeys gobbled in the undergrowth. Up ahead, the river took a hard left.

"Tom, look, isn't that amazing?" I said, turning sideways to see if he was looking, "See the way the hills disappear into the clouds?"

I whipped out the disposable camera from inside a Ziploc bag and took a picture.

What both of us failed to notice was the seemingly insignificant ripple in the water about ten feet ahead. As I sealed the camera back into a baggie, we flipped over as fast as I yelled, "Shit!"

Tom and I sputtered to the surface and laughed at the sudden dunking.

Our laugher was tinged with concern.

"Go there now," Muan yelled. He pointed to the piece of shoreline where we could get out of the water. Trying to reboard the kayak in the river was not possible or safe. The fast moving current and fallen trees could quickly become a lethal combination.

Muan zipped about, collecting our jettisoned belongings. The Silent One caught our kayak and pulled it to shore. Slipping about on the mud, we eventually got it upright and ourselves back on board. Humbled, we continued on, paying more attention to the river.

At lunchtime, we stopped on a rocky shoal in the middle of the river. Muan struggled to build a fire to cook a duplicate of yesterday's lunch as rain thwarted his best efforts. At one point he used a big stick to prop his kayak over the tiny flames. We applauded his efforts when he finally served lunch. By the time we finished eating it, the rising river had engulfed the 16-foot-wide shoal and put out the fire.

TO ENTER THE LAST CAVE, we would have to swim across the strong current of one stream before it pushed us over a modest waterfall, only to then swim up another stream that flowed out of the cave. I was intrigued, but decided not to go because I was worried I would freak out in the confines. The Silent One went off to chat with a friend, Tom went off to explore the third cave with Muan, and I reclined on a wooden bench by the river.

The shoreline was full of the yellow and red kayaks of other explorers. A wizened old couple sold junk food from a makeshift bamboo stand. I did not resist buying a Snickers. In the river, a determined young man tried to master 360-degree rolls with Muan's Dagger kayak. Each time he positioned his paddle and spun upside down, he got stuck. Each time, his amused friend flipped him right side up again.

Not everyone on the river had a safety backup. Earlier, Muan said that a few days ago a lone woman rented an inner tube for about $1 and went tubing without telling anyone that she did not know how to swim. No one kept an eye on her. She fell out of the inner tube and, in spite of her life preserver, she drowned. It seemed like such a senseless way to lose her life.

AT THE BOAT PULLOUT IN Vang Vieng, Tom and Muan straddled the kayaks on top of the roof of the truck for the short ride back to the outfitter office. I was required to ride in the cab next to the Silent One. My *Lonely*

Planet guidebook mentioned that this was due in part to a "deep-seated superstition that women's bodies should not intentionally occupy a physical space above a man's for fear of damaging men's spiritual status."

Tom and I rented a room at the Doukkhoun Guesthouse, a two-story, whitewashed building with a flat roof. Posted on the wall of the terracotta-tiled patio were notices from the proprietor and the government. Both ended their messages, "With love and good hope."

Costing 30,000 kip ($3.10), our immaculate room had two single beds, a private bath and two windows covered with metal bars. The wiring for the fan and the ceiling light snaked along the walls, doorways and ceiling. The sign by the door read, "Please don't burning candle in the bedroom. Except the lights out but you must blow out when you go out of the room."

After dark, the only light on the main street came from business windows. A lone man sold crepes full of banana and chocolate syrup from a cart, just like the vendor at Forodhani Gardens in Zanzibar.

As rain started to fall, Tom and I ducked into a restaurant. There were wooden tables and chairs in the center of the room. Short tables surrounded by floor pillows sat on risers along the outer walls. Two color TVs were mounted high in the back corners. Dinner came with two movies. The first was *Indiana Jones and the Raiders of the Lost Ark*. Odd coincidence that on the river shoal earlier that day, Tom and Muan had been mock fighting the scene where Indiana shoots the sword-wielding bad guy in the bazaar.

We had ham and onion pizzas. My mint tea was served in a chipped Minnie Mouse ceramic mug. Dessert was a mango crumble. Before a James Bond movie started, a plump little rat ran down the bamboo-lined wall about eight feet from our table. Tom and I ignored it, but the rodent horrified the young German woman who shared our table.

I WOKE UP WITH MURDER on my mind. A rooster started crowing about 6 a.m. and kept at it for the next two hours. Even through my earplugs, it was grating. Trying to be a good travel companion, I let Tom sleep while I plotted ways to kill the damn bird.

Our morning was slow going. When we finally caught a pick-up truck back to Vientiane, our fickle friend the sun made a hasty departure. Passengers came and went as we headed south. Same kind of ride. Same hard benches. But there was a twist. The truck stopped, money changed hands, and we were herded from our truck to the back of another. We had been sold. The original driver headed back north. This exchange happened two more times by the time we reached Vientiane.

By late afternoon, Tom and I had settled into separate rooms back at the Phonepaseuth Guesthouse. Afterwards, we joined a couple of hashers, a young British expat and his Thai girlfriend, at an open air restaurant on the bank of the Mekong River. On the distant shore was a Thai village. In the no man's land between shorelines, a lone fisherman stood on a shoal tending a line.

The sun set in a glorious wash of colors as dishes arrived at our table: dumplings, satays and curries. During the meal, a beetle with a shell as smooth and brown as a chestnut landed on our table. Before we set it free, we pondered how it would taste if roasted.

On to Khawp Jai Restaurant for more drinks, where we crossed paths with a boisterous group of young American men who invited me to roadtrip with them to Hanoi, Vietnam. Minus the prospect of a 20-hour bus ride, their roadtrip sounded exciting, but I declined. I wanted to go to Luang Prabang with Ott.

AFTER STARTING THE DAY with banana bread and coffee at the Scandanavian Bakery, Tom and I wandered around the public market. The second floor was packed with brilliantly lit display cases of silver and gold jewelry.

"We buy gold or houses if we have extra money," Ott had explained when we were in Luang Prabang.

I modeled jewelry for Tom as he shopped for presents for his girlfriend. No surprise that I ended up buying a silver and garnet charm for myself.

In the afternoon, Tom and I said our farewells, and he left to go back to Bangkok. It was the right time. I was having fantasies about what would happen if we started a relationship (one where he did not smoke). I got the impression he wanted to leave before he did anything he would regret. We hoped to cross paths again in Bangkok, but it was not meant to be. The luck predicted by our two fortune sticks had run its course.

Sticky rice and Adam's apples

Vientiane and Luang Prabang, Laos

AT 7 A.M., OTT AND I BEGAN the 11-hour, 300-mile-long bus ride to Luang Prabang along Route 13. The roof of the bus was stacked high with suitcases and colorful plastic mesh-covered bales. Every seat was occupied. Still more passengers perched on short plastic stools in the aisle. I was astonished by the crowd, while Ott was indifferent. Even though the bus was a coach-type affair, rather than a school bus, I still had to sit sideways or with my knees bent high on the back of the seat in front of me.

I confess that it did not take long for me to grow irritated with the old woman in the seat in front of me. She wanted the top window down, so she could throw out banana peels, trash from her snacks and cigarette butts after she smoked. I wanted the window up because I got soaked when the rain blew in, about every half hour. Each time the rain started, I would gently tap her on the shoulder, smile and push the window back up where it stayed for about five minutes. The window on the bus went up and down as the wheels on the bus went round and round.

Having slept through the first bathroom stop, I was eager for the next one after we passed the turn for Vang Vieng. The stop turned out to be in the middle of a barren nowhere. Without a word, the men got off the bus and walked past the front of it. Ott waved me off to join the women, who walked to the right of the bus door and down the slope where little bushes came up to their knees and my mid-calf. There was nothing to stand behind. My aching bladder gave me no choice but to follow. Bad day to wear khaki pants.

The other women easily hiked up their sarongs and squatted to do their business. I picked a spot a little ways from them, and, hoping not to blind anyone with the whiteness of my backside, dropped my pants and underwear as I squatted down.

Seconds later my feet started to itch and burn. Something was wrong.

Bending to the left, I could see dozens of tiny black dots swarming my feet. I did not see a mound of any sort, but there the bugs were and there

I was, oh so compromised as the other women headed back to the bus. I tried stomping my feet to shake them off. No luck. They would bite my hands if I tried to brush them off. Time for a last resort. I peed on my feet and washed them away.

I hastily pulled up my clothes as I crabwalked away from the spot. I shook my feet like a cat with wet paws as I headed back to the bus. I smelled incontinent.

THE BUS STOPPED IN A SMALL TOWN so passengers could grab a bite to eat at roadside stands. Ott and I bought bowls of cooked pork bits and green beans served over noodles. This region obviously favored pork products. The farther north we traveled, the more sows and piglets I saw grazing along the side of the road or penned under homes.

In the next town we passed through, a bus like ours had smashed head-on into an industrial truck. The injured and dead had been removed, but both vehicles needed to be towed away. People and traffic just flowed around the crash site as if it was nothing more than a mound of dirt. Life went on.

The road we drove along, Route 13, the only road to Luang Prabang, had first been paved in the 1990s. The former unpaved road limited travel to the dry season, and even then it had unpredictable use. That lack of access helped preserve the city's unique blend of cultures and architectures—French Colonial and Lao traditional. Most of the old colonial buildings now standing—including 679 historic structures—were built between 1920 and 1925.

Luang Prabang's 16,000 loosely gathered residents formed a metropolis on the banks of the Mekong and Khan rivers. Thanon Phothisalat, one of the many names for the main street, was lined with row houses painted white and spotted with sky blue or russet red shutters and doors. Wide sidewalks bloomed with terracotta pots full of geraniums.

A majority of the locals wore casual Western clothes, though the women preferred *pha sin* [long, wraparound skirts]. Most people traveled by foot, bicycle or motor scooter. There were few farangs to be seen.

Ott and I rented a room in a narrow wing of a guesthouse for 30,000 kip ($3.10) a night. The simple room had a barred window, a ceiling fan, twin beds of high-density foam and plywood design, a polished concrete floor and a solid wood door that locked with a padlock. I had a sneaking suspicion that the room had once been a horse stall. The communal bathroom and kitchen were next to the lobby.

The proprietors, a petite old couple with crinkly faces, were eagerly polite. Their limited English had a French accent. The husband slept on a cot in the open lobby at night, surrounded by heavy-framed, black-and-white, life-sized portraits of his solemn ancestors wearing dark suits and high-neck dresses. Each person held a stiff posture—straight back, shoulders squared, arms to the sides and lips pursed. I guessed the portraits were taken with film that required a long exposure time. During our stay, I asked the proprietors if I could take their picture. Pleased, they automatically assumed the same rigid positions.

Ott and I walked over to the public market. A young woman played with a white lap dog that had pink stripes dyed into the fur on its ears, forehead and paws. A matronly woman flicked beads on an abacus to calculate a sale. An elderly seamstress wore a long-sleeve shirt, a *pha sin*, a chunky wristwatch and a purple touk-style hat with black, green and magenta diamonds. A Vietnamese woman, armed with a bucket of tools and a plastic stool, gave clients like Ott a curb-side pedicure for 4,000 kip ($.42).

The food section of the market was a dirt alley lined with plywood tables, each covered with bright plastic tablecloths. Stalls were shaded by canvas patio umbrellas or sheets of corrugated metal weighed down with scraps of lumber. Idle vendors swooshed plastic bags tied to the ends of bamboo canes back and forth over their food to keep flies away.

For dinner, we bought prepared dishes piled high in large ceramic bowls. Pork ruled as the most popular meat available. I bought several finger-shaped sausages for about a dime each.

"Do you want to try one of these?" Ott teased, pointing to grilled sparrow-looking birds.

I scrunched up my face and shook my head.

"Graeme will not eat them either," she laughed.

A lanky young woman with a prominent Adam's apple sold me some potato curry. Her short black hair was pulled back into pigtails. Her crudely padded bra made her tight pink T-shirt oddly lumpy.

"*Katoey*?" I asked Ott after we had walked away.

She smiled and nodded as we walked over to a young woman who hand-peeled, cored, sliced and bagged whole pineapples on request. We bought one for about a dime. During our stay, we always kept pineapple in the communal refrigerator for Ott's late night cravings.

A matronly woman wearing a pink floral apron worked at a cart that seemed like Luang Prabang's version of Dairy Queen. She built dazzling sundaes made from oddly shaped bits of brightly colored gelatin, fruit pieces and sweet beans. One customer sat on a nearby milk crate as he slurped the last drips of coconut milk from his bowl. I saw no place to wash dishes. Hopefully, the woman washed them at home before reusing them. I bought steamed banana leaf bundles stuffed with sticky rice, ripe banana, palm sugar and coconut milk. Yet another reason to love Laos.

OTT WOKE UP ABOUT 6:30 a.m. to start her big paper-buying day—a big change from Tom, who could sleep until noon if given the chance. Our first task was to buy plane tickets back to Vientiane at a local travel agency. I tried to buy both our tickets with a Visa card so I could have Ott's cash, but that was strictly forbidden. Visa was only accepted for *farang* tickets. No explanation was provided. That was just the way it was. How East African, I thought.

When Ott said we would visit paper factories, I had visions of industrial equipment, automation, warehouses and workers in uniforms. In reality, the first one looked like a struggling home business. Its front yard was bricked over and tufted with weeds.

"Please wait here until I wave to you. If they see you, they will think I am buying paper for you and will charge *farang* prices," Ott said quietly before she crossed the street. I waited in the *tuk tuk*, scratching the bites on my feet.

After buying 10 kilos of posterboard-sized sheets of handmade paper, Ott waved for me to come inside the cramped living room that served as the retail office. Richly textured paper goods—wrapping paper, paper bags and blank-paged books bound with hand-spun cotton string—were stacked all over the place.

I bought three medium-sized books, but, when it was time to pay, I broke a golden rule Ott had taught me. Rather than setting my 19 bills on the counter so that the saleslady and I could count them together, I thoughtlessly handed them to her. Sure enough, one of them disappeared when she turned her back to me by the cash register.

"One more please," the woman said to me so politely, so innocently.

It was a 50-cent ripoff, but theft none the less.

Ott fought back the tiniest of grins.

I would not make that mistake again.

As we were leaving, two women started to make paper on the porch. We stopped to watch them. They each submerged what looked like a window screen into a shallow tub of water. Then they mixed in handfuls of pulp until the water looked like runny gravy.

With artistic skill, they placed delicate flower petals, bamboo leaves and fern fronds into the mix. Satisfied with the results, they slowly lifted the screens out of the fibrous water. Water drained through as the fibers formed a layer on the screen, one that would become a sheet of paper when it dried out in the courtyard. So unique. So simple. So labor intensive.

The second factory was a more commercial enterprise. The metal-sided building with industrial-grade grinding equipment and stacks of red five-gallon buckets gave production a jump start, but workers still had to process hundreds of screens by hand.

Few women were working due to the rain. Like the Nepalese who made enough bricks to last through the rainy season, this factory had stockpiled sheet paper. Inside a windowless wooden shed, Ott patiently handpicked dozens of delicate sheets of paper. Some she resold to me later.

After dropping our purchases off at our room, we visited the former Royal Palace of King Sisavang Vong and his family. It was prominently positioned on a palm tree-lined walk between the main road and the Mekong River. Built in 1904 during the early French Colonial era, the spacious T-shaped palace inspired awe to the point that it made us whisper.

We walked barefoot on cool, hardwood floors through reception halls, throne rooms, galleries and royal bedrooms. How many thousands of bare feet had walked these same floors? The vastness of the rooms and the sparseness of furnishings made the palace's few decorative touches more pronounced—family portraits, Italian marble stairs, gilded Ramayana screens, carved elephant tusks and the king's chair for riding elephants. Silver and china gifts to the royal family were displayed in groups according to whether they came from capitalist or socialist countries.

The palace grounds included a separate kitchen building, a royal barge shelter, a conference hall and a bigger-than-life statue of the king. Gilded, seven-headed dragons greeted visitors at the religious pavilion.

Motivated by a brief period of sunlight, Ott and I climbed the steps of Phu Si, a steep hill that rose up in the center of town. On the way up, I pointed out a snake that slithered away into the grass.

"Seeing a snake is a good omen," Ott said solemnly. "It might be a god reminding us to be humble."

From the top of the hill, the whole city lay at our feet. We could also see hundreds of yellow plastic crates stacked on a river dock.

"They are full of empty beer bottles," Ott explained. "They go back to Vientiane to be reused."

I wondered if people in Luang Prabang drank more beer than water.

After dinner I went to check my email. Outside the internet café, I added my shoes to the pile of worn sandals before entering the narrow building. Inside, *farangs*, locals and a couple of monks sat in straight back wooden chairs in front of the PCs.

I could not help but notice the frustrated man sitting next to me, making dramatic hand gestures at his computer screen. He seemed about 30 years old, with dyed blonde hair and dark roots, brown eyes, and a tanned, lean build. He reminded me of a former boyfriend, but what I noticed the most was how incredibly good he smelled. The scent was a delightfully clean combination of soap and cologne.

"She might hear you better if you type what you're trying to say," I joked after a couple of minutes. He flashed me an embarrassed smile.

"She doesn't understand," he said with a British accent. "And I'm having trouble putting my thoughts into words."

"That can be a deal breaker," I said turning back to my computer, thinking that was the end of the conversation.

"My name is Oliver."

"Hello, I'm Kristine."

"You are an American."

"And you are …"

"German," he said pushing back his chair. "I am going across the street for a beer. Would you like to join me?"

"Sure." Ott had already turned in for the night.

We sat at a sidewalk table and talked about travel.

"I am here with my friend Stephan," he said after I explained my connection with Ott. "We're going to Kuang Si Falls tomorrow. Would you two like to go with us?"

Before I could answer, the proprietor approached our table, set down the bill and waited for payment. "We closing now. Thank you for coming."

It was exactly 11 p.m. Lights were turning off all down the street. Even though it was a Friday night, it was time for all business owners to go home to their families.

"We're staying at that guest house," I said to Oliver as we walked down the dark main street. I wondered how to get in touch with him again. It was not like I could give him my phone number.

Oliver laughed. "That's where we are staying."

FORTIFIED BY FRESH MANGO SHAKES, our Lao-German-American foursome took a bumpy 45-minute tuk tuk ride along a dirt road through the rolling countryside to visit Kuang Si Falls. From a gravel parking lot, we ambled along a trail through the woods. Our chatter competed with the birds. We gave no thought to the nearby two-story-tall chain-link fence until a tiger charged out of the undergrowth towards us.

The fence seemed such a flimsy barrier between us and the ripples of muscles under her glossy coat of burnished copper and black stripes.

We stood still.

She looked at us.

We looked at her.

She lost interest, licked her fur and walked away.

"What was that? I mean … I know it is a tiger, but what is it doing here?" I asked no one in particular.

Oliver and Stephan shook their heads and talked in German to each other. Ott just smiled as if the unexpected was to be expected. We later learned that the young tigress had been confiscated from poachers when she was a cub, along with her two siblings, who had not survived.

The Kuang Si Falls was a play-at-your-own-risk, nature-made amusement park. There were rocks to climb on, blue-green pools of water to splash in, and a crude trail through the woods to the top of the waterfall. There, we waded out into the shallow water and peered over the edge. Inches from our toes, the water dropped several stories down.

LUANG PRABANG STILL HAD more than 30 of its original temples. Bellies full of pineapple and French toast, Ott and I walked that morning to Wat Xieng Thong [Golden City Monastery], the most magnificent one of all.

Along the way, we saw monks at a wat hanging out newly washed robes on a clothesline to dry.

"Do the monks share all the robes or do they have their own robes with their names on them to tell them apart?"

"You ask funny questions," Ott giggled and shrugged.

Wat Xieng Thong had no shortage of understated elegance. The temple grounds, mostly covered with square paving stones, included a collection of small stupas, a drum tower, a boat shelter and a reclining Buddha sanctuary. The pale red plaster exterior of the Tripitaka Library building was inlaid with glass mosaics of pastoral Lao life. Blue elephants marched through fields of golden pineapple sprouts.

The gilded doors of the Royal Funerary Carriage House were works of art in themselves. On one panel, maidens with intricate headdresses, Mona

Lisa smiles, ample breasts and hands clasped together in prayer rose from of golden flames. Inside, we looked at a funeral carriage (think small ark with wheels), family urns and odd bits of salvaged wooden architectural pieces. Everything sat in the open, vulnerable to theft and collecting dust. Only the royal stick puppets were stored in protective glass cabinets.

The main *sim* [chapel or sanctuary] seemed to be 80 percent draping, brown-tiled roofline and 20 percent golden supporting wall.

"The roof is like the wings of a mother hen protecting her chicks," Ott said quietly as we entered the building.

By now I was used to seeing Buddhas and shrines, but I was not prepared for the interior's intense sense of gentle peace. It was almost palpable. We sat on the floor in silence and basked in the feeling.

Afterwards, Ott negotiated a *tuk tuk* ride for us to the nearby village of Ban Phanom, known for silk and cotton weaving. In an airy one-room, wooden co-op building, women artisans sat on raised platforms behind piles of their work—mostly silk and cotton scarves and shirts. My appearance—a *farang* on a slow day—brought much excitement.

"Madame? Madame? Madame?" They called sweetly, vying for my attention. I visited each one and murmured praise for their detailed work. After Ott discreetly gave me advice on price ranges, I bargained for two silk scarves and a vest.

As we shopped, ominous clouds filled the sky. The wind blew as thunder boomed. The woman on the back porch kept sliding a shuttle through a loom as an intense rain came down and then just as quickly moved on. The joys of the rainy season.

When we returned to Luang Prabang, we walked past a vacant lot where a crowd conducted a brisk trade with little books and tickets piled on top of folding trays and crude plank tables.

"They are selling lottery tickets," Ott explained. The grand prize was 500,000 kip, roughly $50.

"I feel lucky. Will you help me buy a ticket?" They were 5,000 kip (about $.50) each.

"We need three numbers," she said.

"The first number should be seven because it's lucky," I said.

"We saw a snake today, and 32 is the number for snakes," she suggested.

We were close. The winning number was 727. I did not think to ask what animal might be represented by the number 27.

LUANG PRABANG HAD A CONSPICUOUS lack of advertising. No billboards, signs or posters glued to public walls and poles. The few neon lights were beer signs in restaurants. This made it that much more impactful when a young man handed me a black-and-white flyer promoting traditional songs and dances at the Royal Theatre in the Royal Palace. Not only did we go to the performance, but we also wrangled Oliver and Stephan into joining us.

The theatre's second-floor ballroom felt like a high school gym without basketball hoops. I loved the perforated ceiling tiles and cone-shaped light fixtures. The audience—where did all the *farangs* come from?—sat in upholstered banquet chairs arranged in four crescent moon-shaped rows. A slip of paper with hand-written row and seat numbers on it was pinned to the back of each chair. There was no stage.

Performers swirled in front of us. Musicians sitting on pads on the floor played unfamiliar drum and string instruments. I liked the name of the "Magical Ritual Minority Dance." While the sounds were often too discordant for me to appreciate, they swept Ott to a familiar place. She sang and gestured along with the music, the way most Americans knew how to perform the YMCA song.

During a Baci Ceremony, a couple of performers knelt in front of each of us and tied two raw cotton strings to our wrists.

"They bring good luck," Ott explained. "Wear the strings for three days and then untie them. Do not cut them or it breaks the luck."

Ott wished for four children. I wished for a husband.

After intermission, the performance continued on the outside lawn with more music and dancing. For the grand finale, a man and a woman wearing blue jumpsuits and red headbands carried terracotta pots full of water across the lawn with their teeth clamped on the rims.

ALL DAY LONG, MY SKIN FELT PRICKLY. I tried not to think about it, to deny the possibility of flea bites or bed bugs or tropical skin diseases. Yet I could no longer deny something was wrong.

In the guesthouse's rose pink tiled bathroom, I took my clothes off and checked my body for bite marks. Nothing. Then I checked my clothes and found dozens of miniscule pointy seeds. I had probably picked them up while hashing in Vientiane, and they had not washed out when I had done my laundry.

As I sat on the Western toilet, I wondered why I had jumped to such extreme conclusions when there was such a simple explanation. I decided to blame the sweltering heat. The state of the bathroom did not help. After a busy day's use, its warm, still air stunk from the used toilet paper piled in the trash can. Tangles of hair and lumps of soap dotted the floor. Ants marched out of a hole in the wall to my right, went around the back of the toilet and disappeared into a hole in the wall to my left. The bathroom and I were both in a sorry state.

IT WAS A GOOD THING Ott brought me along to Luang Prabang. She was only allowed to check in 20 kilos of luggage for the return flight to Vientianne yet she had 30 kilos of paper. One bale had to be checked in under my name.

While waiting in line to validate my plane ticket, I met a man originally from Washington, D.C., who was on his way home to Japan. On a whim, he gave me his remaining 45,000 kip. I did not win the lottery, but I still had good fortune.

When Ott and I arrived at the spartan Wattay International Airport in Vientiane, Graeme picked us up. Since the workmen had finally finished the renovations at their house, Graeme and Ott invited me to stay with them at their ranch-style house. It was my last night before going back to Bangkok.

As he drove home, we passed five horses roaming the streets, grazing where they wanted, with no obvious caretaker. They reminded me of the cows that wandered the streets in Nepal.

"I had a job interview today," he proudly announced.

"Doing what?" I asked.

"Teaching people how to drive properly," he said. "Most locals learn to drive by winging it. That's probably why car accidents are the No. 1 killer here."

According to Graeme, the lackadaisical attitude toward safe driving coincided with the local life-is-cheap attitude. Why spend time, money and effort on driving programs when accident victims were going to die somehow anyway?

"It is so easy to have someone killed here, like *farangs* after their local wives get their names on the deeds to the house and car," Graeme continued. He was on a roll. "Sometimes they file charges against the *farang* husband when he goes to his home country for a visit so that he can't get back into Laos. The wife and her family don't need him any more because they have control of his belongings."

This low value of life was new to me. I peeked a look at Ott, but she seemed lost in her own thoughts. That evening, she confessed that she had been so tired and had craved so much pineapple because she was pregnant with her first child.

"Those Baci Ceremony strings work fast!" I joked when she told me.

RIDING WITH OTT ON HER MOTOR SCOOTER, we started the morning with a trip to a Federal Express office. I wanted to buy a cardboard packing tube to hold the handmade paper I bought. A good plan gone wrong. The salesman refused to sell me a box for any price because I was not shipping anything anywhere.

Later, Graeme proposed a reason for the salesman's decision.

"Laotians are so used to being told what to do and how to do it that they can't think outside the box," he said. "That salesman couldn't see that breaking the rule still supported the company's bigger goal of making a profit."

Our next stop was a food market, a sprawling cluster of wooden tables shaded by blue plastic tarps. The meat section was fascinating and repulsive. Flies were prolific. Grayish balls of raw ground meat aged on metal trays. Dozens of dead chickens, turkeys and geese hung from the rafters. Catfish and eels squirmed in rusted washtubs. Quarter-sized clams spread their shells apart, revealing red-feathered flesh as they died from lack of water.

Ott bought fish filets to cook for lunch before I left town. I wish I had eaten one before she pointed out the kind fish it was. It had an ugly bulldog face and motley green and brown slimey skin. Fortunately, it tasted much better than it looked.

When it was time for me to head back to Bangkok, I could not thank Ott enough for her time and hospitality.

"Congratulations on your baby, and you two have a safe trip," I said hugging first Ott, then Graeme. "If I ever make it to New Zealand, I will look you up."

CROSSING FROM LAOS BACK INTO THAILAND was a piece of cake, or perhaps I should say a scoop of sweet sticky rice. With the help of a gawky German man who spoke English and some Thai, I even caught a ride in the back of a truck with other locals from the Thai border to the Nong Khai train station rather than pay for a *tuk tuk*.

There was nothing around the station but open countryside and a small strip of open-air businesses. In the sweltering heat, I passed the hours until the next train to Bangkok by people-watching.

I could not help but notice one man who shuffled by. His dark crew cut rippled along the deep ridges in his disturbingly large head. Only a whisper of Asian heritage showed through thick facial features. One arm hung limp at his side. One leg did not bend as he moved. Judging by his age and the look of his worn but clean clothes, someone was taking care of him with much love.

The weary looking men who lived in the abandoned boxcars on the other side of the train platform were not so lucky. They wore ratty undershirts and flicked cigarette butts onto the tracks. Their homes were nothing more than clotheslines and shoddy bedding. There seemed to be no music, no laughter, no women, no joy in their worlds.

At 6 p.m., all activity at the train terminal stopped. We solemnly faced the royal portrait while the national anthem played. That was when I noticed a young traveler sleeping against the train station wall. His hair was a matted mess. A heavy gauge silver ring swung from the underside of his nose. His clothes and backpack were threadbare. He looked feral. Perhaps he had drifted so physically and psychologically far from his past that he had crossed a point of no return.

Temple for the well-heeled

Bangkok, Thailand

MY LAST PASS THROUGH BANGKOK was two days long. Once again, I stayed at Keith's house. The highlight was when Maggie and I signed up for a boat tour along the Chao Phraya River. It was a peaceful, efficient way to avoid the city's ever-present traffic congestion. Under the boat's canvas awning, we sat with dozens of tourists at lacquered tables. An attendant served us bottled water and chilled, wet wash cloths to help combat the muggy heat.

As we motored up the river, we passed buildings of all shapes and financial status—squat, weathered shacks on pilings, towering high-rise hotels, pointy temples, even an Italianate villa with a caved-in roof. On a monstrous digital billboard, athletes kicked soccer balls to promote Coca-Cola.

From a distance, Wat Arun [Temple of Dawn] looked like a brownish set of nesting dolls. Walls and castle towers surrounded smaller, higher walls and towers. Up close, its surfaces were intricately plastered with millions of bits of aquamarine, rose pink, russet red, navy blue, sage green and butter yellow bits of porcelain—a brilliant, artistic use for the tons of broken porcelain ballast dumped by decades of Chinese ships picking up cargo.

Our next stop, the Royal Barges National Museum, floated on a small canal near the Grand Palace. Back when the river was the main means of transportation, thousands of royal barges carried the king, queen and other members of the royal family.

Since the beginning of the 1900s, the royal barges have been built, burned by Burmese attackers, rebuilt and used for ceremonial reasons only, confiscated by civilian or military governments during political coups, and bombed by the Japanese during World War II. The few dozen surviving barges, fragile with age, are only brought out for processions on rare occasions.

The museum houses eight barges, including the largest and most important one. Built in 1911, the Suppannahong [Golden Swan] measures 160 feet long and 10.3 feet wide and weighs 15 tons. She required a 77-man crew.

Our last tour stop was a meager one-hour visit to the Grand Palace, which was established in 1782. Our allotted time was cropped even shorter when Maggie failed inspection by the fashion police posted just inside the Viseschaisri Gate. We knew to wear clothes that covered our legs, but the backs of her heels were bare. Evidently, the narrow heel strap of my Teva shoes conveyed proper modesty. Ten minutes ticked by as we stopped at the shoe stand strategically located across the street.

Once inside, we dashed past manicured lawns and dodged slow-moving, camera-happy visitors as they explored more than a hundred royal residences, throne halls, temples and government offices. We gave appreciative glances at dramatic spires, statues, gilded temples and water fountains as we raced to the Royal Monastery of the Emerald Buddha. With a secretive past like the Golden Buddha, this mysterious gem of religious faith was first discovered in 1434 inside a plaster cast when an abbot noticed plaster on the statue's nose had flaked off.

We removed our shoes, tucked away our cameras and joined the masses filing into the monastery ordination hall. The walls were covered with murals depicting milestones in Buddha's life and spiritual teachings. Visitors sat knee-to-knee on the floor, an audience for the Emerald Buddha, who held court from a gilded, multi-tiered throne. About the size of a toddler, he was carved from a single block of green jade or jasper quartz or possibly nephrite jade, depending on which source I believed.

"I heard that they change his clothes with the seasons," Maggie said as we put on our shoes and headed back to the boat.

"Does his fashion sense lean toward classic, modern or couture?" I asked with a smile.

That night, I went to a hashing event. Because Keith's house, the trail start and the airport were all about 45 minutes apart, I planned to camp at the airport after the hash until it was time to catch a 6 a.m. flight to Tokyo, where I would catch another flight to Hawaii. But then I ran into Heath, the American who had been at both of the Bangkok and Phuket hashes.

"I've got a flight to Tokyo about an hour after your flight," he said. "Want to crash in my hotel room? There's a spare bed, and we can share a cab to the airport."

Thinking it would be more comfortable and save me money, I accepted. It was an offer I should have refused.

I could not sleep, so I had to just lay quietly in the dark for hours while he slept. We did not leave the hotel until 4:20 a.m. due to his time-consuming morning habits. There was a manual luggage search at the airport entrance. At the check-in counter, there was a 500 baht departure fee that I had not expected and could not pay with a credit card. The currency exchange booth was closed for a staff break. When it finally reopened and I got the money I needed to pay the fee, I had only minutes to spare before the flight crew sealed off the plane for departure. I paid dearly for being cheap.

The hostess with the leastest

Oahu, Hawaii

OF ALL THE PLACES I HAD TRAVELED so far, I had the most expectations for Hawaii. They are the most remote of all islands—2,500 miles from the mainland United States, but television had brought glimpses of it into our family home in Georgia when I was a teenager. Black-haired hula girls with floral halos and swaying grass skirts. Heavyset men playing ukuleles. Bronzed surfers in low-riding board shorts catching waves. Elvis rocking the social scene with his hips. Magnum P.I. solving crimes. It was a land of pineapples, macadamia nuts, orchids and words with an abundance of vowels, like humahumanukunukuapuaa, the state fish.

Before I left home, I planned to spend 12 days in Hawaii, the time split between two homes on the island of Oahu. The first home belonged to a man I met at a hashing event in Austin, Texas. I remembered him as an outgoing soul with a handsome, tanned face that conveyed a mix of Japanese and Hawaiian heritage. He had dropped my favorite line, "If you're ever in the neighborhood," so when I started plotting my trip, I followed up on his invitation.

Imagine my surprise when a man with pale English features greeted me at the Honolulu International Airport with a fragrant lei and a kiss on the cheek. I had been emailing a man I had obviously met, but not the one I remembered!

"Hello," I said, quickly adjusting to the change.

"Aloha!"

Dave and his wife lived in a narrow house that staggered up one of the incredibly steep sides of Manoa Valley. The pitch on the driveway was impressively close to 45 degrees. Though the home was modest by size and number of rooms, I was sure it was worth a fortune. The valley view from the living room balcony included the distant skyline of Honolulu against the azure ocean.

My lack of sleep and time changes took their toll. I crashed in the guest bedroom and slept into the late afternoon. In the evening, I took a cab to an upscale restaurant and bar where some hashers were supposed to be meeting. Toying with my drink, I waited and watched well-dressed patrons swirl around me. I was tickled by the familiarity of my surroundings. Once again, I was literate. Money was green. Toilet paper could be flushed. Tap water was safe to drink. Menus made sense.

But there was a price to pay. I had lost my ability to tell locals from travelers from tourists. And staying at a private home made me even more disconnected. The women I saw at the bar traveled in packs and were not open to conversation with a stranger. The one man who talked with me was seeking more than conversation.

The hashers never showed up, so I went home after paying for a drink that cost more than a day's travel expenses in Laos.

AFTER DAVE AND HIS WIFE LEFT for work in the morning, I took a public bus to the premiere Ala Moana Center, where about 200 shops clustered around plant-filled courtyards. It had everything from beachwear to high fashion, food courts to fine dining. Tourists swarmed the Hello Kitty merchandise at the San Rio store and the colorful, hibiscus-print shirts at the Hilo Hattie shop.

From the shopping center I ranged on foot to Ala Moana Beach. School groups played on the park lawns while tourists sunned on the sand and played in the surf. I loitered about, disturbing white pigeons and morning doves. Amazing to think that the northeast trade winds keep the average temperatures in Honolulu between 72° and 78° F all year long.

In the midst of this idyllic scene, I was sad to see a homeless man riffling through garbage cans. He wore layers of soiled, tattered clothes. His exposed skin looked like brown leather. His pale eyes were vacant. I had never considered that Hawaii would have vagrants. What twists in his life brought him to such destitution here? Besides the weather, was it more or less difficult to be homeless in Hawaii than a city like Chicago?

A school teacher held a homemade sandwich in a baggie out to the homeless man, but he shied away. She set it down at the base of a tree and returned to her students. Comfortable in the shadows of her attention, he eventually picked it up and ate it.

When I got back to the house, I relaxed on the balcony. A cloud of mist floated over the ridge behind the house and wafted down into the valley, dumped rain drops, and rolled back up over the ridge—all in about 15 minutes. The mist seemed alive, as if the advance and retreat were a playful attack.

I HAVE TO SAY THAT I HAVE NEVER stayed in someone's home and felt less welcome by the hostess. She left rooms as quickly as I entered them. She only spoke to me when I spoke to her first. She kept conversations short. She did not ask me any questions. She showed zero interest in my open-ended dinner invitation. Dave offered no answers when I made delicate inquiries about the cause of her poor reception. I only mention it because it drastically changed my plans. I left the next day for Hauula and did not return.

HAUULA WAS A SMALL TOWN wedged between the emerald-green, erosion-rippled foothills of the Koolau Mountain Range and the ocean on the northeast coast of Oahu. I joined a couple of dozen hashers who had pitched tents in a shoreline campsite. Fronds on the palm trees rustled with the constant breeze. Nearby, the beach disappeared under a roaring surf. To my surprise, a hasher named Scooby was there. He was at my going-away party in Charlotte. He was a sign that I was getting closer to the end of my trip.

The activities of the Aloha Hash House Harriers were familiar, but the trail included steep hills, spectacular ocean views and a magical evergreen forest of pale light. I was startled when we ran into two men with threatening knives and aggressive dogs. It was pig-hunting time.

Sunlight faded away during the trail-closing ceremony, followed by drinking, singing and swimming. There was also some unexpected kissing with a new hasher buddy named Mike, a fair-skinned, military-employed young man. We were an unlikely pair. I was a woman, months from being 40 years old, who was freely traveling around the world. He was a husband, not yet 30, with three small children and a stack of divorce papers on the back seat of his red VW van.

SINCE I NOW HAD TO PAY for hotel rooms, I decided to fly over to the Big Island for four days until it was time to return to Oahu to stay with other friends as planned. But first, a recuperation day to counter my lack of sleep and too much beer. I asked Mike to drop me off at the Pacific Marina Inn near the airport, where I got a room with a polyester bedspread and industrial-grade carpet.

"You know, I can hang out with you today if you want," Mike said, putting down my pack and sitting on the end of the bed.

"No, thanks," I said, standing by the open door, "but it's been great meeting you, and thanks again for the ride."

Mike got the message. He hugged me goodbye and left, frustrated that I felt no need to consummate our encounter. For me, sex was not to be treated as casually as a handshake. If I was not emotionally close enough to a man to comfortably give him a key to my house or my credit card, then I had no business sharing my body with him.

GETTING TO THE BIG ISLAND the next day was like running an obstacle course. I read that I could get a discount coupon for inter-island plane tickets at an airport ATM, but it turned out that I had to have a plane ticket to get to the area where the ATM was located. I ended up trekking around the airport for 30 minutes until I found another machine that dispensed coupons. The effort saved me $50.

Airport security picked me for an intense security inspection. It was the first time I had seen security personnel use white circles of paper that reacted to explosive residue. They even swiped my Teva shoes.

I was all set to fill a standby seat on the 9:20 a.m. flight when the arrival of a flight attendant's friend bumped me to the 11:45 a.m. flight. Sometimes the cost of freedom was time.

At least there was decent people-watching. A petite Japanese woman in a fitted navy blue suit walked by holding a pole with a red velour lobster on top. A gaggle of senior Japanese tourists followed her like ducklings. A matronly woman in a loose floral muumuu, a wreath of flowers around her head, sang traditional Hawaiian songs. Her backup band played an electric keyboard and guitar. A clean-cut young man in blue scrubs, handcuffs and ankle chains shuffled into the waiting area between two burly men. Another crack in my pre-conceived Hawaiian illusion.

Aloha, sticker shock

The Big Island, Hawaii

OVERCAST SKIES AND A SHORTAGE of rental cars clouded my arrival in the small town of Hilo on the eastern side of the Big Island. Working my way down the strip of car rental booths by the parking lot, I found each one was either out of rental cars or only had astronomically expensive SUVs available. Just when I started to panic, Thrifty Car Rental came to my rescue with a red, mid-sized car for $144 for three days. My plan was to drive clockwise along a series of main roads that formed one big circle around the perimeter of the island.

I am an American at heart. I know this because of the rush I felt starting the engine and driving off after three months of not driving. Such liberation. Such control. Such convenience. No old woman to fight with over a window. Even surfing on the radio was thrilling, though there were few stations to pick from.

The less-than-stellar weather in Hilo was no surprise. It has about 278 soggy days a year, which produce about 129 inches of rain. That is nothing, however, compared with Mount Waialeale, on the island of Kauai. Called the wettest spot on Earth, it has an average rainfall of 444 inches a year. Compare that to Kawaihae on the Big Island, which gets about nine inches a year. On the bright side, the rain keeps tourism from taking over Hilo's quaint, traditional feel.

The pace was laid back, the streets were quiet, and the buildings were low and far back from the crescent-shaped bay. On the outskirts of Hilo, I passed by a cemetery that draped down a gently sloping hill. Many of the gravestones were cropped obelisks engraved with columns of delicate Japanese script. Some were weathered dull gray with age; others shone with the high gloss black of newness.

Most likely, many of the older stones memorialized people who all met the same fate on April 1, 1946. At 7 a.m., a tsunami, traveling 2,500 miles from Alaska, wiped out Hilo's bayfront area known as Little Tokyo and killed 159 people. The community that grew in its place met the same fate 14 years later. Giving up the fight with nature, Hilo turned the waterfront property into park land.

My first stop after leaving Hilo was the Akaka Falls State Park. I walked along a path that meandered over hills, through dense forest and bamboo stands, and linked several waterfalls. I decided that Hawaii took tropical foliage to an astounding new level of intensity. It was a color study of hundreds of shades and textures of green.

The first waterfall I saw, the 100-foot-tall Kahuna Falls, seemed impressive until I reached Akaka Falls. Frothy white water hurtled 442 feet down the side of a moss-covered, black stone wall until it crashed into a dark pool below. The misty air was exhilarating.

I drove on to Lava Tree State Park. A sign in the parking lot warned visitors to stay on the paved path that wove around buckled ground and narrow fissures. Lava that had once flowed through this area became a layer of unstable igneous rock, eventually hidden by a thin layer of top soil. As if to prove the point, there was a sinkhole, big enough to swallow an SUV, next to the parking lot. A high chain link fence around it kept curious people at bay. I resisted the temptation to throw a rock into it and count how long before I heard it hit the bottom.

Within the park, randomly placed stones sprouted from the ground. Some looked like stocky cannons filled with rainwater and moss. Others were tall and decidedly phallic. All tickled the imagination. These sculptures were formed in 1790 when lava flowed around trees and burned them until there was nothing left.

Back in the car, I drove to the tiny town of Volcano and the Holo Holo In (not sure why it was spelled "In" with only one n). It was a large house-turned-hostel owned by an artist and his cats. For only $17, I rented a bed in a room of bunk beds. The communal kitchen was decorated with maps where guests marked their home towns and wrote messages of goodwill.

"Hello. That smells really good," I said to a couple who were sipping wine as they waited for their spaghetti noodles and sauce to cook. I had been so busy trying to find the hostel that I had not made dinner plans.

After we introduced ourselves, I learned that Tim and Tally were glass blowers from Australia. They were the only two other guests at the hostel.

"So I'll trade you some impressively good bread for some of your spaghetti," I suggested when it was obvious they had enough to share. Earlier that day at a convenience store, I had discovered mini loaves of Captain Cook banana bread with pineapple, coconut and macadamia nut honey. I practically inhaled the first one in ecstasy. The second loaf did not last much longer. There was one loaf left.

"It's like eating a piece of Hawaii," I said.

"Deal!" they replied.

As we ate, we talked about travel in general and the challenges of connecting with other travelers in Hawaii.

"Even though I'm technically among my fellow Americans, I feel more alone here than anywhere else I have traveled," I said.

"We've found it hard, too," Tallie said. "We try to talk with people, see if they want to hang out with us, and they're not interested. They're either locals who act like it would be a waste of their time or tourists who keep to the people they came with."

"Well, I'm available. Want to hang out with me tomorrow?" I asked. "I thought I'd spend the day at the Hawaii Volcanoes National Park."

"We have to go back to Honolulu tomorrow so we can fly home," Tim said sadly. "But we want to go out and look at the lava tonight. Want to come with us?"

"Absolutely."

With visions of glowing red lava blasting into the night sky like fireworks or oozing in undaunted waves down a mountainside, I grabbed my hiking boots, camera, flashlight and jacket, and piled into the backseat of their car.

"I think you turn here," Tally suggested once we entered the park.

"OK," Tim said. He made the left turn and drove down an unmarked road through dense trees.

"Oh, I don't remember seeing trees like that. Do you?"

"No, we better turn around," Tim said. "It must be the next turn or the last one."

We were lost, and before we could find our way, it was time to go home. The hostel had a 10 p.m. curfew.

As I settled into my bunk that night, I discovered that my blue turtle sarong was missing. Distressed, I charged a phone call to the Pacific Marina Hotel.

"Hello, I stayed at your hotel last night and left a blue sarong in the room," I said. "Did the cleaning people find it?"

"I'm sorry. I don't know," said the front desk clerk. "If you give me your name, we'll hold it for you if we find it."

I climbed back into my bunk and cuddled a shirt, pretending it was the sarong. The missing fabric had become my blankie. In addition to its practical uses, it brought a comforting consistency to all the places I had slept. I was going to cry if I did not get it back. I felt as despondent as Tom Hanks' Castaway character when he lost his soccer ball friend Wilson.

ESTABLISHED IN 1916, the Hawaii Volcanoes National Park represented 70 million years of volcanic activity. It was home to Mauna Loa, the world's most massive volcano, and Kilauea, the world's most active volcano, which was why the park had no consistent size.

After a quick visit to the visitor center as its first guest of the day, I drove along Crater Rim Drive. The first two stops were both intriguing and offensive. At the Sulphur Banks, cloudy vapors that reeked of rotten eggs wafted up from a pile of powder-covered rocks as sulfur dioxide and hydrogen sulfide escaped from deep within the ground. Signs warned that the fumes were hazardous to young children, pregnant women and the elderly. At the nearby Steaming Bluff, more smelly vapors rose from small fissures in the hillside covered with scrubbrush that defied the elevated ground temperatures.

My third stop, the Jaggar Museum, was named after Thomas A. Jaggar, former head geologist at the Massachusetts Institute of Technology. He developed ways to study earthquakes associated with volcanoes. In 1911, he led a group of geologists who lowered the first thermometer into the nearby Halemaumau crater when it was still a lava lake. It registered 1,832 degrees F before melting. According to legend, the crater was home to Pele, goddess of fire and volcanism. Her Hawaiian name, Ka wahine 'ai honua, means "woman who devours the land."

The museum featured historical photographs and displays of past and present research equipment. It was mesmerizing to watch seismometers record real-time tremors and tiltmeters record changes in the slant of the land around the park. I could not feel the ground move as I watched a thin black line zigzag along the paper. I was torn between wanting some major activity to occur and fearing that it would.

One display case showed types of lava. Under the right conditions, lava formed Pele's hair, thin strands of volcanic glass. A single strand could be two yards long, and the wind could blow it miles from its source. Pele's tears, small tear drop-shaped bits of volcanic glass, often formed at one end of those strands. Enticing as these geological formations might be if I found one, I knew better than to take one home. It was common knowledge that taking rocks from the islands brought bad luck. As a result, thousands of pounds of rock have been shipped back to Hawaii because people blame their homeland misfortunes on their vacation souvenirs.

In the museum parking lot, a sign cautioned drivers to be on the look out for nene. A flock of the chest-heavy Hawaiian state birds happened to be hanging out by the museum. They looked like first cousins to Canadian geese.

What started out as a cool and cloudy day turned sunny and Winnie-the-Pooh blustery by the time I walked over a flat plateau to the safety railing at the rim on Halemaumau Crater, a vast geological pockmark. A helicopter would look like a fly sitting on its surface.

For many decades, the crater was a constant lake of bubbling lava. Then in 1924, it violently exploded and cast out massive boulders, some of which still sat along the rim. After that eruption, the crater was 1,345-feet deep, but has been gradually filling back up as a result of numerous short-lived eruptions, the longest lasting about eight months.

Just beyond the safety railing, someone had left two offerings for Pele—leis of delicate magenta orchids and a bunch of green bananas. Both were intensely colorful against the landscape of gray and black.

While the caves in Laos triggered some deep-rooted anxiety about being underground, a walk through the Thurston Lava Tube, named after a publisher who helped create the park, only brought a smile to my face and visions of Dune sandworms to my thoughts. The tube was formed about four centuries ago when lava flowed down the east side of Kilauea's summit. The tube could easily fit an Airstream travel trailer, and it was illuminated with evenly spaced lights.

Next on my agenda was the Kilauea Iki Trail, a four-mile hike that descended through a rainforest and crossed the mile-wide crater floor. In 1959, the plain was a bubbling pool of molten lava with record-setting lava fountains spraying into the air. Today, the jagged surface of the crater floor looked like it had been crumpled by an earthquake. Stunted shrubs with crooked branches and bright red, pompom-like flowers sprouted up between rocks, oblivious to the heat and lack of soil. Tufts of steam wafted out of tiny fissures. The ground was warm to the touch. Lava still lurked somewhere not too far below my hiking boots. It brought new meaning to the phrase "flirting with disaster."

After a steep climb back up the far side of the crater, the trail looped around the rim until it returned to the parking lot. This section of trail introduced me to more of Hawaii's native plants, including football-sized clusters of frilly yellow orchids and an astounding number of ferns. My guidebook said there were about 170 species in Hawaii. The Hāpu'u ferns ranged in height from knee high to a stunning 40 feet tall. Young Hāpu'u shoots were covered with so much velvety down that in the 1800s, people sold it as stuffing for pillows and mattresses.

Mid afternoon, I drove down a steep landscape of tall, straw-colored grass and black, weather-worn swells of ancient lava. The road soon turned to follow the shoreline, only to abruptly disappear under an old lava flow. Like other visitors, I parked my car along the road's grassy shoulders.

Where the road ended, a large wooden sign, sensibly attached to a moveable stand, read, "Danger. Hazardous fumes. Steep cliffs. Rough surface. Hot lava. Flashlight required after dark." In the background, the world seemed composed of three colors—a vast black plain of jagged rock, the pale blue of the sky and the intense azure of the ocean.

Under a blazing sun, visitors of all shapes, sizes and ages followed a trail of reflector tags. They crossed iridescent flat ledges, pillowy mounds, crinkled ridges and jagged boulders. The people heading back toward their cars looked wilted but pleased.

"Don't follow the reflectors," a woman said to me as she walked by. "Look for clumps of people."

Just like I did while trekking in Nepal, I kept my eyes on the uneven ground as I walked. I stopped moving when I wanted to look around. After about 10 minutes, I veered toward a cluster of people pointing fingers and taking photos. Nearby orange-red lava oozed out a crack. Seconds later, its surface lava changed to an iridescent silver color.

Even at a distance with a strong wind to my back, the heat from the 2,100-degree lava was incomprehensible. The closer I got to it, the more painful it was to inhale. To take close-up pictures, I held my breath, dashed in, took a few shots and ran away. As if it were my first zebra, I over-photographed every ooze and ripple of this newest bit of Hawaii.

Farther along the trail, I joined the people who gawked at an area where lava had formed a mercurial-looking stream. We oohed and ahhed as fresh lava kept breaking through its surface to form silvery pillows that broke apart as more lava pushed forward to create more new mounds.

"Who's got the hotdogs?" one man joked.

"Marshmallows would be good," said a woman.

"If you like them burned," said another man as lava cremated the last clump of grass in sight.

As more people gathered at the lava flow, a lively, senior-aged woman had a learning experience. She started walking across the silvery crust that was only minutes old. People on the other side yelled against the wind and frantically waved to her. She realized her mistake and hurried to the far side. She was only a couple steps from safe ground when the thin crust gave way. For a few seconds, the side of her foot was inches from glowing molten lava. This was not good.

She finished her stride to safe ground. Compassionate people quickly sat her down and poured water on her foot.

"I don't know what I was thinking," she said flustered. "I didn't realize that lava was so new."

Even though the lava had not touched her skin, the heat from it vaporized the cuff of her jeans, the side of her Keds tennis shoe and a portion of her white sock. I peeked to see if her foot was charred black. Surprisingly, the seared flesh was powdery white. She showed no signs of being in pain. Was she in shock or had the heat burned away the nerves in the side of her foot?

I heard later that she was on a geology course field trip, of all things, and hours before had changed from heat-resistant boots to the more comfortable shoes.

Walking back to my car, I passed a wildlife officer striding to the scene as another officer stood with the people at the first flow.

"Some folks bring drama," he said when I told him about the lady. He added that the park received up to two dozen injury reports a day, ranging from minor lacerations to burns to heart attacks. "Others bring entertainment."

"How so?" I asked.

"This one guy brought a tin pan of Jiffy Pop popcorn taped to a long stick," he answered. "It was fun to watch him try to pop it. He almost had it the first time, but the lava melted out the bottom of the pan. But he got it right the second time, and we all helped him eat the popcorn."

By the time I hiked back to my car, it was late afternoon, and I realized I was not much smarter than the woman who burnt her foot. I was wiped out by the heat. I had not worn a hat. I had set off across perilous terrain without water, snacks or sun protection. I wore nylon shorts that could not protect my legs from sunburn or scrapes if I fell.

There was only a half a Nalgene bottle of warm water in the car. Bless the nearby vending truck where I bought a cold bottle of water.

My last stop in the park was Pu'u Loa [Long Hill], one of the largest concentrations—more than 15,000—of petroglyphs in Hawaii. Most pre-dated Western contact. Ancient Hawaiians had no written history, so the meanings of the petroglyphs were not well understood. They could be religiously significant or the doodles of dreamers. The majority showed human forms and dots (shallow holes) surrounded by shapes like circles and spirals. A few featured fish, starfish, hooks and insects.

The dots were part of a Hawaiian custom specific to this lava field. When a baby was born, the *piko* [umbilical cord] would be brought here, placed in a dot and covered with a rock. If the *s* was still there the next day, it was a sign that the child would have a long life.

After leaving the park, I went to Panaluu Beach Park, my first black sand beach. By the parking lot was a commemorative plaque of a long-haired woman riding on the back of a sea turtle. It honored Hawaii's sea turtles and Kauila, a turtle who could turn herself into a young girl. The local people loved Kauila because her spring gave them drinking water, and she watched over and played with their children.

The palm trees along the shoreline looked even greener against the black sand of the beach. The sand covering my bare feet looked like coarsely ground black pepper. I half expected to see shapely women in grass skirts dancing, but the beach was empty. A lone sign read "Turtle nesting. Please do not touch turtle." False advertising. Not even a turtle track in sight. I knew it was off season to see a whale while I was in Hawaii, but I was determined to see a sea turtle.

As I walked, I mused about my life. I had always thought that when I got to be 40 years old I would have all the answers. I would know myself. I would be savvy about the rules of the social playground. Facing that milestone birthday in about eight weeks, I had to admit that I had fallen far short of these expectations. The best I could say was that every year I learned how much more there was that I did not know. As I got back into the rental car, I decided that was okay as long as I kept growing.

As a red sun sank below the horizon, I drove along the coastline through small rural towns, pastures and old lava flows toward the city of Kailua-Kona. It was the largest vacation destination on the island. The verdant landscape gave way to concrete and advertising. The traffic grew congested. The closer I got, the less I wanted to be there.

IN THE BRIGHT MORNING SUN, I joined a flock of overly fed and glaringly pale tourists as they shuffled aboard a 51-foot catamaran for a half-day snorkel trip. Coming from Southeast Asia, where so many of the people were petite, I was startled by the number of overweight people I had seen in Hawaii. I expected most of them to be athletic and outdoorsy. The first native Hawaiian-looking family I had seen struggled against their fat to get in and out of a pickup truck. The hefty teenager was crunching his way through a family-size bag of Doritos and drinking a 64-oz Pepsi.

At the Pawai Bay Marine Preserve, worn lava rocks cluttered the underwater landscape. While there were no reefs teeming with invertebrate life as shown in the promotional brochure, there was a hefty eel, schools of yellow tang fish, spotted puffers the size of grapefruits, purple and green fish, and my first wild octopus. Still, no turtles.

After the snorkel trip, I spent the rest of the day driving across the northern side of the Big Island. From Kona, I headed northeast, passing one of the most intense rainbows I had ever seen. It arched over velvety fields of green grass, part of Parker Ranch.

Founded in 1847, Parker Ranch was one of the oldest and largest—more than 175,000 acres—cattle ranches in the U.S. Its history began in 1809, one generation after Captain James Cook first encountered the Hawaiian islands. A 19-year-old sailor from Massachusetts named John Parker jumped ship and hid until it sailed away. He ended up befriending King Kamehameha I, the monarch who united the Hawaiian islands into a single kingdom.

After a stint at sea during the War of 1812, Parker returned to Hawaii with a state-of-the-art American musket. He was given the privilege of being the first man allowed to shoot some of the thousands of maverick cattle that roamed Hawaii's remote plains and valleys. They were the progeny of the five head of cattle given to Kamehameha 21 years earlier.

Due mostly to Parker's efforts, salt beef eventually replaced the increasingly scarce sandalwood as the island's chief export. As the desire for beef increased, so did Parker's fortune and influence. In 1992, following the death of Richard Smart, the ranch's last owner, Parker Ranch was left in a trust to benefit the Waimea community.

The weather turned gray and rainy as I headed south toward Hilo. The scenery included homes with sky-blue hydrangeas, towering hardwood trees, sugarcane fields, dense fog, torrential rain and mongoose racing into a forest.

I booked a room at the Wild Ginger Inn just after dark. For a few extra dollars, I splurged to get one with cable TV. My days of stylish $15 rooms were gone, but I had *Law and Order* and the calming sound of the rain. I was on the Big Island in Hawaii. Life could be a whole lot worse.

WHEN I RETURNED THE RENTAL CAR at the airport, I cringed when I handed over my credit card yet again. I was charging expenses at a fast clip, but kept denial well in hand. When I started the trip, I had left a stack of pre-addressed envelopes containing $100 checks to VISA. A friend of mine mailed one each month to the credit card company to cover the minimum payments until I got back. I did not want to know about the outstanding balance until I got home.

I also kept blinders on when it came to my checking account. If I knew how low my funds were getting, I knew I would start basing all my decisions on money rather than the experiences. That would take the joy out of the trip and prevent me from doing things I might never get the chance to do again. Worst case scenario, there was money from the sale of my house that I had sworn I would not touch.

Back in Honolulu, I took a taxi straight to the Pacific Marina Hotel.

"Is this it?" the reception asked, passing my blue turtle sarong over the counter.

"Oh, thank God," I said, snatching it up and tucking it into its designated pocket in the backpack.

From there, I went on to the University of Hawaii at Manoa campus to meet Kim, a woman with long legs and deep brown eyes. Her husband Charlie was a goofball of a man who was much smarter than he let on. I met them both through hashing in North Carolina. They had since moved to Hawaii as part of Charlie's military career. While they both had hectic schedules, they had graciously offered their guest bedroom in their ranch style house for the next week.

Comforted by the warm reception and the return of my sarong, I was ready to explore Oahu.

Red plaid fish

Oahu, Hawaii

"LET'S PLAY TOURIST," I thought, focusing the day downtown Honolulu. Getting off Bus 52, I started with the stately Kawaiaha'o Church. It was one of the few remaining churches that offered services in the Hawaiian language.

The history of the New England-style building, widely known as the "Westminster Abbey of the Pacific," began in April 1820. The first contingent of Christian missionaries arrived on Oahu after enduring a five-month journey from Boston, Massachusetts. Their initial houses of worship were four huts made from pili grass. In 1836, King Kamehameha III called a meeting of chiefs to build the first Christian church. Construction began a year later on what was to become Punchbowl Street. For the next five years, workers collected and placed more than 14,000 coral reef slabs, many weighing more than 1,000 pounds each.

These days it is quite prestigious, expensive and difficult to arrange wedding ceremonies at Kawaiaha'o Church. As a result, many new couples have their wedding photos and videos taken at the church and their ceremonies performed elsewhere.

I watched an Asian-looking couple stand by the church's front door. The groom looked stiff in his black tuxedo. The bride, encased in a size-zero, full-length, white gown, looked shell-shocked. She teetered on high heels. Her delicate, perfectly manicured hand held a vice grip on the groom's elbow. An elderly man in a cardigan sweater and slacks showered them with white flower petals as they slowly walked down the church steps. A photographer and videographer captured the brief procession. The session ended. The old man gently swept up the petals.

The next couple assumed the position by the front door, and the process began all over again.

I walked over to the Ali'iōlani Hale [House of Heavenly Kings], the former government seat of the Kingdom and Republic of Hawaii, and the current home of the Hawaii State Supreme Court. It was originally designed as a royal palace for King Kamehameha V, but the building was not completed until after his death.

Out front, a bronze cast of King Kamehameha I greeted visitors. In 1879 in Rome, Italy, American artist Thomas R. Gould sculpted the original statue of the deceased ruler. It depicted a man with a muscular physique wearing a helmet of rare feathers and a gilded cloak of yellow feathers woven into a fine mesh net. The spear in his left hand symbolized the ability to defend oneself and one's nation. His right arm was extended, palm up, in a gesture of aloha.

Gould sent his sculpture to Paris, France, where it was cast in bronze. Sadly, the bronze statue was lost in a shipwreck off the coast of South America during its move to Hawaii. The sunken bronze statue was eventually recovered and placed on the Big Island. I was looking at the second cast of the original sculpture. A third cast, commissioned when Hawaii became the 50th state in America on Aug. 21, 1959, stands in the U.S. Capitol in Washington, D.C.

After a quick peek at Iolani Palace, America's only royal palace, I went to the Hawaii Maritime Center, located on Pier 7 in Honolulu Harbor. It highlighted aspects of Hawaiian history, including early canoe-faring Polynesians, the history of surfing, the golden age of the trans-Pacific luxury liners, and the impact of World War II.

The center was also home to the world's largest known marlin, which once weighed a whopping 1,805 pounds, and a giant humpback whale skeleton displayed as if it was preparing to make a deep dive. The 159 bones, which came from a carcass that had washed ashore, ranged from inch-long digits to a 12-foot-wide, 750-pound skull.

The admission ticket also gave me access to the *Falls of Clyde* docked next door. It was the world's only surviving four-masted, full-rigged, iron-hulled ship. Built in 1878 in Scotland, the 266-foot-long ship spent her first years sailing to Asian ports. In 1899, she became the first four-masted ship to fly the Hawaiian flag and served as the largest ship in its sugar trade. After the turn of the century, she brought petroleum to the islands. She came to rest in Hawaii in 1963. With low ceilings and tiny sleeping rooms that should have been called closets, the ship was obviously not built for comfort, hygiene or tall people.

On Pier 8, I plugged quarters into a vending machine that sold fish food pellets. When I started dropping them into the harbor water, I saw more fish in more sizes, shapes and colors than I did on the half-day $89 snorkel cruise on the Big Island. Go figure.

The fish were not the only ones eating well that morning. I thought about buying a pint of Ben & Jerry's ice cream, but decided to wait until I finished my trip. It would be my version of a champagne toast. Instead, I bought an extreme Rice Krispies treat that contained white chocolate, dark chocolate, marshmallows and chunky peanut butter. The sugar rush was stunning.

Missing someone to share the day with, I spent the rest of the day wandering around Chinatown, said to be the oldest one in the United States. Tiny shops sold produce and colorful trinkets in crates along the sidewalks. I ate *manapua*, delicious steamed buns stuffed with barbecue pork. One butcher sold crabs that looked like hand-sized red lice.

It was impressive that historians could trace the first arrival of Chinese people in Honolulu to two ships that arrived in 1788. As Hawaii's sugar industry grew, plantation owners looked to China for cheap labor. The country was relatively close, and Chinese men wanted the work. The first contract laborers had five-year contracts to work in harsh field conditions for $3 per month. For many, that was still better than what they left back home.

EACH MORNING AXEL, THE FAMILY LABRADOR, felt the need to abscond with one of my belongings. Today he sauntered off with my bra and presented it to Kim and Charlie. Yesterday they had received one of my bath gloves. Ah, the language of love.

Thus began a lazy day as we three dinked around the house, ate pastries, cleaned the car and watched a movie. Eventually, we drove to the North Shore. During the winter, wave riders and spectators flocked to its towering waves—prime surf spots with names like Graters, Pounders and Tumbo Land. But this was the off season, so the surf was calm at Pupukea Beach Park, where we stopped to go snorkeling. The sand, with multicolored, pinhead-sized grains, sparkled like mosaic art.

In the water the invertebrate life was sparse, but the red fish with white dots were amusing. Just as I was about to go back to shore, something swam by to my right. A sea turtle! Its half-barrel, olive-brown shape glided from one rocky ledge to the next. I could hear its beak rasping against the rocks as it grazed on algae. It looked small enough that I could wrap my arms around it, though hugs were out of the question. Perhaps it was young. I slowly followed it, using up the film in my underwater camera, until it swam out to deep water. Our brief encounter felt like a great first date.

That evening, Kim, Charlie and I went to the Haleiwa Ali'i Beach Park for the Sunset Festival. In the postcard-looking setting, families enjoyed live music, food and carnival games. The best thing we ate were *malasadas*. These fluffy doughnuts were surely a close cousin to the beignet. Alas, there were no SPAM-based foods, even though Hawaii is the No. 1 consumer of the pink canned meat.

I RENTED A CAR SO I COULD SPEND the day exploring Oahu along Highway 72, which runs along the southeast coastline. At a scenic overlook, I watched board surfers and wind surfers dance on white-edged waves out in the ocean. Cue the theme song to *Hawaii Five-O* in my head.

I was happy sitting on the retaining wall until a guy walked up and introduced himself. Ross looked late 40s, not homeless dirty but definitely weathered shabby. He rambled on about how grand it was to live on Oahu, as if he was my personal tour guide or real estate agent. Then he ranted about nonnative people taking over the island.

As he rambled on, I kept an eye on my car. How easy it would be to keep me distracted while someone else broke into my car.

"Oh, did you grow up here?" I asked him.

"Nah, I was raised in Scranton, Pennsylvania."

"Well, have a nice afternoon." Time to move on. No doubt there would be another scenic spot without someone like Ross to spoil it.

After watching a photo shoot of a model by Kawaikui Beach and eating a Hawaiian shaved ice, a tropical version of a snow cone, I drove on to Hanauma Bay Beach Park. I planned to go snorkeling, but the weather was stormy, and the waters looked choppy. I continued on to a lookout about a mile down the road. Beyond its parking lot, giant waves crashed against cliffs of lava rock as two solitary men cast their lines into the ocean.

A U.S. Coast Guard helicopter roared overhead, and a teenager in the parking lot pointed a handgun at it, pretending to shoot it out of the sky. It took me a few fearful seconds to realize it was just a realistic-looking plastic toy. I wanted to slap him and his mother, who thought it was amusing.

At the nearby jagged precipice of black rock called Halona Point, there was a stone monument that honored people lost in the ocean. Across a small cove from the monument, I could see the Halona Blowhole in a black rock ledge jutting out over the ocean. I watched as ocean waves slammed into the shoreline, forcing water through underground fissures and caves. Sometimes the water came out of the foot-wide blowhole as a whispery mist. Other times there were hiccups of froth. Just when I was lured into thinking the blowhole was relatively harmless, a column of water rising more than two-stories tall roared out of it.

On the hillside above the blowhole, the observation deck and parking lot were blocked off by fire trucks, police cars and ambulances.

"They are trying to rescue someone," a stranger said as people gathered to watch the scene. Men in bright red rescue slickers roped themselves together and edged their way toward the blowhole. In the turbulent ocean, more rescuers on jet skis dashed around the base of the cliff as waves bashed them around. I left before they recovered the body.

According to a newspaper article I read later, a young man from California—showing off for a girl—straddled the blowhole in spite of the warning signs. A gush of water blasted him into the air, and he fell into the blowhole. He drowned as water smashed him into the walls of the underwater passages. He was on vacation with a sibling and his mom, celebrating his high school graduation and a scholarship to college.

I drove along the highway as it rose and fell toward the north side of Oahu, then detoured onto the Pali (cliff) Highway. This narrow road linked the North and South Shores by cutting across the Koolau Mountain Range. The Nuuanu Pali Lookout, nestled in the spine of that range, was one of those "can't miss" spots that blow tourists away—literally. Trade winds often turned the lookout into a wind tunnel.

Rain surged from sprinkles to blustery torrents as I peered out from the 1,200-foot-tall cliff-side perch. The sweeping panorama included two small towns, the lush coastline and the decaying remnants of the Old Pali Highway. This highway replaced a cobblestone carriage road that had replaced a horse trail that had replaced a footpath.

The area was also the setting for one of the most significant battles in Hawaiian history. In 1795, Kamehameha I and his army invaded Oahu and fought with troops led by Kalanikupule. The fierce battle gradually forced Kalanikupule's men to retreat up the valley and to jump from the cliff to their deaths. That explained why hundreds of human skulls and bones were found during construction of the former highway.

MY LAST FULL DAY IN HAWAII started at the Waikiki Aquarium. It featured more than 420 species of aquatic animals and plants, plus frenetic groups of school children. One tank held only a tray of bean-sized, aspic-looking eggs—baby Palauan chambered nautilus. My favorite creatures looked like feather dusters that disappeared into shells shaped like Pirouette Rolled Wafers when spooked.

Sunning near their private pool, two Hawaiian monk seals perfected their lethargy. These animals are one of the most endangered marine mammals in the world—fewer than 1,400 remain in the wild—and one of the two endemic mammals found in Hawaii. (The other is a bat).

In a round concrete tank on an outside courtyard, mahi mahi fish swam briskly around and around. Obeying a higher calling, they tilted each time they passed the public viewing window, a natural inclination to keep their dorsal fins toward the perceived surface sunlight.

From the aquarium I made a quick drive around Diamond Head, arguably the most famous volcanic crater in the world, then drove over to Hanauma Bay Beach Park. The park draws more than one million visitors a year, and I could see why. The surf of the open ocean raged hundreds of yards away, but the calm waters in the bay were perfect for snorkeling.

I put on SPF 45 sunblock and a chambray shirt over my swimsuit, and then dog-paddled into another world. A Dr. Seuss-designed fish—red and white plaid—greeted me. Wafer-thin fish with chocolate-colored stripes paraded by. Peacock blue, cat-sized fish grazed rocky outcroppings. Fish shaped like little black boxes with white dots hovered on tiny fins. The pencil-thin fish were so narrow they were almost two-dimensional. While it was interesting to watch fish trapped inside the aquarium, it was thrilling to swim with them in their natural habitat.

The fish in the bay could have entertained me for days, but hours later, when I went to get a drink out of my backpack, I knew it was time to go. Without the cooling effects of the water, I could feel that the back of my legs were burned. This did not bode well for tomorrow's flight to Alaska.

WITH A FEW HOURS LEFT before my afternoon flight, I decided to take a submarine ride. The Atlantis Submarines ticket office and boarding dock were at the edge of the Hilton Hawaiian Village—a swanky mega-resort complex. Guest rooms were stacked in towers separated by pools, water features, restaurants and boutique shops. It was interesting to wander through the complex, but it felt contrived. Did they really need courtyard ponds with pink flamingoes? The birds looked like sad versions of the ones I had seen in Lake Nakuru.

I rode with a couple of dozen passengers on a shuttle boat to the 100-foot-long submarine moored in deep water. A *Love Boat*-perky uniformed crew directed us to either side of the white plastic bench that ran down the center of submarine's interior. Each seat had its own umbrella-sized window to look out.

As the submarine gently descended, colors faded away outside the window. Reds were completely gone by 60 feet. At the bottom, at 113 feet, we could only see blue water and the dark shapes of three turtles, one sting ray and dozens of small fish. Three boat wrecks and a pyramid made of chicken wire sat on the sandy ocean floor to help establish a new reef. The landscape was alluring, like a desert.

Before I returned the rental car at the airport, I tried to visit the *U.S.S. Arizona* Memorial. It commemorated the site where the Japanese attacked Pearl Harbor on Dec. 7, 1941. The memorial was located on the surface of the water, above the final resting spot for most of the ship's 1,177 crewmen who lost their lives on that fateful day. The first-come, first-served admission tickets were sold out by the time I arrived, but I did get a ticket to explore the *U.S.S. Missouri* docked at nearby Ford Island.

Built in a New York naval shipyard, the "Mighty Mo" was launched in 1944. She reached the high point of her career on Sept. 2, 1945, when Japanese representatives came aboard to sign surrender papers, marking the end of World War II.

Walking toward the ship, I was overwhelmed by its sheer vastness. It was a world of its own. A fact sheet noted that she weighed more than 60,000 tons. She had guns that could fire a 2,700-pound shell up to 23 miles. Impressive when I considered that a vintage Volkswagen Beetle weighed about 1,900 pounds. In her prime, Mighty Mo's galley served more than 6,000 meals a day, and her crew drank 50,000-100,000 cans of soda each month.

And for all of her size, the crew quarters of the "Mighty Mo" were impressively compact. Rows of narrow bunks were stacked four deep. They were better than the accommodations on the *Falls of Clyde,* but not by much.

After I returned the rental car, I settled in at the boarding gate at the Honolulu International Airport. An impressive number of people around me wore newly purchased shirts and dresses with hibiscus flowers and sportfish motifs.

While my two weeks in Hawaii were not what I expected, they were enjoyable. I was grateful to the hostess who forced me to change my plans, but I was sad not to have connected with more people.

As I realized that the confines of island life were not for me, an airline attendant announced that passengers could upgrade their tickets to first class for $250. I was startled to see how many people signed up for the offer. That much money could fund a month of travel in Laos.

American goodness slightly chilled

Seward, Alaska

WHILE MY COUSIN VIRGINIA GAVE me a warm welcome, Alaska did not. My beach-appropriate T-shirt and shorts were no match for the windy 60-degree F weather. Time to bulk up, to put on khaki pants, socks, layers of shirts and my North Face jacket.

Virginia had driven from her home in Fairbanks to pick me up at the airport in Anchorage. Five years older than me, she shared the family female traits of height, broad hips, generous spirit, travel hunger and strong will. One of my earliest memories of her was when she glued pearls to her earlobes because her parents would not let her get her ears pierced.

"I am so excited to see you! I can't wait to show you some of Alaska," she said as we got in her red Toyota truck. "And Seward is a perfect place to celebrate the Fourth of July." The 125-mile drive south along the Seward Highway wove around mountains and along the shores of the Turnagain Arm of the Cook Inlet.

"Never go out there," Virginia said as she pointed to the chocolate-colored mud flats that lined the shore. "People go out there, get stuck in the mud and drown when the tide comes in." The tide was the second highest one in North America.

We made a pit stop in the small town of Girdwood for coffee and to meet up with Virginia's friend, Polly. She was traveling back to Alaska from Arkansas with her sister and two strapping teenage nephews.

The cozy shop offered grand coffee choices. My best packaging award went to Deadman's Reach with the motto, "Served in bed, raises the dead." It was recommended for "morning jumpstarts, long-haul truck driving, cramming for exams, winning races, inspiring great ideas and noble emotions, making it 'til quitting time, deadlines and pure coffee pleasure."

SEWARD WAS FOUNDED in 1903 as an ice-free port to serve the Alaska Railroad. The small town went about its business until 1964 when it was leveled by the Black Friday Earthquake. Alaska is no stranger to earthquakes. It has about 50 quakes a year, more than all the other 49 U.S. states combined. But this 9.2 magnitude shock caused fires and tidal waves that destroyed more than 90 percent of the town.

The town was laid out on a grid roughly seven by nine streets, wedged between the shore of Resurrection Bay and the steep slope of Mt. Marathon. Over the years, its popularity grew. Now it receives visitors from cruise ships, the Alaska Marine Ferry system and trains from Anchorage.

This weekend, Seward's population would swell from about 2,800 residents to more than 30,000 people, so Virginia had made reservations for us at a guesthouse. The two-story, wooden home on a hill overlooking downtown was surrounded by a plush lawn. Its lovingly tended garden was fragrant with lilac bushes, tea roses and columbine. These signs of spring conflicted with the crisp weather that smelled of pine needles and wood smoke. Seward had an average summer temperature of 56 degrees F.

I shared a room with Virginia's friend, Priscilla, a vibrant woman like Virginia.

"So you really drove here all the way here from Pennsylvania?" I asked after claiming a twin bed.

"Yes, with Magnificent Bart," she said, explaining he was a silky black cat who traveled in a spacious pet crate in her truck. "I'm moving to Fairbanks for a job."

"What do you do?"

"I am a colonel in the Army."

My esteem for her jacked up a few notches.

We three wandered around town. Every souvenir shop focused on a wildlife theme. There was a line of jewelry made from pecan-shaped moose droppings. Some T-shirts featured illustrations by Ray Troll, famous for his salmon humor. One showed why men should not fly fish while naked. The salmon was about to eat the man's private angler off.

"So you two have known each other since high school?" I asked Virginia.

"Her mother was one of my teachers in high school," she said. "We lost touch over the years, but then I heard her on the radio."

"Why were you on the radio?"I asked Priscilla.

"They were interviewing me because I was about to be shipped out to Desert Storm."

THE FOURTH OF JULY began as a bright and glorious day. Even our guest house breakfast was patriotic. The pancakes were topped with blueberries, strawberries and real whipped cream. Cool breezes nudged puffy white clouds across a crisp blue sky. People (and often their dogs) declared their American pride with red, white and blue clothes, face paint and hair spray. Sidewalk sales featured artwork and handicrafts.

"We're not in Kansas any more," I joked with Priscilla. The nearby street fair booth was giving away free gun locks and literature on how to can moose and caribou.

Today was also the 75th running of the infamous Mt. Marathon Race, one of the most grueling footraces in the world. The tradition began in 1909 when a couple of miners bet on how fast they could run to the top of the 3,022-foot peak and back down. Conditions along the steep route were treacherous—tangled roots, mud, snow and unstable patches of loose jagged rocks called scree. The winning miner took one hour and two minutes to complete the course.

These days, there are four races. The first was a toddler course about the length of a street block. Race numbers covered whole chests on chubby-kneed entrants. Parents shouted encouraging words. Little girls twisted their pigtails. Little boys sucked their thumbs. When the whistle blew, some young racers shot down the course. Others scrunched up their faces and cried big tears, much to their parents' amusement.

Afterwards, there were three races up and down the mountain: juniors, women and men. The junior race ended with a touching moment. A leggy teenage girl ran the last stretch of the course while carrying a small girl who was too tired to finish the race. Yards before the finish line, the teenager set the girl down. They joined hands and crossed the finish line together. This was my first taste of Alaskan spirit.

Nina Kemppel won the women's race. The 31-year-old, four-time Olympic skier from Anchorage, finished the course in 55 minutes, four seconds. It was her seventh consecutive title.

When the male racers stampeded out of town and up into the evergreen forest, many were bare chested. Some had no discernible body fat. Most wore gloves to protect their hands and duct tape around the tops of their running shoes to keep rocks out. One man was dressed like Elvis Presley in a powder-blue jumpsuit with a sequined cape. Another sported a massive Mexican sombrero. A free-spirited man hung his race number from his nipple rings.

When the men disappeared from view, we walked across town to the end of the race course, making a pit stop at a lemonade stand along the way. The budding entrepreneur showed promise and flair. The poles that held up a neatly hand-lettered banner were wrapped in red, white and blue electric tape and topped with American and Alaskan flags. The candy bars and lemonade cups were arranged in neat rows on a piece of plywood covered with aluminum foil. Sales were brisk.

As we passed the town hospital, the mountain summit towered directly over the emergency room sign. It could be a busy day for the staff. The end of the race was a steep shoot of scree and rocky crags that spilled out onto a dirt-encrusted snow bank next to a paved street. A large crowd, ambulances and paramedics gathered at the finish line. Who would be the front runners? Who would fall in pursuit of a speed record?

A low murmur grew as racers headed down the slope through the trees. Trails of dust rose from their heels as if they were Road Runner cartoons. Wild screams and applause greeted the first racers who made it across the finish line, all unscathed. Finishing in 46 minutes and 17 seconds, 35-year-old Brad Precosky of Anchorage won his fourth consecutive title.

The rest of the racers, not out to set speed records, slowed over the snow bank to entertain the cheering crowd with comical victory dances. Bloodshed seemed minimal. There would be no overtime for the emergency room workers.

We strolled around town until it was time to watch the Fourth of July parade. Politicians waved to the motion of elbow, elbow, wrist, wrist, wrist. Bearded riders throbbed along on Harley Davidson motorcycles. A brass band performed on a flatbed trailer. Seniors drove vintage Ford automobiles. War veterans strutted in their uniforms. Youngsters waddled by in giant detergent boxes to promote the laundromat. Dignitaries, seated high on glossy convertibles, tossed candy to the crowd. The scene was so small town Americana that it felt almost unreal, like we had stepped into a movie set.

And then we ate.

"Let's eat there," I said pointing to the street fair booth that sold baskets of golden fried chunks of local halibut and sourdough corn fritters with honey butter.

"You'd think we ran the race the way we're eating," Priscilla noted. Afterwards, we looked for the church ladies who sold slices of homemade pie.

Seeking a relaxing place to digest our meals, we watched the 6:45 p.m. showing of the movie *Unfaithful* at the vintage Liberty Theater. Red-striped candy cane lawn ornaments flanked the stage. A close cousin to the ballroom in Luang Prabang, Laos, the ceilings were covered with square particle board tiles and cone-shaped light fixtures with colored light bulbs shone up the side walls.

It was still light outside when we left the theatre. The sun was below the horizon, but the sky was bright.

"Would you take my photo?" I asked Virginia as I sat on an old snow pile from the previous winter, which had yet to melt. "I can't believe it's 10:47 p.m., and you won't need a flash."

"Welcome to Alaska," she laughed, enjoying my sense of wonder.

We meandered through a traffic jam of cars heading out of town as we walked to the bay to watch the midnight fireworks show.

RVs lined up along the bay's shoreline. Resourceful campers used old washing machine liners as fire pits along the beach of black slate chips. I was layered up as if snow was about to fall, but some teenagers paraded around in T-shirts, shorts, halter tops and flip flops. Just looking at them made me shiver.

By midnight, the sky had mellowed into a ceiling of navy blue with a ribbon of orange glowing along the horizon. The fireworks sparkled against a backdrop of mountain silhouettes. Explosions ricocheted across the bay and back. We all applauded the grand finale, and as we headed home at 12:45 p.m., the sky finally turned starry black.

It was a splendid way to end a daylong birthday party full of camaraderie, competition, food and playfulness. America is a vast land of disparate people, but this holiday always seems to bring us all together.

A 586,000-square-mile outdoor asylum

Seward to Fairbanks, Alaska

TIME TO HEAD TO ANCHORAGE, but not before I accidentally set off the fire extinguisher inside Virginia's truck while loading it with our stuff. A billowy cloud of white powder filled the back of the truck before I figured out what I had done. Thankfully, my cousin was a forgiving soul.

We drove along the Seward Highway for a couple of hours until a mother moose nonchalantly strolled across the road. Cars from both directions stopped. Her knobby-kneed calf hesitated where the marshy lowland met the pavement. Spooked, he ran back into the high grass. The mother noted his decision, but started to graze.

As Virginia and I waited to make sure that neither one was going to cross the road, I marveled at how intimidating the mother was in spite of her amusingly bulbous snout. Her species, the third largest mammal in North America, is known for cantankerous dispositions. For example, an Alaskan park visitor was riding a bicycle around with a bell tied to the handlebars just to warn moose about her presence. The plan failed. She startled a mother moose with two nearby calves. The woman tried to abruptly turn the bike around and fell off it. She got up and ran into the woods. The moose stayed at her heels. When the woman fell again, the moose struck her with a hoof, breaking the woman's wrist.

Our drive to Anchorage included a brief stop at the Begich, Boggs Visitor Center. It offered all kinds of information about glaciers and Alaskan wildlife, but what caught my attention were ice worms chilling out on a chunk of glacier at the welcome desk. They were twisted, pubic hair-looking creatures.

Ice worms only live in a coastal region between Washington and Alaska. One valley is home to seven or eight worm colonies, each with millions of residents. The worms spend their lives on ice, feeding on the algae and hiding in crevices during the warmer parts of the day. They die in temperatures below 20 degrees F or above 40 degrees F. The heat from my finger would burn one to death if I touched it.

When we got to Anchorage, we met up again with Priscilla and Polly (from the coffee shop in Girdwood) to go to Mr. Whitekeys' Fly By Night Club for dinner and a show. In the parking lot, there was a scraggly tree branch decorated with cans of SPAM. Posted inside the club's front door, a letter from Hormel demanded that the club cease and desist featuring SPAM in their shows. Next to the letter was Mr. Whitekeys' reply, requesting that Hormel cease and desist taking itself so seriously. These were signs of things to come.

There was a bar along one wall. We sat at a round table near the stage. We ordered a round of Moose Milk cocktails—a creamy blend of banana, coconut, Godiva chocolate liqueur and rum served with a swirl of chocolate syrup on top. The menu included SPAM nachos and SPAMadillas (quesadillas made with Spam)—after all, Alaska was the second largest consumer of the canned meat—but our tastebuds were won over by the Thai nachos. Who could resist fried wontons topped with mozzarella cheese, shrimp, snow pea pods, pesto sour cream, sweet hot chili sauce and minced cilantro?

We tapped our toes to the music performed by the SPAMtones. We laughed at the hilarious woman performing a reverse strip tease, layering on her husband's grungy clothes after he left her to go fishing. We cheered for the woman who modeled shapely evening wear made from blue tarp and duct tape. I quickly learned that these were two Alaskan essentials.

The crowd roared with laughter as an actress stepped onto the stage wearing a voluminous blond wig, an impressive bosom, a cowgirl dress and a three-foot-long, silver-sequined salmon around her hips.

Virginia explained, "There is a kind of salmon named Dolly Varton."

My favorite line in the show was, "If it's tourist season, why can't we shoot them?"

THE NEXT DAY PRISCILLA AND POLLY headed on to Fairbanks, and Virginia's friend George and his daughter, Astrid, joined us. Astrid was a bubbly, intelligent high school student with black hair and dark eyes. George, an astrophysicist by profession, had a mop of curly brown hair and a penchant for untucked Hawaiian print shirts.

We four headed north on the Parks Highway that connected Anchorage to Fairbanks, 359 miles into the interior of Alaska. The passing landscape was fairly flat, full of evergreen trees and measured by white mile markers. Dusty tracks from dog sleds and off-road vehicles paralleled the road. Buckshot holes perforated most road signs.

Random campgrounds helped break up the monotony along the road. RVs lined up like well spaced teeth along shorelines. One broad river was thick with fishermen dressed in green rubber waders and copious amounts of red plaid wool.

"What's wrong with those trees?" I asked. Patches of black spruce trees tilted at unnatural angles. Some were 45-degrees to the ground.

"There was permafrost under them—dirt that stays frozen year round," George explained. "If it thaws, the dirt shifts, and the trees tilt."

But the curiosities of permafrost were no match for the gorillas at Mile 52. A brown one with disproportionately long arms. A black one wearing a pink bikini. A third one wearing a red flower lei and calico boxer shorts. These hot air balloon figures invited traffic to stop for a visit at Gorilla Fireworks, where a Batmobile sat by the front door.

The lemon yellow building was a pyrotechnic freak's paradise. If it glowed, sparkled, exploded, smoked, screamed, whizzed, boomed or cascaded, Gorilla Fireworks had it. Products had inspiring names like Goliath, Saturn Missile Battery, Space Flyers and One Bad Momma. Need lots of firecrackers? Buy a 16,000-count case.

It was love at first sight when our foursome pulled into Talkeetna, population of 360. It was like stepping back in time. Buildings along the four-block main road, the only paved road in town, were built with clapboard and logs. Antlers poked out from random walls.

In the past, the town flourished as a miner's supply center, a riverboat station and the headquarters of a company that built railroads because the town was located where the Susitna, Talkeetna and Chulitna rivers converged. More recently, it has become a starting point for anglers, hunters and outdoor adventurists, particularly Denali mountain climbers. We had yet to see the elusive mountain peak due to cloud cover.

We checked into the rustic Roadhouse Inn for the night. Each of its narrow, wood-paneled rooms had a bed, a nightstand and a light. There were no televisions or phones. The shared bathroom was down the hall. A massive stone fireplace anchored the communal living room full of deep couches and overstuffed chairs. There were board games and books for entertainment. A flier promoted a gun raffle as a fundraiser.

At a local bar, we drank Moose Drool brown ales when a homemade looking flying machine flew by, barely clearing the trees along the road.

"We're too early to go to the Moose Dropping Festival," Virginia noted, which set off a comical discussion about throwing techniques. Alaskans seemed to have a quirky, yet appealing, sense of humor.

THE WELCOME SIGN TO FAIRBANKS declared that it had the coldest heart in Alaska. Average temperatures ranged from -15 degrees F during the winter to 73 degrees F in the summer.

According to the book, *Good Time Girls of the Alaska-Yukon Gold Rush* by Lael Morgan, if I had arrived about 1905, I would have been asked "Are you a lady or a whore?" by the city attorney who met females coming off each incoming boat. "If you are a lady, pass on. If you are a whore, $17.50." The fees could average $1,200 a month!

Virginia lived in an A-frame house, previously owned by her uncle, Jimmy Bedford, on a parcel of densely wooded, gently sloping land. Over the years, she transformed the ramshackle bachelor pad into a comfortable home with electricity, indoor plumbing, central heating, hardwood floors, and a modern kitchen with countertops set high for a tall woman. I learned later that there was no garbage collection service in this part of town. Virginia took her trash to a gravel lot full of dumpsters, where dumpster diving was a popular past time.

The unattached garage next to the main house had extra electrical outlets for plugging in cars.

"We install heating pads on the car engine blocks, oil pans and batteries to keep them from freezing," Virginia explained. It was a clear indication that there would be no Alaskan winters for me.

A fierce squirrel stood on top of the round woodpile in the front yard. His body jerked up each time he barked at me. When I got closer, he hightailed into a dark recess but continued to harass me. He did not sound alone in there.

The squirrel had good reason to be defensive. People killed them to protect their homes from the damage the rodent caused by chewing, stealing and nesting.

"A friend of mine had to climb up into a tree to get chess pieces out of a squirrel nest," Virginia said. I later discovered that squirrels liked to eat seeds out of pinecones inside the 1958 Ford truck parked next to her garage. They left a pyramid of rust-colored pinecone petals under the steering wheel.

I was tickled to be "roughing it" with Astrid in the one-room cabin on the other side of the gravel driveway. It had electricity but no plumbing. Its best feature was a screened porch with a spring-hinged door that made a pleasing whack when it slammed shut. The vintage couch was a perfect place to scribble in my journal and read books with my feet propped up on a burled oak stump. A downshift in travel gears, this was my home for the next four weeks. I would wake up in the same place every day and leave my stuff unpacked. It was time to hang out.

The cabin contained twin beds, office furniture, storage boxes and enough books for a small library. When we needed a bathroom, we could walk to the main house or use the red-walled outhouse lined with two-pound M&M bags (a surprise decorative touch from Virginia's neighbor, Ron). Toilet paper was kept in an upside-down, five-pound coffee can to keep squirrels from stealing it.

"So are you going to use the outhouse?" I asked Astrid, who wrinkled her nose in distain.

"Absolutely not," she said.

During my stay I used it a number of times for novelty's sake. I always left the door wide open, so I could enjoy the wooded view while I did my business.

No matter which bathroom we picked, it was never dark when we skipped to the loo because we slept through the few hours of darkness every night.

CHRISTMAS WAS 169 DAYS AWAY, but Astrid and I started our morning with a visit to the town of North Pole and the Santa Claus House, the epicenter of holiday kitsch. The few men we saw were husbands sitting on benches patiently waiting as their wives shopped.

Reindeer (domesticated caribou) grazed in a pasture next door.

"Did you know that only female reindeers keep their antlers in winter?" I asked Astrid as we reached through the fence to stroke the surprisingly warm velvet on their antlers. "That means all of Santa's reindeers were female."

Afterward, we went to the University of Alaska Fairbanks' Museum of the North. Giant cedar totem poles by the front doors told stories through expressive carvings painted coal black, sky blue and salmon egg red. Crest poles recorded family history. History poles chronicled the life of the clan. Memorial poles honored individuals. Legend poles illustrated folklore or real experience. If I had a memorial pole, it would probably include zebras, giant tortoises, leeches and Snickers bars.

As Astrid and I wandered the museum halls, we learned about the region's ecology, cultural traditions and history-making events. There was something for everyone. Native Americans. Polar bears, walrus and whales. The evacuation of Japanese Americans to camps during World War II. The influence of the Russian Orthodox Church. The Alaskan Highway. The largest display of gold nuggets in the state. Blue Babe, a steppe bison who died from a lion attack about 36,000 years ago.

In the UAF auditorium, students demonstrated traditional games played by the Inuit. These aboriginal groups lived in coastal areas of Canada, Greenland, Alaska and Northeastern Siberia. These groups endured nine months of snow, three months of total darkness and freezing temperatures around minus 30 degrees F during the coldest months. The deceptively simple games challenged each player's physical strength, agility and endurance, often necessary for survival under these conditions.

We winced and cheered as the students bounced on the hardwood floor on their knuckles, knees or butts. They played tug of war with round straps linking their ears together. They knelt on the floor with their butts against their heels, only to jump (no pumping) as far as they could but still land on both feet. The most comical game required contestants to strap a loop around the back of their necks and behind their knees, forcing them to crouch down. With their hands clasped behind their backs, the two contestants bumped, hopped and crab-walked against each other until one was knocked to the ground. The winner sat on the loser.

"We're screwed," Astrid and I agreed. We would both die if left to our feeble abilities.

We also watched a presentation about the northern lights, a topic more than appropriate because Fairbanks is one of the best spots on earth to see them. These auroras are mysterious waves of color—Granny Smith apple green to Meyer lemon yellow to Cherry Kool-Aid red—blazing, rippling and curling across the sky.

While the northern lights have always had spiritual interpretations, the UAF professor explained that they were a mesmerizing phenomenon created by the sun's energy.

"When those particles hit the earth's atmosphere as part of a solar wind, their energy converts to light," he said. The intensity and appearance of the northern lights varies, but in Fairbanks they can occur any time between late August and early April. Odds were high that I would not see them during my visit to Alaska.

Before dinner, I went for a run along the forest-lined road near Virginia's house. A dead dragonfly laid by the side of the road. Proving that I was getting the hang of the local humor, I plucked off one of its wings and taped it to the cover of my journal when I got back to the cabin.

"See how big the mosquitoes get up there," I said later to people who had never been to Alaska.

AT THE MAIN ENTRANCE of Denali National Park, a sign asked visitors to unload their guns before entering the park. At the visitor center, Astrid and I caught the 11 a.m. Blue Bird bus for an eight-hour wildlife viewing ride up to the Eielson Visitor Center and back. Most of the gravel road was limited to bus, bike or foot traffic.

Everyone on the bus buzzed with excitement. Hopes of dramatic wildlife sightings danced through our heads. We were armed and ready—cameras, extra batteries and film, telephoto lenses, binoculars, field guides and wildlife checklists. It reminded of my Kenyan safari except that we had layers of wool, fleece and Gore-Tex clothing to keep us warm as the weather vacillated from sunny and warm to overcast and cold.

"So we have drinks, snacks and sandwiches right?" I asked Astrid who nodded. "There's no place to shop for the next four hours." It seemed downright un-American.

Statistically speaking, the park has 39 species of mammals and 167 species of birds. The grizzly bear commands visitor attention, but scientific attention most likely goes to Denali's lone amphibian—the adult wood frog. Their body temperatures fluctuate with their surroundings to the point where they freeze solid each year. Afraid of snakes? No worries. Every inch of the 6,075,030-acre park is reptile free.

Miles and miles we bounced along, hoping someone would call out a wildlife sighting. It was funny to see a bus full of adults (including me) get downright ecstatic over a hare.

Everyone was scanning the scenery out the side windows of the bus when the bus driver called out "Caribou!" We laughed when we realized it was sauntering down the road in front of the bus. Its hide was a mangy transitional mess of short summer coat and woolly winter fur. Our cameras clicked away despite the rear-end view. The caribou eventually ambled off the road when another bus came in the opposite direction.

Down in the valley, we spied moose grazing on the tender water plants in kettle ponds. Retreating glaciers created these ponds when large chunks of ice broke off, indented in the land and then melted, filling the indents with water.

Our thoughts turned to bears when we saw a sign cautioning visitors not to leave the road for the next five miles. The bottom corner had been chewed off in spite of outward-pointing nails.

We drove on, searched, waited and snacked. Just like on the East African safari, nature would not perform on demand. My excitement waned, our early start time caught up with me, and I nodded off a few times.

Perched on a tundra slope, the Eielson Visitor Center was a welcome respite from the bus. From its parking lot, trails led to the high ridges overlooking the Thorofare River and to the low pastures by the river's shoals. On clear days the center offered a breathtaking view of Denali, the crown of the park, and the 600-mile-long Alaskan Range. Unfortunately, clouds blocked the view during our visit. I did not mind. I still had glorious memories of the Himalayas.

Our last wildlife sighting of the day trip was the biggest.

"Bear," someone yelled. The distant grizzly looked like a plump, golden Star Trek tribble on a grassy slope. Through binoculars, we could see where its fur gradually darkened to brown on its legs. My guidebook explained that the long guard hairs on its back and shoulders often had white tips, giving the bears a "grizzled" appearance, hence the name "grizzly bear." It was too far away for us to tell if it was one of Alaska's sumo-size male bears, weighing more than 700 pounds thanks to a salmon-heavy diet.

The visitor center guide book advised hunters to carry bells so that bears can hear them coming and pepper spray to chase bears away. However, Virginia had told us a joke tied to this advice.

"How do you tell the difference between black bear scat and grizzly bear scat?" she asked. "Black bear scat is full of berry seeds. Grizzly bear scat is full of bells and smells like pepper."

DURING OUR FEW REMAINING DAYS together, Astrid and I continued to explore Fairbanks.

We went on a river cruise with about a hundred senior citizens on a sternwheeler riverboat. It was designed to operate in less than four feet of water, perfect for the shallow, ever-changing Alaskan rivers. At one point, the boat dropped us off to watch a series of presentations, including one about sled dogs. I expected plush, stocky dogs, but learned that true racers had short coats and lean bodies. By weighing less than 60 pounds, they were less likely to fall through frozen snow.

We went to Gold Dredge No. 8, a National Historic Site. The mine's giant steam engines ran from 1928 to about 1958 in Goldstream Valley, where prospector Felix Pedro had discovered gold and started a gold rush. But that was inconsequential. We were there mainly so Astrid could hang out with Polly's nephews, Frank and Mike. They were hard at work dumping handfuls of dirt into pans and sloshing it around in a trough of muddy water. Because gold was more than 19 times heavier than water, it sank to the bottom of the pan as the water whisked away the dirt. Alas, Astrid's flirtatious moves could not compete with their gold fever.

We went to Pioneer Park, a 44-acre complex that included an amusement park, a mini golf course, a salmon bake restaurant and several museums. A vintage poster beckoned women to come to Alaska and the Yukon. It noted that a pioneer woman could pay $119 for all the clothes she would need—including a rubber blanket to wrap them all in to keep them dry.

The park also included Judge James Wickersham's first house, which he built using lumber he carried on his back from the sawmill a few blocks away. In 1900, he became the first judge in the new district that covered some 300,000 square miles. The district had no roads, so he covered his circuit by boat in summer and dog sled in winter. In 1901, he completed a 45-day, round-trip journey of more than 1,000 miles by dog sled to preside over claim-jumping disputes.

One evening when Astrid and I got home from a day of exploring, Virginia and George were rendering marbled chunks of bear fat in a cast iron frying pan on the back porch. It was a stinky affair.

"What a bear eats affects how the bear fat tastes," explained Virginia. "The fat can be fishy if the bear has been eating salmon."

Virginia used the bear lard to make an apple pie crust. Astrid, George, Virginia and I compared the bear fat pie crust with one made with Crisco shortening. Not bad. The lard crust was slightly gamey and had a denser texture.

Days later, Stan, the hunter who gave Virginia the bear fat, sent an email alert.

"Three bears are roaming the area," he wrote. "They have eaten a two-day old colt, and a yearling is missing. Everyone should keep their guns handy."

Some aspects of Alaskan life were as foreign to me as some aspects of Maasai life.

When Astrid and George left to go back to Seattle, it was lonely without them. And quieter. Once when I was in the shower, I heard blood curdling screams coming from the living room. I dashed out to rescue Astrid, only to find her in ecstasy over the appearance of Britney Spears on the *Oprah Winfrey Show*.

VIRGINIA AND I PICKED UP GOODIES from Bun on the Run. The aptly named bakery was housed in a kidney-shaped camper parked in a shopping center lot.

We took them over to Virginia's friend, Yvonne, who was stuck on a couch. Her leg was encased in a lime green cast and propped up on a pillow. Yvonne told me how her casual weekend hike had gone wrong.

"The trail was a big circle, so my friend and I hiked away from each other—I went clockwise, and she went counterclockwise—for a little wilderness alone time, and then we met at the trail's halfway point, about 14 miles from the start," Yvonne said with a sigh, knowing it would be a long time until she went hiking again.

"The next day we split up again to finish the trail and planned to meet back at the car. I'd gone about a mile when I fell on a patch of ice. I knew it was bad, but I didn't know how bad," she said as she cast her eyes down, no doubt reliving the pain. "I was still above the tree line, so I had to drag myself for miles before I found a branch I could use as a cane.

"But I made it back to the car, and we went to the hospital. Good thing we didn't try to take my boot off," she said. "I had broken my leg just above the ankle, and the pressure from the boot kept me from bleeding to death."

She was tough.

I needed to be that tough. My trip was coming to an end, and I was starting to freak out about it. During one of my runs, I was swarmed by mosquitoes and conflicting thoughts. I wanted to go home. I had no home. I was uncomfortably full of experiences. I did not want to stop traveling. I did not want to go back to Charlotte. I did not know where I wanted to go. I hated the thought of getting a desk job. I needed money.

At least my cousins Tamara and Todd, the missionaries from Tanzania, had found direction. They had returned to the United States, and Todd had accepted a job working with a ministry organization in Minneapolis. Not only did this position fulfill some of the family's personal and spiritual goals, but it also reunited them with family and neighbors because they had lived there before.

Call it God or karma, something seemed to be leading us by opening and closing doors of opportunity.

"Finish the trip, Kristine," I told myself as I continued to make my sweaty way to the top of a hill. "The answers will come when it's time for them to be here."

That evening, Virginia and I went to watch one of her friends perform at Pioneer Park's Palace Theatre and Saloon. Kit was the piano player for a musical show about the history and colorful characters in early and present-day Fairbanks. Seniors were packed in tight rows in the audience.

The skits were hilarious, particularly the one that featured a nutty professor teaching B.S. 101: Outhouse Architecture and Décor. He pointed out how the winterized (fur-lined) toilet seat also made a good airline logo. (The Alaska Airlines' logo features a Native American man wearing a fur-lined hood shaped just like a toilet seat).

BEFORE BED, I FINALLY TOOK my last Lariam pill. (My physician had prescribed that I take the medicine until a few weeks after I left Southeast Asia.) I dreamed about flushing dinosaur toys down a toilet and eating cake on a grassy hillside with actress Meg Ryan. I was absolutely ready to say goodbye to the weird dreams.

JEAN LESTER HAD SOMETHING I wanted. The magnificent painting captured peonies in full bloom. Each blushed in rich lipstick-colored shades of pink, rouge and magenta.

I had grown peonies at my house in Charlotte, North Carolina. I loved the way the heavy blooms bowed in the rain, the sensuous curves and folds of the petals, the colors that ranged from shy to confident. With her decades of experience, Jean captured all of these nuances with her brushstrokes. Alas, I had no money to buy her art.

"I haven't worked on it in days," she explained as we stood in her studio, naturally brightened by skylights. "I'm letting it ripen."

She explained that every few days she gave it a few dabs of paint until her artistic sense deemed it done.

Virginia, Jean and I chatted through the afternoon over hot tea. At one point, we compared our decades of experience with love.

"So, finding a good man, one who feels worthy and right, is based significantly on timing," I concluded. "You cannot search for them. They just appear."

"Yes," Virginia and Jean agreed.

That evening, I went with Virginia to a dinner party. Eight other people sat around the communal table, surrounded by walls decorated with crazy quilts made by the hostess. Eventually someone asked about my future plans. It was clear I had passed the mile marker between "What are you going to do on your trip?" to "What are you going to do after your trip?"

"I'm trying to be quiet and let my inner voice tell me where to go when it's ready," was all I could say. But the lack of direction was fertile ground for fear. The newspaper declared that the stock market had had its third worst crash in history. "Maybe grad school, but I definitely don't want to go back to Charlotte. I want to live someplace new."

"Come here!" they suggested.

"I don't think I could handle the winters, but I am tempted."

The more social visits I made with Virginia, the more I realized how everyone was both fiercely independent yet strongly connected to a vibrant social network. I expected cable TV to have a stronghold on locals because of the long, dark winter months, but that was not proving true. They had hobbies and read books. They had activities for every season. The wilderness was an extension of their family rooms.

VIRGINIA'S NEIGHBOR, RON, was an older gentleman with white hair tufted like a horned owl and chunky black-rimmed glasses. I never saw him wear anything other than jeans and white T-shirts with the sleeves ripped off. He arrived in Alaska in 1975 to work on the Alaskan Pipeline and bought his property in 1977. From the looks of it, he had never thrown anything away since then. He was delighted when I asked for a tour of his yard.

It began with the largest building, a monstrous two-story, wood-sided box with solar panels and rows of tiny windows. The first floor was supposed to be a workshop. The second floor was supposed to be a combination library and ballet studio (leftover from a former girlfriend era). Neither project was finished. The downstairs was haphazardly filled with piles of tools, construction materials, furniture and magazines. There were dozens of coffee cans and Breyers ice cream cartons full of gun cartridge brass and wheel weights. I opted not to climb the ladder in the empty elevator shaft to see what was upstairs.

Ron's bachelor pad was a shed just wide enough for a raised bed with storage underneath. Next to the bed was a potbelly stove, jerrycans of water, and a honey pot—a polite name for a five-gallon bucket topped with a toilet seat.

"You don't have a kitchen or shower," I said.

"I've got a hot plate, and I usually have dinner at the all-you-could-eat bar at the grocery store downtown," he explained. "And the laundromat rents showers."

Ron's lifestyle seemed odd, but I soon learned there were quite a few people living in rustic cabins who had similar habits.

I opened the door of a Volkswagen van (also called a Twinkie-mobile by one of my new Alaskan friends), which had not been moved in years. It was dirty and rusted, and the tires were flat.

"The owners are looking to sell it," Ron said. "You want to buy it?"

The door of opportunity swung wide open, but that kind of adventure would require both money and mechanical abilities. I had neither, but that could change. "I'll have to get back to you on that."

We walked past a welding shack covered with chains, an outhouse packed with paint cans, a small building that served as Ron's study and a white radar dome that looked like a small igloo with a spike on top.

"I like to tell people I keep my ice cream in here during the winter," he said, patting a four-tier filing cabinet that just sat out in the yard.

Scattered about the woods were other curious things. Ron pointed out aluminum kegs with octagon-shaped seals, which were used to transport rare earth ore from Russia, and sewer pipes made of wood and wire, which made them tolerant of Alaska's temperature fluctuations. There were piles of oak dunnage beams once used to keep Alaskan pipeline construction materials from smashing around inside moving railroad cars. There was a row of purple school lockers, a 1910 Dunn marine engine and five pickup trucks for parts salvage. Segments of 65-, 90- and 150-pound railroad rails were dated 1896 and 1920.

We walked around a pile of bowling balls, the bottom half of a mannequin and the hopper for a sawdust-burning stove to see his Civil War field cannon replica.

"There are six other cannons like this in town," he said proudly. "We like to get together and shoot them off."

This yard, with its 14 critically placed fire extinguishers, was perhaps the sign of a rich man in Alaskan terms.

"We should remember that these folks are performing a major service for future archeologists," noted a new Alaskan friend when I told him about the yard. "If we are too tidy, there will be no record of our society."

EVEN THOUGH ALASKA WAS THE LAND of trucks and sport utility vehicles, boys will be boys, so it was no surprise that there were some impressive performance automobiles on the road. For example, Virginia's friend, John, arrived in a 1972 silver Porsche 911 to take me to the annual Red Green River Regatta.

This event was based on the philosophies of the *Red Green Show*, a PBS comedy. The show gave hilarious insight into men, their egos and other inflatables. Red Green, host of the show, believed that, "If women don't find you handsome, they should at least find you handy." According to Red, the handyman's secret weapon is duct tape, so all vessels in the regatta had to be constructed with at least one roll of duct tape.

In the launching area, participants put last minute touches on their vessels. Extraneous decorations ranged from racks of moose antlers to an armadillo dangling from a fishing pole. Onlookers were quick to offer suggestions to improve floatability.

One humbled father learned a lesson in physics with his young son when their rowboat, perched on empty 55-gallon drums, flipped over seconds after leaving the shore. It was too top heavy. One mariner served burgers from a charcoal grill to fellow passengers who sat on patio furniture. A Viking warship (with a cardboard exterior) sailed confidently downriver, guided by sailors wearing horned helmets. One boat's gunnels had sunk under the water, but her crew continued to paddle on with their snow shovels.

Even though the event was not a race, participants still earned prizes for Best Use of Duct Tape and Most Ludicrous.

Winner of the popularity vote was definitely the float that featured a swing set stuck into logs of foam. Two blonde women in duct tape-covered bikinis and high heels sat in the swings, daintily kicking water while their men did the real paddling with snow shovels.

RON AND I SPENT ONE MORNING TIDYING up a part of Virginia's wooded yard, organizing construction debris left over from various projects. Ron, of course, relocated a truckload of scrap wood, doors and windows to his yard.

After lunch, three of Virginia's friends stopped by for a visit. Peter worked in the petroleum industry on the North Slope, an area between the Brooks Mountain range and the northern shoreline of Alaska. Jane was an electrician who had also worked in that area but now lived in Oregon. Arthur was her housemate and personal assistant when he was not taking extreme kayaking trips. He was a handsome man with a quiet disposition, though I questioned his sanity: he did not eat butter.

The threesome helped us cut down a tree and stack a wood pile. There was that Alaskan sense of community again.

One thing led to another, and I was off with Jane, Peter and Arthur to visit a portion of the 800-mile-long Alaskan Pipeline. At one point it moved more than two million barrels of crude oil per day from the North Slope to tankers on the southern shore of Alaska. The 48-inch-wide pipe crossed three mountain ranges and more than 800 rivers and streams as it zigzagged down the state.

That night Virginia and I went for drinks at the Pump House Restaurant and Saloon overlooking the Chena River. We met up with a few of her friends including Kit, the piano player from Pioneer Park.

"Are you going to write a book about your trip?" he asked.

Kit's question stunned me. In spite of the fact that I had worked editorial jobs for two decades, I had never considered doing that. The trip had been about me seeing the world and breaking my life out of a rut, but perhaps others would find my tale an enjoyable read. What an obvious thing to do.

I traveled around the world based on Larry's idea. I wrote a book about my trip based on Kit's idea. I wondered when I would I start coming up with my own ideas.

DURING A DINNER PARTY at Virginia's house, we settled into chairs and couches with plates of food on our laps. The conversation wandered from topic to topic like a bee in an English garden.

Visiting from Australia, Rob described mice plagues in his home country.

"Females reach sexual maturity at about six weeks of age, and they need less than three weeks to birth a litter of up to 13 mice," he said. When they were not birthing babies, the mice ate newly planted seed crops, spread diseases, gnawed on everything—even electrical wiring, and contaminated grain stores with urine and droppings. "In one town they recorded about eight mice per square yard."

Teresa, originally from Poland, was a testament to the strength and courage of the human spirit. She was destined to die in a WWII concentration camp, but the train she was on was turned back by American soldiers. She eventually ended up in Alaska, where she thrived and built a strong network of friends, a house and several outbuildings.

"But I've lost my bottom teeth somewhere in the house," she confessed as she ate only soft food. We scheduled a search party for the next morning.

Priscilla (my roommate in Seward) recalled a motorcycle rider she met at a rest stop.

"He was a burly man, complete with whiskers, leather vest and faded denim jeans," Priscilla said. "A senior citizen asked the rider if U.S. dollars were accepted in Alaska. So the biker said, 'Alaskans prefer dried fish and shiny beads, but they will accept dollars if they have to.' The senior thanked him quite seriously and went back to his RV."

Pleased that the meal did not include carrots, coconut or cheese, neighbor Ron was content to just listen to the conversations. He did become quite animated, however, when the topic turned to using a modified stun gun to treat insect and snake bites. Evidently, electrical currents can break up venom.

Paolo, a burly, Italian-looking man who kissed me hello on both cheeks when we met, talked about how he used aerial photography and GPS to locate Incan ruins. When I mentioned that I had shipped some of my journals back to the United States, he was horrified that I had not made back-up copies.

"They are irreplaceable, and you CANNOT trust the postal system," he declared. "I sent a mummified llama fetus to my mother, and it took three years for it to arrive."

"And why did you send your mother a mummified llama fetus?" we all wanted to know.

"It a Peruvian thing," he shrugged. "If you place it under the foundation of your house, it helps keep earthquakes away."

These were the funny, smart, adventurous people I wanted in my life, to inspire me, to help me push my boundaries. Why did they have to live in a place that was so damn cold in the winter?

Where did that come from?

Barrow, Alaska

OUR ALASKA AIRLINES BREAKFAST TRAYS included slips of paper with Bible verses printed on them. Mine read, "I will be glad and rejoice in you; I will sing praises of your name, O Most High," It inspired me to make a little prayer of my own, to ask that my sense of mental numbness and travel overload would go away. I wanted the rush again of exploring a new place totally unlike any other place I had been before. God heard me.

Virginia and I were flying to Barrow, 340 miles north of the Arctic Circle, to spend the night. The small town was the most northern city in Alaska and the United States, and the ninth most northern city in the world.

As the flight progressed, the landscape below flowed from rolling evergreen forests to mountaintops that looked like white crumpled paper to barren, grassy tundra polka-dotted with mirror-smooth lakes. Bow down, Minnesota—Alaska was a land of 10 million lakes. Three million were larger than 20 acres in size. No wonder the Barrow Birding Center provided an impressive checklist of 185 species.

When we arrived, the temperature was 49 degrees—balmy, considering that local temperatures were below freezing about 324 days a year. Later, our guide said the hottest weather he had ever experienced was a sweltering 79 degrees for a few hours. He and his mother had fled in a boat to the ice floes until the heat wave had passed.

The map of Barrow (population 4,500) was simple. No roads lead to Barrow. All roads in town come to a dead end. The longest road is 14 miles long. The only pavement in town is the airport runway. No license plates are required. The one stoplight in town only change from green to red when school children push the crosswalk button. All buses have GPS tags so passengers could track them via a live cable channel. This allows them to wait inside until the bus arrives.

Downtown sat between the airport and the ocean. Most buildings looked like one-story box houses in washed-out primary colors. They were heated with natural gas captured from local gas fields. Each house sat on pilings and had a mechanism for dispersing heat so that the house did not thaw the permafrost below it and sink into the resulting mud.

Grass-free yards were cluttered with snowmobiles, oil drums, engine parts and spare lumber. I was startled to see fringed strips of baleen that had once been a part of a bowhead whale's mouth, strips of raw meat draped over racks, and gutted eider ducks hanging from porch railings. The air was so dry that it sucked the moisture out of the meat before it went rancid. Traditional hunting and subsistence practices remained at the heart of the community.

We met up with our Tundra Tour guide, Bunna Edwardson, and his tour bus full of seniors. He had sparkling black eyes, black hair that hung down his back, a quick smile, a strong compact body, and a love for sharing his Inupiat history and culture. Even though we were all bundled up against the cold, Bunna only wore a windbreaker, a T-shirt and jeans.

As we rode in the bus to the edge of town, Bunna cleared up a fallacy.

"Eskimos do not rub noses," he said, laughing when we all pouted. "That was something Hollywood made up."

Our first stop was a series of wide gray-brown embankments made of soil and tiny pebbles. Looking out toward the ocean, we saw an artistic study of blues and whites. The wind had driven thousands of pieces of ice against the shoreline for as far as we could see. They ranged in size from a snowball to a fire truck. Many giant pieces were carved into mushroom shapes as waves ate away at their bases faster than the sun could melt their tops. All of the pieces swayed ever so slightly in the water.

Behind us, the tundra spanned out to the other horizon as a carpet of golden yellows, light greens and reddish browns. There were no trees or shrubs; they had no way to survive the brutal winters or the frozen ground.

We got back on the bus and continued past the Imaiqsaun Cemetery. It contained recent burials, plus human remains excavated from local archeological sites, including the "Frozen Family." In 1982, an eroded shoreline revealed a family of two women and three children who died about 450 years ago.

"The family had been starving. There was animal leather in their stomachs," Bunna said. "We think they were crushed to death by ice the wind had pushed ashore."

He also pointed out the ancient village of Utqiagvik, once a collection of sod houses. In 1994 archeologists discovered the frozen body of a young girl in one that dated back to the year 1200.

"When someone died in a house, it was tradition to leave the body in the house and seal it off," Bunna noted. "The family then built a new home."

After the tour, Virginia and I ate lunch at Pepe's North of the Border Restaurant, one of the handful of restaurants in town. Owner and operator Fran Tate led us to our seats. As a one-time guest on the Tonight Show, she surprised Johnny Carson with an oosik, a three-foot-long bone from a walrus penis. Tate also had a business delivering water around town. Water sold for 14.5 cents per gallon in Barrow, compared to 7 cents a gallon in Fairbanks.

The restaurant offered mostly Mexican food. We ate halibut but looked to see if the menu offered whale meat tacos or seal enchiladas.

"If whale tasted so great, it'd be farm-raised by now," a friend joked with me later.

After checking in at the Top of the World Hotel, we took another tour with Bunna. It began at the Utqiagvik Presbyterian Church. The white building with blue trim was built in 1898 to serve the influx of Yankee whalers who began arriving in 1854. More than 2,000 whaling ships from New Bedford, Massachusetts, sailed into arctic waters during the late 19th and early 20th centuries. Many Alaskan natives, particularly the Inupiat, crewed on the ships, hunted for food to feed the whalers, provided fur clothing and sheltered shipwrecked men. The mingling of whalers and locals explained the dozens of Browers, Leavitts and Hopsons listed in Barrow's current telephone directory.

The whalers were after bowhead whales, the only baleen whales that spent their entire lives near sea ice. Measuring about 60 feet long and weighing more than 120,000 pounds, these ocean dwellers rely on their blubber, sometimes 18 inches thick, for insulation and food storage. Mankind's desire to own that blubber decimated the whale population.

"In London in the 1840s, they installed 5,000 street lamps that burned whale oil," Bunna noted.

Fortunately, by the early 1900s, the whaling industry had, for the most part, collapsed due to a shortage of whales, the replacement of baleen with steel in corsets and whale oil substitutes.

Our tour group laughed at the facetious Barrow National Forest. Someone had hauled a tree trunk to town and topped it with baleen fronds so that it resembled a palm tree from a distance. It was not the only public display of humor. There was also a carved totem pole with a white porcelain toilet perched on the top. Alaskan humor thrived in spite of the weather.

The white golf ball-shaped structure on a platform behind it, however, was no joke. It was a DEW (Distant Early Warning) Line station, one of 63 radar and communication stations spread along a 3,000-mile route in the 1950s to help protect the U.S. and Canada from air attack.

Our afternoon tour ended at the Inupiat Heritage Center, a modern building designed to take advantage of as much natural light as possible. Based on the concept of *qargi* [community house], it contained a museum, meeting and performance spaces, a library and artisan workshops. A gracefully arched, life-size replica of a bowhead whale hung from the ceiling in the lobby.

We met with locals who were selling handmade crafts. I bought a mask the size of my palm from an artist's granddaughter. The face was translucent caribou hide with contours for the eye sockets, nose, cheekbones, lips and chin. The eyelashes and eyebrows were made of gray seal fur. The wispy gray fur circling the face and the yellowish fur bangs were from a black wolf.

"Wolves are not native to Barrow, but we can trade to get the fur," explained the granddaughter.

An exhibition in the museum featured photographs taken in 1887 by Herbert L. Aldrich, a 25-year-old reporter for New Bedford's *Evening Standard* newspaper. Believing he was about to die from tuberculosis anyway, he sailed with arctic whaling fleets for the better part of a year. His photographs were among the first ever taken on a whaling ship at sea and of the native peoples of coastal Siberia and Alaska. Aldrich lived to be 87.

"So, who wants to get in the water?" Bunna challenged the tour group. "I'll go with you, and if you go completely under water, you'll become a member of the Polar Bear Club."

"I'll do it!" Virginia said. No surprise there.

"And I will photograph her triumph for posterity," I said, as if responsibility would cloak my cowardice.

Virginia went to the hotel to change into a red tank top and black shorts. When she returned, she got down to business. With Bunna at her heels, she waded into the frigid water, dodging some large chunks of ice, dipped completely in the water, popped back up and rushed to shore. She made it look so simple, but I was not buying it.

"The water takes your breath away," she said. As the numbing shock from the frigid water wore off, she began to shiver.

Virginia beamed as I took a photograph of her with the soaking wet Bunna and Fran, who presented her with the sacred membership patch.

"A dry Eskimo is a happy Eskimo," Bunna said as Virginia scurried back to the hotel for a hot shower.

To the north of town the land narrowed and formed Point Barrow, where the Chukchi Sea from the west met the Beaufort Sea from the east. This was polar bear territory. Not the friendly, cuddly Coco-Cola spokes-bears, but 1,200-pound carnivores that could make a meal of a walrus. The boundary between the town of Barrow and Point Barrow was marked by a wooden billboard with a mixed message: "Welcome to Barrow, Alaska. Danger! Polar Bears." Buckshot obliterated the rest of the sign. As if to emphasize the point, a bearded seal skeleton lay in the dirt nearby.

That night, we went with Joe the tour guide past the sign. He talked and looked like Dave Barry and was son of Fran the restaurant owner. His colorful background included stints as a national hockey champ, a KFC manager, a water delivery man and a cook at a Mexican restaurant.

The sun coasted just above the horizon as we rode in his Humvee, and the conversation touched on alcohol regulations in Barrow.

"In the 1970s, residents decided to close all the bars and liquor stores," Joe said. "In 1994, they banned all alcoholic beverages, hoping that would wipe out alcohol-related violence and public disturbances."

The Sober Life Movement, a group of Inupiats in support of the ban, said felony assaults dropped by 86 percent, fights by 61 percent and drunk driving by 79 percent after the ban took effect. Yet in 1995, residents overturned the ban.

"Now we have a 'damp law,'" he said. "We can bring booze to town and share it with our friends, but we can't sell it."

We soon drove past what looked like an abandoned roll of brown shag carpet half buried in the sand of tiny gray pebbles.

"That was a dead whale that washed up on the shore," Joe explained. "Polar bears won't eat it. They won't eat sick animals."

In another place, we saw a bleached white bone the size of a car hood but with unfamiliar curves and holes. It was the top of a whale skull.

In the distance I could see a jagged pile of something. As we grew closer, my fascination and horror grew. The pile of whale ribs, vertebrae and skull plates dwarfed our Humvee. A yellowish resin from leftover flesh glazed the bones. It looked as if a monster had thrown up its last meal.

And yet, for all the carnage, there were no flies and only a rich, earthy smell.

During spring whale hunts, locals butchered their kills far out on the ice. Carnivores scavenged the remains until they fell into the sea when the ice broke. During the fall whale hunt, however, there was no ice. The whale was brought to shore for butchering, and the remains were deposited at this site via a bulldozer to help keep bears out of town.

Alas, there were no polar bears. One had been seen the day before our visit. Another came the day after our visit. A month later, the *Fairbanks Daily-News Miner* reported that an abnormally large number of polar bears were crowding Point Barrow. Visitors saw 40 to 50 bears instead of the usual five or six. With men and polar bears, it seemed, timing was everything.

WHILE WE WERE SLEEPING through the night, the wind changed direction and blew all of the floating ice out of sight. It seemed like magic. Poof, it was gone, leaving two vast plains of unbroken blue—water and sky—punctuated by a full moon. I could see why people once thought the earth was flat and you could fall off the edge at the horizon.

While Virginia had her morning coffee and checked work emails, I wandered around town. Barrow was quiet. Only a few people and two trucks passed me by. All the stores seemed owner-operated with one massive exception, the A.C. Value Store. I walked its aisles, checking out a few prices: six-pack of V8 juice, $9.25; five-pound bag of sugar, $7.29; a quart of Miracle Whip salad dressing, $7.19; milk, $8 per gallon; and cherries, $8 a pound. The store also carried ropes, dry sacks, couches and, in the frozen food aisle, a Honda TRX 450FM all-terrain vehicle for only $6,899.

Down the street from the supermarket, children played on a merry-go-round and primary-colored jungle gym. Barrow mothers could rarely tell their children to be home before dark. The sun did not set for about 12 weeks between May and August, and it did not rise for about 12 weeks between November and January.

Bunna spent his morning taking a family of three on a private tour, but he invited Virginia and me to join them all for lunch at Brower's Café. The cafe was housed in the oldest building in the Arctic region.

Minutes after we sat down, it was obvious why Bunna had invited us. The family was aloof and hard to read. They offered no playful banter or inquisitiveness about Barrow's culture. It was as if they wanted to check the town off a bragging list.

The father was a successful business owner, the kind who probably had his black dot portrait published in the *Wall Street Journal*. When I mentioned my safari, the father said they had gone on one as well.

"We had a service staff, so it was a pleasant experience," he said.

The mother appeared to be the perfectly groomed trophy wife who hardly said a word unless spoken to. The college-age daughter came across as arrogant with her rigid posture, designer clothes, gold jewelry and harsh opinions.

"With access to modern food distribution," she said, eating an imported steak as she protested against the meat curing in the yards around town, "Subsistence hunting is not necessary."

They were polite but dismissive toward us—perhaps due to our casual clothes and laidback attitudes—as if Virginia, Bunna and I were peasants or dishwashers. I tolerated it throughout the meal, discreetly making silly faces at Bunna when I could. As lunch ended though, I gave up. When the daughter name-dropped her Ivy League university, I could not resist stepping into the verbal boxing ring of accomplishments.

"I graduated from Purdue University and was a medical writer at the Mayo Clinic," I said. "But right now I'm taking a break and traveling around the world." I refrained from adding By. My. Self.

The father's eyes squinted ever so slightly as he reevaluated me.

"And Virginia, she's a technical services director on global computing projects."

Nice right jab, followed by a left punch.

Virginia and I said our goodbyes and grinned as we left.

After lunch the family cut their tour short because they were bored, so Bunna drove Virginia and I out of town to see wildlife.

"Look over by the wood pile," Bunna said. Puffy fox kits preened in the sun, but trotted away when we got too close. "We trap them for fur, but we don't eat them. They carry rabies."

When we talked about my trip, I mentioned that a Maasai man had offered 50 cows for my matrimonial hand.

"I'll give your father whale blubber, halibut, salmon and access to our family fishing camp," Bunna said as I laughed at the thought of my parents' reaction to getting a cooler of whale blubber in the mail.

"I'll let him know," I replied.

Before Virginia and I left town, Bunna and five new tourists plunged into the frigid sea water. I waffled about joining them, but chickened out again. I did, however, bare my feet, roll up my pants legs and wade calf high into the water around two rust-colored jellyfish with ruffled tentacles. I only stayed in the water long enough to pose for a photo.

Quyanaqpak! [Thank you for visiting!]

Boys, bugs and beavers

Fairbanks, Alaska

ARTHUR THE EXTREME KAYAKER moved into the second twin bed in Virginia's cabin where I was staying. A few days before, when Virginia proposed he stay for a couple of weeks to help work on the yard, I had wondered if she was giving romance a chance to blossom. I was game. His witty, laid-back style was fun to be around. But if he snored, out to the porch couch he would go.

Over the next few days, Arthur and I mixed yard work with visits to local attractions.

We went to the Big Dipper Ice Arena to watch some of the annual World Eskimo-Indian Olympics. My favorite game was the two-footed high kick. Competitors kept their feet together as they kicked forward at an elevated target ball about the size of a grapefruit. Jesse Frankson won first place by kicking a ball that hung 8-feet, 2-inches off the ground. He was six inches short of the world record. Historically, this jump signaled that a whale had been caught.

At the 134-acre University of Alaska Fairbanks Large Animal Research Station (LARS), we met our first musk ox. He looked like a short-legged, woolly cousin to a water buffalo. The brown outer layer of his wool coat was made of coarse guard hairs that extended almost to the ground. The under layer was a soft, light gray wool called *qiviut* (a great word for Scrabble). It was among the world's warmest and most sought-after natural fibers—softer and warmer than cashmere and angora wool.

The musk ox stood absolutely still. No grazing. No chewing. No turning his head to look at us. The only time we saw him break his Zen-like stance was when the LARS presenter rattled a bucket of grain pellets laced with molasses. Just like people, he would move for snacks.

"Musk oxen conserve energy by not moving, and this trait is one of the ways their species survives in the Arctic cold," explained the presenter. "These guys seem most happy at 40 below."

That trait, however, got all of Alaska's musk oxen killed off by people by the 1930s. Musk oxen only returned to the Alaskan wilds when a new herd was imported during the Great Depression. Thirty-four transplants survived an astonishing cross-continent journey from Greenland via boats, trains and dog sleds.

Arthur and I also went to the Tanana Valley State Fair.

"I'll make you a deal," he said when we got there. "If you wear your hair down while we're here, I'll buy you a caramel apple."

"With nuts?"

"Yes."

"Deal."

I normally wore my thick red hair up in a loose bun all the time because it trapped heat against the back of my neck in an irritating way, but he had gotten to know me well enough to know I was willing to suffer for something sweet.

The most novel part of the fair was the horizontal plywood roulette wheel. Gamblers bet on which hole a live mouse would disappear into after it was set in the center of the gently spinning wheel. No payoff until both the wheel and the mouse stopped moving. The crowd roared as the wheel turned and the mouse scurried. It ducked into one hole, only to pop up and run to another, fueling the excitement. We walked away with less money and more smiles.

When it was time to leave the fair, Arthur could only find a caramel apple without nuts. A man of his word, he found some peanuts in Virginia's kitchen and stuck them all over the apple before he handed it to me. He liked me. And I liked him too, but not in a romantic way. I wanted to fall for him. He even drew a peony for me because I still pined for Jean's painting. But there was no chemistry. Without it, he had no chance, even if I could logically reason why he would be a good guy to date. It sucked.

NO BETTER WAY to spend my last day in Fairbanks than searching for abandoned log cabins in the wilderness with Paolo the cheek kisser, Virginia and Arthur.

We drove out of town, parked on the side of a road and began our adventure. Paolo was armed with a global positioning system, two compasses, an aerial map, and survey maps.

"Always carry two compasses and not the flip top kind because flipping the top up gets annoying after a while," he said as if he were addressing a novice Scout pack. "And keep in mind that compasses can be as fickle as kids in love."

We high-stepped down a steep clear-cut. Perhaps a corridor for a new power line, it was crisscrossed with branches to prevent erosion. Within minutes, every mosquito from miles around came to suck our blood. They filled the pine-scented air with a constant hum of wings. We thwarted them as best we could with clothing and a thick coating of insect repellant (Alaskan cologne) over every exposed inch of skin.

When we reached denser woods, Paolo blazed a new trail or followed narrow animal footpaths. We ducked under branches, zigzagged around trees, and skirted pebbly mounds of moose manure.

In a small clearing choked with wild rose bushes and raspberry briars, Paolo gave a hopeful yell when he found a section of vintage barbed wire. Like a hunting dog that had caught a scent, he darted off in search of a cabin while we stood around picked and ate berries. We had to be quick about it to keep the mosquitoes out of our mouths. Paolo came back defeated a few minutes later.

We trekked downhill for another hour until we reached a valley and two intriguing ground covers. In one area, a super plush layer of moss covered the forest floor. It was like walking across dense foam padding. The second landscape looked like a richly textured plain of chocolate browns, blush reds and sage greens innocently speckled with tiny yellow flowers. But this area, known as a muskeg, was a dangerous combination of dead plants, treacherous pockets of decomposing muck and grass-covered mounds of dirt shaped like round foot stools. We either sank in the muck or fell off the wobbly pillars. It was the perfect place to break an ankle.

As the sun turned the bright day into a sweltering one, we found a cabin foundation near a riverbank. Only a few logs and stove parts remained. Nearby we found vintage cans with their soldered lids crudely peeled back and a rusty, log cabin-shaped syrup tin. Amazing to think that Alaskan pioneers carried their food supplies for great distances through the wilderness, when people now fought over parking spaces near the fronts of stores.

When we finally found a whole cabin, it was a tiny, one-room beauty with a branch propping up one of its sagging walls. Inside, sunlight seeped through gaps in the chinking, illuminating a packed dirt floor, a small potbelly stove and a rickety stick ladder to a narrow sleeping loft about five feet off the ground. On the raw plank table were a metal fork, a tin plate, a dog-eared romance paperback book and some candy bar wrappers. Had the cabin been recently used as a clubhouse for children or a love shack for teenagers? I could not fathom spending a long dark winter in such a cramped space with no indoor plumbing.

Arthur and I stopped to take a refreshing dip in a small pond as Virginia and Paolo continued on. I took off my socks and boots and, fully clothed, slowly eased my way into the pleasingly cold water. Bubbles fizzed to the surface as my steps disturbed decaying vegetation on the bottom. Indifferent to the cold, Arthur stripped down to his boxer shorts and strode right in. Little did we know that we were not alone.

We were both about waist deep in the water, scooping water with our hands onto our necks and arms, when a turf war broke out. Two menacing beavers appeared. They swam slowly back and forth, leaving V-shaped ripples on the glassy water surface. After a quick eyeballing, they violently slapped their paddle-flat tails against the water. These dog-sized rodents declared war. This was their pond.

We conceded to their authority, but we realized we had another problem.

"We just washed off a lot of our insect repellent," I said. "We have to wait until Virginia comes back to get more."

Just because Virginia, Arthur and I were with a consummate explorer did not guarantee that we would or could take the most direct route back to the truck. Our daytrip, richly fueled by the spirit of adventure in the morning, had become a tiresome chore by late afternoon. We had underestimated our water needs and overestimated our stamina. Once we reached the truck, our first stop was a Tesoro Station for bottles of Gatorade.

When we got home, we dined on king crab legs and watched a National Geographic Society documentary that included footage of Paolo and his discovery of an Incan village site under a Spanish mission in Peru.

Paolo's running commentary gave a more realistic view of the experience.

"A local man had to convince the villagers not to kill our film crew," he explained. "They seriously believed the crew was going to kill or steal their babies."

After I sadly said goodbye to Arthur, who was about to leave town, I settled into the couch on the cabin porch for the last time. I was caught between wanting to stay in Fairbanks and forging ahead with my trip. I had met so many supportive, accepting people. I was inspired by the strong women. I loved the attention from the men. I could have a love affair with Fairbanks, but never make it my permanent home. I knew from two miserable winters in Minnesota that Alaskan winters were out of the question. Another case of poor chemistry.

Crabby growers, not showers

Juneau-Douglas, Alaska

ON THE FLIGHT TO JUNEAU, Alaska, I finally saw the peak of Denali in all its brilliant, snowy glory as it poked through the top of the clouds. I was beginning to think it was mythical, like the jackalope or the short-furred trout, said to be caught with Velcro lures.

Time to visit Joleen and her sister, Rachel. I had met these two Alaskans in North Carolina when they took a break from visiting relatives to attend a hashing event. They ended up staying at my house for a night, and, before they left the next day, Joleen extended an invitation to stay if I ever came to town.

"Hello!" Joleen gave me a big hug at the Juneau International Airport. She was still the athletic, outgoing woman with curly blonde hair that I remembered. "I'm so excited you're here."

"Thank you so much for having me." I never thought I would have a friend who liked to eat moose tongue and heart.

We piled into her car and headed toward the downtown cluster of buildings wedged between a forested mountain side and the Gastineau Channel, but soon took a hard right over an impressively arched bridge. From its high point, Joleen pointed to the monstrous white cruise ships that lined Juneau's docks. Each year, more than 700,000 cruise ship passengers visit the city, which only has a permanent population of about 31,000 people.

"We call the passengers newlyweds and nearly deads," Joleen joked. "They're usually on their honeymoons or retired."

Joleen lived on the far side of the bridge in the town of Douglas on Douglas Island. She parked the car by the jovial crowd partying in her small grassy front yard. Most wore T-shirts and jeans. They grilled burgers and swilled healthy doses of Vitamin R, the nickname for Rainier Beer.

"What's the occasion?" I asked.

"It's a sunny day," Joleen laughed as if the answer was obvious. "The Southeast Alaska Rain Festival runs January 1 through December 31, so we celebrate the sunshine the few days we see it."

The area averaged 222 rainy days and 278 cloudy days per year. At least the average daytime temperatures ranged from 44 to 65 degrees F in summer and 25 to 35 degrees F in winter.

Joleen introduced me around. Her quiet new husband, Pete, gave me a strong handshake. Heather, his daughter from a former marriage, waved at me. This spritely young girl had inherited her Cherokee mother's luminous black eyes and straight black hair. Joleen, Pete and Heather lived in the basement of a modest but comfortable house along a ridge. Their friend Mikie and her son Mike lived upstairs.

"Joleen told me about your trip. That's very cool!" said Mike. This from a man who worked as a fly-fishing guide half the year in Alaska and the rest of the year in Peru.

"Well, thank you, though it's not like I walked to the North Pole or swam the Amazon River," I said, eating grilled halibut. "Perhaps this trip is a sign that I am a weak woman—not strong enough to hold down a job for long."

We both had a good laugh.

I met a couple of four-legged residents.

"This is Razz," Pete said, proudly ruffling the fur of a white German Shepherd as it leaned into his leg. "He's worked and played hard all his life. When he was a young pup, he was attacked by wolves, but survived."

The handsomest dog in the house, however, was Cujo, a half-chow and half-golden retriever mix with the plushest of rust-colored fur coats.

A neighbor arrived with a 25-gallon bucket of crab legs. For a woman born in Missouri, I have a surprising appetite for crab. It was all I could do not to grab the bucket and run to a defendable corner where I would eat it all.

By the time I started eyeing a plate of brownies, Joleen introduced me to Kevin, a single father with an 11-year-old son. He had a lanky build and dirty blond hair.

"So my brother and his girlfriend are in town from Arizona," he said. "In a couple of days we're going to take a ferry up the Inside Passage and drive over to Whitehorse in Canada, just to check it out. Joleen thought you might like to come with us. Would you?"

"Absolutely," I said.

BELLIES FULL OF HALIBUT AND CRAB, Joleen, Heather, Cujo and I walked along a paved trail through the nearby woods that masked the remains of what had once been the massive Treadwell Mine.

"You have to be very careful if you leave the path," Joleen warned. "There are a lot of collapsed tunnels and unsealed shafts that you can't see under all the plants."

When the mine was active, the land had few trees, hundreds of men worked at all hours, boardwalks linked the buildings, and St. Bernard dogs hauled laundry and groceries to homes. There were only 48 hours of relief per year from the thunderous mining ruckus: the Fourth of July and Christmas. On the remaining days, 859- to 1,020-pound stamps slammed down on gold-bearing rocks as ore cars screamed and clattered along iron rails.

Pierre Erussard first staked the claim on Douglas Island in April 1881, but months later sold it to John Treadwell for less than $400. It turned out to be gold bonanza, and Treadwell eventually sold his shares for more than a $1 million. Sadly, his fortune was not enduring. After he lost it all through bad investments, he filed for bankruptcy with a debt of almost $3 million.

In the end, the prosperity of the mine collapsed, literally. Workers had been removing tons of ore from below the water level when, in 1917, a 200-foot-tall geyser shot out of the ground as tons of seawater flooded three mining shafts in less than four hours. The fourth shaft was spared, and production limped along for another five years before the mine finally closed.

Not far from the trailhead, a porcupine crossed our path. The waddling cushion of long black and white spines looked sinister. Cujo sounded an alarm bark, eager to pursue and defend, but Joleen forced him to heel until the animal clamored up a tree and hid in the shadows.

"Cujo got in a fight with one a while back. He lost," Joleen said as Cujo growled. "He had so many quills in his face, we weren't sure he would live."

The porcupine was not the only prickly thing in the woods. Devil's Club plants, that could grow up to 8-feet tall, had tiny thorns shaped like crochet hooks on its stalks and the undersides of its platter-sized leaves. My hand brushed against a leaf, and a thorn impaled the pad of my thumb.

Joleen watched me try to scratch it out with no luck.

"Nice try," she said, "but you have to wait until it pusses up so you can squeeze it out."

I would not need to learn that lesson twice.

Throughout the forest there were an unusually large number of fallen trees.

"The Taku winds do that," Joleen explained.

The local mountains compress these ferocious winds so they hit Juneau at speeds of more than 60 miles per hour. The unofficial record was more than 200 miles per hour.

"They can break windshields on cars," she added.

It was dark by the time we returned home. My days of endless sunlight had come to an end. We put sheets on the couch (a Chesterfield if I spoke Canadian like Pete) for my bed. It sat next to a built-in wall safe made by the Victor Safe and Lock Co. of Cincinnati. I wondered if the house's original owners were miners.

BASKING IN THE GLORY of a second brilliantly sunny day, I joined Joleen's brunette sister Rachel and her two visiting college friends, Cathy and Teresa, as they toured around Juneau.

Our first stop was Franklin Street, which should be renamed Tourist Alley. It led from the cruise ship terminals to the heart of downtown. Professional crossing guards managed the waves of pedestrians and discouraged jaywalking. One shop sold $129 real fur coats for Barbie dolls and plastic moose-shaped keychains that could be squeezed to make rubber poop balloon out of their backsides.

By the waterfront was a memorial dedicated to lost commercial fisherman, including Joleen and Rachel's brother and Rachel's fiancé. Both were lost in 1986 when they went with a friend to check crab traps. They vanished in a sudden storm.

"All we found was a life preserver and pieces of the boat," Rachel said.

Our next stop was the Last Chance Mining Museum, located high in the woods on the mountainside above Juneau. The mine had produced more than $80 million in gold.

A lethargic Saint Bernard greeted each of us with a nonchalant sniff before he went back to sleep. The former compressor building felt damp like a cave and smelled oily like a car engine. For me, the high point of the museum was a black-and-white photo of two men sitting next to the biggest gold nugget ever found at the mine. It was the size of a deformed pumpkin. Talk about motivating.

After we toured the Taku Smokeries fish processing plant (that processed more than six million pounds of fish each year), we ate lunch on the waterfront patio of the Twisted Fish Co. Alaskan Grill.

"Does anyone really buy the Alaska Crab Cocktail?" I asked. The menu listed it as a bucket of 10 jumbo Alaskan king crab legs served with a basket of fresh bread knots for $89.95.

"I think it's a joke," Rachel said as she winked, "but if tourists want to order it, why not sell it to them?"

Priceless.

As we ate, a nearby cruise ship spewed forth a flood of passengers. Many stopped to have their pictures taken with a bald eagle mascot for $10 a photo. All seemed oblivious to the real bald eagle perched on the street light less than 10 feet away.

I FELT LIKE AN ELVIS FAN going to Graceland that afternoon. We four went with Rachel's friend, John, to check his crab trap. A lifelong fisherman, he had calloused hands and worn Carhartt work clothes. He probably had extra salty blood and the homing instincts of a salmon.

We layered on extra clothes before boarding his boat. There was only a light breeze at the dock, but it turned into a biting wind as the boat picked up speed down the channel. Not that we cared. We were happy women riding in a boat on a beautiful day.

John stopped the boat when we reached a battered white buoy with his name on the side. It was attached to his crab trap line. He put the line in a winch and then manually turned the winch arm around and around to raise the trap from the deep water. It was hard work. The trap, a heavy cage of rebar and chicken wire about five feet square, had been sunk to a depth of about four hundred feet.

"So these scientists came out here with fancy underwater cameras, and they found this huge mountain of crabs in one spot," he chuckled. "Took them a while to figure out that the crabs were eating a whale carcass."

I wondered if I loved crab so much because it tasted like whale.

The trap finally broke the surface of the water, and John swung it onto the deck. We tossed aside a slimy gray flounder to get to three defensive crabs, who were not happy about the daylight or the fresh air. One was a wee babe about the size of my hand. We chucked him back into the water. We had our eyes on the two larger crabs. John laughed as we childishly nudged one to see how it moved. We took turns, carefully avoiding the wicked front pincers, picking up one by its back legs for souvenir photos.

The crabs looked potentially tasty, but John shook his head.

"You can only keep them if their back shells measure seven inches or more," John said. "We caught ourselves a couple growers, not showers."

This isn't television

Admiralty Island, Alaska

DID GOLDILOCKS GET DRESSED in a dark room lit only by the light of a VCR readout and dash to the Driftwood Lodge by 7 a.m. to see bears? I think not, but I did.

It was the start of my $495, one-day adventure, arranged before I left home, to visit Admiralty Island. Any anxiety I had over spending that much money evaporated the moment the floatplane lifted off the water.

Thomas was the pilot. His gentle demeanor belied what must surely have been nerves of steel. Juneau was notorious for plane-rattling weather conditions. I rode shotgun. Behind us were tour guides Jeff and Claire, two other clients (Tom and Patty), and a stack of yellow rubber rain overalls and boots. The couple's son felt under the weather, so he stayed back at their hotel. I would have to be in a coma to miss this experience.

Through the plane's headphones, Tom Petty sang about free falling as we soared over the Gastineau Channel toward Windfall Island, part of the Admiralty Island National Monument (an impressive 955,921 acres). The view below was breathtaking. Mendenhall Glacier slowly carved out a valley. Little tributaries spider-veined mud flats. Blue-green water defined spits and islands where shorelines gave way to deeper water. Avalanche chutes furrowed through dark green forests.

The floatplane gently landed on the water and purred over to the shallows of Windfall Island. As we waded to shore, a salmon jumped into the air. A deer bolted into the forest. Little waves lapped a shoreline crusty with plum-colored mussels and barnacles. Leafy strands of yellow-green seaweed caught on our boots as we walked to a rack of kayaks.

"What are those?" I asked Jeff. Plump dry sacks dangled from ropes over high tree branches like giant red and yellow holiday ornaments.

"Emergency rations and gear in case we get stuck here," he explained as we carried our kayaks to the water. "The weather can be fickle when it comes to flying. Wish we had that stuff when 9-11 happened, and all the float planes were grounded."

We casually paddled over to Admiralty Island. Wildlife ranger Paul, armed with a walkie-talkie and a rifle, gave us a warm welcome. His job was to enforce rules and minimize human-bear interaction.

"Please go where and when I tell you to go. Be as quiet as possible. Keep your pack within your reach at all times in case we need to leave quickly," he said as he packed our lunches in a cache box and buried it in the beach sand. "Do not carry anything that can be perceived as food, even gum or fruit-flavored lip gloss."

As Jeff instructed, we tethered our kayaks to a line and floated them back out into deep water.

"Otherwise the bears might think they are toys and start playing with them," he explained.

Alaska natives call Admiralty Island "Kootznoowoo"—the fortress of the bears—for good reason. There is about one bear per square mile, the densest population anywhere in the world.

"We usually see at least one bear on this trip," Jeff said.

With big eyes and jumpy thoughts, we followed bear tracks the size of dinner plates along the shoreline. I wondered, a little too late, if facing such a large animal without the security of a truck was such a smart thing to do.

We stopped at the viewing area. It was a small gravel lot—about the size of four parking spaces—fringed with thigh-high grass and stocked with two logs to sit on. There was nothing to draw a bear's attention except us.

In front of us the broad estuary of Pack Creek flowed past a thick wall of forest. Next to us was a green field, and behind us was the decaying remains of a cabin. Known as "the bear man of Pack Creek," Stan Price lived and studied there for 40 years in harmony with the bears he came to cherish.

"Price was pretty much a hermit, but sometimes he would row his boat all the way to Juneau for supplies. It's about 30 miles away," said Jeff. "He had a big garden over there, surrounded by an electric fence. The bears zapped themselves quite a bit trying to get to it."

We sat on the logs and waited. Would the bears be a no show like the polar bears in Barrow? Dozens of seagulls and black ravens sailed the air currents and swooped down to grab scraps of dead salmon. Young bald eagles, still in mottled brown feathers, practiced their maneuvers. Their distinctive white hoods had not grown in yet.

There was movement by the creek. Two lumbering bears came out of the woods. We did not need binoculars to figure out how huge they were and how vulnerable we were. They dinked around, splashing the water, scratching their backs against boulders and swiping at salmon. One took a couple of bites out of a fish and tossed it aside.

"See how he's only biting the head and the belly of each fish?" Jeff whispered. "He's eating the high-protein parts—the brain and the salmon eggs. The bears have been eating salmon for weeks now, so their mouths are probably very sore from all the sharp fish spines."

Tom, Patty and I started to whisper about moving inland when we had not seen a bear for an hour.

"Remember, this isn't television. Life is all around," Claire the tour guide whispered.

We quickly turned around and saw a baby bear tugging on a chain in the Price cabin ruins. Logic dictated that if there was one baby bear, another bear was close by. Sure enough. A second baby bear waddled into view. If there were two baby bears, momma must be close. And she was. She rose up from a bank of tall grass seconds later, a massive tower of fur, fat and muscle. A potential killer, she had an endearing face and round, woolly ears like a teddy bear.

With momma bear in the lead, the threesome ambled their way across the grassy plain toward Pack Creek. Officer Paul motioned for us to be ready to leave, but they ignored us. Momma bear caught a salmon and tossed it to a cub, who gnawed on it. The other cub vigorously dug a hole in the dirt.

Not long after the family ambled away, we stood up to stretch our legs as a new bear swam around the corner of the island, up the creek and out of sight. I thought only polar bears went swimming.

We retrieved our box lunches and walked out to the end of a sandbar to eat them, hopefully downwind from any bears. To keep warm, I put on my rain gear and burrowed down in the sand behind a boulder. The wind had grown brisk as the sky had clouded over. I was cold and wanted a hot pizza, but I could not be happier about the bears we had seen.

We had a few hours before we needed to head back to Juneau, so we headed inland to a bear observation platform. We passed the bear-chewed remains of a wooden post that had once been a sign-in board for visitors. Bears had also worn the bark off a nearby tree trunk by scratching their backs against it. Their favored spot was sticky with sap and fuzzy with fur.

We followed a narrow path through a lush old-growth forest. Spruce and hemlock formed a canopy high above the rolling landscape. Once towering cedar trees lay on the forest floor. Their root balls formed one-story tall dirt mounds. In some places the leafy undergrowth was smashed flat to form kiddy pool-sized circles.

"Odd place for a crop circle," I joked.

"The bears plop down and eat everything within their reach, and then maybe take a nap," Claire explained.

I had done that more than a few times in my life.

"Bears will eat just about anything," she continued. "Acorns, bugs, berries, frogs, even moose and caribou if they can get it."

We picked and ate wild blueberries and golden salmon berries as we walked, careful to avoid ones spattered with what looked like white paint.

"Eagle poop," Claire said.

We lost our appetite, however, when we crossed over the last hill. The air turned foul with the smell of rotting fish.

We climbed up a ladder to the bear observation platform, where we could see dozens of dead fish along the shoreline of a river. Live salmon kept their distance from a clever bear sitting in the water.

When it was time to head back to Juneau, I grinned the whole way. I felt like I had just lived a PBS nature special.

Bottles of sadness

Whitehorse, Yukon, Canada

BY 4:45 A.M., JUNEAU'S WEATHER had returned to normal—cold, rainy and windy—as I caught the Malaspina ferry with Kevin, his son Jesse, Kevin's brother Brad and Brad's girlfriend Ty. We were cruising up the Inside Passage via the Alaska Marine Highway to Skagway. Joleen had helped me dress for the cold weather by loaning me her wedding coat. Instead of buying a wedding dress that would be worn once and boxed away, she celebrated the occasion with a new Helly Hansen cream-colored wool coat with chocolate brown stripes.

As our six-and-a-half-hour ride commenced, the sky lightened from pitch black to kitten gray, revealing a small world hemmed in by fog. So much for the route's spectacular views of five glaciers and abundant wildlife.

We sat on the observation deck with nothing much to see. Jesse wandered off, and Kevin entertained Brad, Ty and me with tales of Alaskan humor.

"Some guys put burning tires in one of the dormant volcanoes to get everybody all hot and bothered about volcanic activity," he said. "Some other guys drove their snowmobiles on some paved roads until the friction set the asphalt on fire."

That sounded less funny and more stupid.

"So you're traveling around the world alone?" Ty asked.

"Yeah, I'm not married, but I've had some good offers along the way." I said, describing the Nkashu Mpai's bride price of 50 cows and Bunna's offer of whale meat and fish.

"Well, I'll offer a lifetime supply of halibut, salmon and king crab when it's in season," Kevin said.

Now we were talking.

"Does your offer include hushpuppies?" I inquired. It was a crucial point in the negotiation. My mom and I both loved the little balls of fried cornbread.

"Sure, why not," he laughed. "Plus, you get an instant son."

"I think you have made the best offer yet," I laughed.

Not only could Kevin catch king crabs, but he could also make them into the delicious dip that we were eating on crackers as breakfast. I would never again like the grocery store dip made with imitation crab meat.

I spent some of time exploring the other areas of the ferry. Outside the cafeteria, a menu from the Malaspina's 1963 maiden voyage advertised a French-fried king crab leg dinner for $3.60. It included a fruit juice cocktail, a salad, a relish tray, a potato and a roll with butter. I confess I also peeked into car windows to see what people had packed. One station wagon was jammed with groceries, and its back seat was sprinkled with round brown bits. The black lab sitting in the driver's seat had raided the 50-pound bag of dried dog food.

When we arrived in Skagway, the small town was tucked into the cleavage of steep, forested mountains. In 1897, more than 20,000 gold rush prospectors and others swarmed through the Skagway cabin settlement until it became a lawless boomtown of tents and shacks.

From Skagway, miners had a choice between two trails to reach Lake Bennett in British Columbia, Canada, where they would sail on to the gold fields around Dawson. The 33-mile-long Chilkoot Trail was the shortest, but toughest, option. Pack animals could not manage the high pass, so men shuttled their gear into Canada on repeated foot trips. The Canadian famine-reduction requirement added to their burdens; miners crossing the border had to bring enough food to last at least a year. The other option was the White Pass Trail. More than 3,000 pack animals, overloaded and unsuited for the trail's rocky terrain, perished on this route.

As the gold rush waned and miners left for home or moved on to new gold strikes, Skagway's leaders recognized the town's tourism potential and turned its gold-rush buildings and boardwalks into a Historic District in 1903. Their plan worked. Each year, the 800-plus residents cater to about a half million tourists.

We decided to explore Skagway when we came back to catch the ferry, so we drove out of town, past the gates that stood ready to block traffic when snow made the Klondike Highway impassable. Dense fog limited our sight to about 15 feet. Red-striped snow plow marker poles popped in and out of view along the steep shoulders of the road.

After we passed through the Canadian border station, the road continued to rise in elevation. The temperature dropped until it felt more like late fall than early August. When the fog gave way to a metallic gray sky, the view revealed an intriguing landscape dictated by harsh weather. The few trees in sight were stunted, with no branches on the windward side of their trunks. Ponds and lakes glimmered in colors that ranged from toothpaste blue to mouthwash green as sunlight reflected off white sediment.

The sun was setting by the time we arrived in Whitehorse. The streets were empty in a desolate way. There was no quaintness, no quirky coffee shops, galleries or enticing bakeries. The store spaces that were not empty sold used furniture, cheap clothes and homemade crafts. We had our pick of rooms at the hotel.

What little I knew of Whitehorse was that it had a history of economic growth and decline due to factors like a copper boom, the construction of the Alaskan Highway, the construction of an oil refinery, and the exodus of military personnel.

We walked several blocks from the hotel to the Yukon River. Below the viewing platform, a drunk Native American man rolled around in the dirt, disoriented and unable to stand up. His equally drunk companion in urine-soiled pants staggered about, flailing her arms and raving that he did not love her anymore. It was a hard slap of reality.

That was not the only sign of alcohol addiction during our less-than-impressive overnight visit. At a small restaurant, Ty and Brad each ordered a Bushmills Irish Whiskey neat before their meals, but their drinks arrived watered down, even after they had them replaced. When they brought this to the manager's attention, he made a sad confession.

"I'm so sorry," he said. "I know what's happened. Someone has stolen the liquor and replaced it with water."

Someone was going to be fired that night.

AT THE YUKON BERINGIA Interpretive Centre, we spent the morning learning about the last ice age. About 12,000 to 15,000 years ago, it had deposited so much water on land in the form of ice and snow that sea levels dropped enough to expose the sea floor between Asia and North America. This created a 1,000-mile-wide grassland steppe called the Bering Strait Land Bridge, part of a larger area called Beringia. While it lasted, many animals traveled across this land bridge, including mammoths, giant short-faced bears, three-toed horses, woolly rhinos, saber-toothed tigers and humans.

The centre had life-sized statues and skeletons of some of the extinct animals. The blue ribbon of weird went to the skeleton that looked like a

Ninja turtle the size of a grizzly bear.

On the lawn, Jesse and I pretended to play tug-of-war over a stick with the statue of a castoroides. This extinct species of giant beaver could grow to about 8-feet long. If beavers were still that big, there would be no swimming in wild ponds for me.

On our way back to Skagway, we stopped at what was left of the town of Carcross, located at the tip of Bennett Lake. Like Skagway, it had been a key stop for Gold Rush miners. Today's Carcross had a beguiling sense of desolation. Narrow-gauge train tracks ran through a downtown that was only a few blocks in each direction. There were no stoplights or fast food restaurants. Signs of the past—old wooden boats, mining equipment, wagons—lay abandoned in people's yards. Nature filled the soundscape: sporadic chirps of birds, the ruffle of wind and the lapping of water against the lake shore. The surrounding green hills were snow-free, but in the distance, mountain peaks and shady valleys still wore winter ice.

The tallest building on mainstreet was the former Caribou Hotel, which started serving guests in 1898 and closed a century later. In 1918, Captain James Alexander, owner of the Engineer Mine, asked the hotel owners to take care of his parrot while he was on vacation. The bad news: the captain was killed in a shipwreck. The good news: Polly lived on and gained international fame for singing opera and using colorful profanity until she died in 1972, when she was 126 years old.

IGNORANCE GOT US INTO TROUBLE at the Canadian border. Kevin had bought two bottles of aspirin with codeine at a convenience store. Codeine is a regulated substance in the United States, so there are laws about how much can be taken across the border. Kevin declared his two bottles without knowing that the regulation had recently dropped to one bottle per adult.

"Sir, will you please pull your truck over there, and come into the office," the polite officer asked.

While they searched the truck, we checked out their display case full of illegal museum-quality artworks they had confiscated. One was a ship made of elephant ivory, complete with lifelike figurines.

Minutes ticked away. The departure time for the ferry drew near.

"Sir, we are going to let you through with a warning," the officer said sternly. "You may keep both bottles since there are four adults in the truck."

When we arrived back in Skagway, the ferry was loading. So much for having a beer at the Red Onion Saloon, built in 1897 as a bordello.

Humor strikes my line

Juneau-Douglas, Alaska

DON AND RYCH, AN EASY-GOING COUPLE who wore baseball hats, trim beards and flannel shirts, invited Joleen and me to go fishing. The day was promising, with crisp temperatures in the mid 60s F, an overcast sky, calm waters and garlands of wispy clouds on the surrounding mountain peaks.

"Have you ever gone fishing before?" Rych asked as Don guided the 30-foot Owens boat away from the dock and down the Gastineau Channel.

"Oh, yes. I fished for bluegill with my dad when I was little. I tried fly-fishing with my grandfather in Colorado, but I only caught one trout and a bunch of sticks. And I caught a flounder in North Carolina a few years back."

Joleen and Rych laughed. The fact that I could name all the fish I had ever caught proved I was a novice.

I stepped into the boat's cabin to check it out. A metal rail kept kettles and fry pans from sliding off the top of the petite metal stove when the boat swayed. Don had glued to the wall a newspaper photo of a polar bear with a bloody shoe in its mouth. (A tourist had gotten too close to the animal's cage at the zoo.) Strips of 32-cent Nixon stamps lined the ceiling next to rolls of navigational charts. A stuffed teddy bear gripping a salmon sat on the dashboard for good luck. A photo of Don, once a commercial fisherman, showed him standing proudly next to a 57-pound halibut.

There was a tiny bathroom with a toilet. Joleen and Rych both agreed that, "If you don't have to pee in a five-gallon bucket, you must be on a yacht."

"Let's get ready to fish," Rych called from the back of the boat. The process was far trickier than baiting a hook with a worm. First he pushed a three-barbed hook through the end of a six-inch-long dead herring (partially dried out so that it would stay firmer longer in the water) until the hook came out of its mouth.

"What's that?" I asked as he squirted something into the herring's mouth before sealing it shut with a small metal clamp.

"Professional-grade garlic oil. Makes the herring more tempting to salmon," he said. I waited for him to confess it was a joke, but he was serious.

Then Rych connected the baited hook line to a flasher—a brick-sized plastic rectangle with holographic reflectors on each side—to dazzle the salmon if the garlic was not alluring enough. The flasher connected to a rigger line with a weight to pull the baited hook and flasher to the preferred depth, about 60 feet. Finally, he cast the line out into the water. We were salmon fishing in Alaska.

We started to bait a second line when the little bell clamped to the end of the first fishing rod tinkled. A fish hit the line.

"Get it, girl," Rych yelled at me.

I grabbed the rod and started to reel in the fish.

"Slow and steady," he advised.

Tension on the fishing line came and went as the fish struggled.

"It must be huge—at least 20 pounds—the way it's fighting," I said proudly.

Joleen and Rych grinned at each other.

When the fish reached the surface by the boat, Rych scooped it up with a long-handled net. The salmon was beautiful. Its greenish-blue back blended into a shimmery silver underbelly.

"It's a keeper," Rych reassured me when it only weighed in at 10 pounds even. "That's a solid weight for a Coho salmon."

Rych clubbed the salmon on the back of the head, assuring me it was knocked out so that I could gut it per his guidance. Yet with my first poke with the knife, it thrashed back to life. I screamed.

As he scrambled to catch the fish, my resolve to be hands-on for the whole fishing experience withered. I set the knife down in front of Rych.

"I'm done. You do it."

Rych shrugged and got to work. He cut out the fish's gills and slit open the fish from tail to head. I flinched with guilt when a sac of blood red eggs fell out of her belly. She was on her way to spawn.

To tease me, Rych put her walnut-sized heart on the railing. It kept beating as he packed the rest of the salmon on ice in a cooler.

"Okay, okay, make it go away," I pleaded until he flicked it into the water.

For such an auspicious beginning, the rest of the day was a fishing bust.

Joleen, Rych and I danced in unison to Uncle Kracker's song "Follow Me" to lure fish to our lines. We only got applause from Don. I suggested using Cheetos instead of garlic oil in the herring. Still no luck.

We swapped town gossip as mist rose from the shoreline forests and bald eagles flew overhead.

"Some of the best stuff around here never makes it into the newspapers, like the folks who do stripper pole dances on their boat masts to amuse and disgust cruise ship passengers," Rych said. "Just because you respect the income the tourists bring, doesn't mean you can't poke fun at them."

After lunch Rych made wedding cake martinis. Mix one shot of vanilla vodka with a squeeze of fresh lemon juice and a dash of dry vermouth. Serve it in a martini glass with confetti-colored sugar on the rim, along with a joke.

"What is the speed of sex?" Rych asked. "68. If you reach 69, you have to turn around."

This was my kind of fishing. Less about catching salmon and more about releasing laughter.

BY DEFAULT, HEATHER BECAME my tour guide for the next couple of days while Joleen and Pete were at work.

"I thought you'd be more fun to hang out with than my grandmother," she said. Thanks, kid.

In a generous act of supreme trust, she took me to a sacred cluster of pine trees downhill from a neighbor's house.

"Fairies pass through here," she said reverently. "Let's build them a hut to sleep in."

Heather picked the site, a small hollow at the base of a tree. I gathered construction materials like twigs, pebbles and fern fronds. Heather expertly arranged them.

"I hope they like this," she said when I handed her a seagull feather. She placed it as a blanket next to the pinecone pillow.

"We can come back tomorrow and see if a fairy used it," she said. Her anticipation was infectious. While I was skeptical about fairies, I started to muse about a chipmunk using the hidey-hole we had built.

The next day, neighbor Wendy dropped by while Joleen, Heather and I were having breakfast.

"Heather, I think there was some fairy activity in the back yard."

Wendy and Joleen exchanged discreet winks.

Heather squealed in delight and grabbed my hand. "Let's go! We have to go see!"

We ran to the shelter and knelt before it. She gingerly lifted the bark roof. Inside, the feather covered three polished stones, the size and color of Jelly Beans, and a shiny cat bell.

"They like it!"

As her dark eyes sparkled with pride, I reminded myself that how I saw things was just as important as what I was seeing.

A SMALL CROWD CAUGHT our attention as Heather and I wandered around downtown Juneau. They gathered at the bottom of a steep stairway that led up to a residential area.

"What are they looking at?" I asked Heather, who just shrugged and rolled her eyes.

"No telling with tourists," she said.

An awe-struck woman, trying to get out her camera without dropping her lumpy shopping bags, explained the mystery. "A momma bear and her two cubs are up there."

"Silly me," I said as we walked away. "I paid hundreds of dollars to see bears in the wild when I could see them downtown for free."

The bears were eventually captured by the local police. A tourist quoted in the newspaper asked, "What are they arresting the bears for?"

Heather and I continued on to the Alaska State Museum.

"If there was a museum about my history," I joked, "it would include metal-wheeled roller skates, eight-track tapes, black-and-white televisions with 13 numbers on the channel dial, air popcorn poppers, and disco balls."

She looked at me as if I was talking in Swahili.

"Do you know what those things are?" I asked.

"Nope."

"Do you care?"

She gave an impish grin. "Nope."

"Bad child, being mean to such an old person."

"You're not that old."

"Bless you. For that, I forgive your lack of appreciation."

In the museum gift shop, a man charged more than $1,500 to his credit card for a woven baleen basket the size of a softball and a few art books.

"I'm late for a helicopter ride over the glaciers," he told the cashier before he hurried away.

"I bet his wife buys Barbie doll fur coats," I whispered to Heather.

We stopped at an ATM on the way home. I punched in a request for $40, and it declined the request due to insufficient funds. I kept my back to Heather as tears welled up in my eyes. The day of reckoning had come. I had spent all of my trip money. I still had money from the sale of my house, but I worried that if I spent it, I might never be able to buy another house. But I had no choice. I still had weeks of travel left, not to mention I needed money to set up a new life somewhere, and there was no telling when I would get another job.

MENDENHALL GLACIER WAS ONLY a short bus ride from downtown Juneau, so one morning Heather and I bartered a trade. She would go with me to see the glacier if we built a fairy hut while we were there. Deal.

I must say from where we stood by the visitor's center, the distant glacier was a bit disappointing. It looked like a dirty wall of blue ice that was crumbling into the greenish-white murky waters of Mendenhall Lake.

"Impressive, huh?" Heather asked.

"You were right about this one, kiddo," I said.

After building a fairy hut with a five-star lake view, Heather and I walked over to the Moraine Ecology Trail. At the trailhead, a sign warned visitors to be wary of bears and how to respond if faced with one.

We followed the curvy trail that meandered through the woods and crossed over streams thick with salmon.

About five minutes later, nature tested my survival skills. An animal came around the bend. A woolly, black bear cub with dark beady eyes and a short snout. I sucked in my breath and tried to recall what the sign said.

"Don't run. Don't freak out. Don't get between a sow and her cubs. Oh, God, which way was momma bear?" I said to myself as I slowly reached for Heather, pulling her shoulder against my hip. Perhaps momma would think we were one big animal. What would I say to Pete and Joleen if I came home without their daughter?

And then I noticed Heather was not afraid. Not one inkling. She just looked up at me with a weird look. I knew she was a wilderness-savvy girl who sometimes carried a knife, but it was a bear for cripe's sake.

I took another look at the cub and realized the error of my ways. It was on a leash, one of those fishing-line thin, retractable leads. It was just a young chow dog. Heather figured out my mistake and laughed so hard tears welled up in her eyes.

"She thought your dog was a bear!" Heather yelled to the dog's owner when he came into sight. His laughter added to my blushing humiliation.

"Careful, young lady," I said, trying to muster a sense of authority. "I have the return bus tickets, and it's a long walk back to town."

It just went to show that I was more fun than Heather's grandmother.

"IN LESS THAN 16 HOURS, I fly to Key West, Florida," I thought as I packed up my stuff and pulled the sheets off the couch. My vague post-trip future was only a couple of weeks away. I was not ready for it, but it had to be done, like an impending surgery.

I wanted to go back to the familiar, yet I did not want to go. The unfamiliar had become familiar. I was both addicted and burnt out by the rush of newness and discovery. I did not want to think about finding a place to live, getting a job, finding out if Roxanne was still alive. I never considered that it would be easier to pry myself away from an established life than to face rebuilding a new one.

As I folded up the turtle sarong, I remembered all of the places it had been—the teal YWCA room in Dar es Salaam, the prison cell-like room in Zanzibar, the swanky cottage in Nairobi, the camp site in Kenya, the guest houses in Nepal, hotel rooms in Thailand, the former horse stall in Laos, and the rustic cabin in Fairbanks.

"Will I ever travel with this again, or will it become a trivial memento of my trip?" I wondered as I tucked it into my backpack.

Joleen took the day off work, and she, Heather and I drove to the end of the scenic Glacier Highway. Interesting fact from a promotional brochure: Alaska has one mile of road for every 42 square miles of land, compared to the U.S. mainland average of one to one.

On the return drive, we visited the Shrine of St. Therese.

St. Therese died in 1897 when she was 24 years old, but during her short life she devoted every minute to the belief that anyone can and everyone should love in "little ways"—with a kind remark, a smile, a prayer—simple but important ways to actively show love. What mattered in life was "not great deeds, but great love." Her devotion embraced one of my core beliefs.

Work on the shrine began in 1935. The original plan included a wooden chapel on Crow Island (a dot of land 400 feet offshore into the Lynn Canal), but a severe storm washed all the construction lumber away. By a twist of fate, the construction foreman happened to be a stone craftsman by trade, so they built the chapel with local stones instead. It was the kind of place where enduring marriages were born and loved ones were sent to heaven with less regret.

The chapel was closed for a private ceremony, so we walked in the dense forest around it. The twisted, shadowy path linked 14 Stations of the Cross that represented scenes from the life of Jesus Christ. The serenity on the tiny island calmed my thoughts. My near future seemed ominous, but it could only come at me one day at a time.

"You survived leeches, you can survive anything," I joked to myself as I left the trail to follow Heather. Black hair flying behind her, she darted about like a small bird, searching for a place to build a fairy hut. I had a choice. I could fret about the unknown or I could bask in the beauty of the island, make a young girl smile with colorful pebbles, and live in the moment.

LAUGHTER FILLED THE FINAL HOURS before my flight. Joleen, her niece, Edra, and I began an impromptu pub crawl at the Triangle Bar. This hole-in-the-wall joint had a pool table, neon beer signs, a black ceiling, sturdy furniture and a picture window that faced the street. Through it we watched a handsome young man sitting on top of a newspaper sales box with a cell phone to his ear.

"He's got to be listening to a girl," I said. "She's doing all the talking. He's not really interested in what she's saying—see how he's kicking his feet, but he's interested in her. He's got a cheesy grin."

Edra and Joleen concurred.

When he came into the bar, we asked him if our deductions were correct. They were. Cody had just come from working upriver at Taku Lodge doing jack-of-all-trades work. During the off-season, he was an extreme skier in Utah.

Cody and a couple of his friends joined our detective group and speculations about strangers continued. Two men in their early 20s, who had not encountered razors for at least a year, were deemed the "The Sasquatch Twins." They kindly posed for a picture so that I could help perpetuate the idea that all Alaskan men looked that scruffy.

Our trio's next stop was the Alaskan Hotel, a narrow, three-story building with Victorian bay windows. It opened for business in 1913 to much fanfare. The management tied the front door keys to a balloon and sent them aloft as proof that they would never close the doors to guests. Their grand intentions failed over the years as prostitution and illegal drugs took root. At one point the hotel was condemned, but subsequent owners had brought it back to a dignified life.

It was open mic night, and young locals crowded the lobby and bar.

The first two acts were forgettable, but the third grabbed our attention from the get-go. The shaggy young man started his act by dropping his jeans down to his ankles. Sporting plaid boxer shorts, he sang fast, catchy tunes while he nimbly picked his guitar. We rewarded his talent with deafening applause.

Excited by this act, the audience was primed for more, but the next two guys quickly killed the momentum. They took too long to set up. They were boring to watch. They played discordant rave techno music. They drove most of the crowd away, including us.

Our last stop was Louie's, uphill from Joleen's home on Douglas Island. Photos of regulars plastered the walls and sporting trophies lined the shelves. Laid-back couples shot pool, played video poker or lounged in padded booths. The jukebox in the corner kept things lively. The no-nonsense lady bartender knew everyone by name, and, no doubt, all of their secrets.

We hung out with Tom (who looked, acted and talked like actor Christopher Lloyd), Wilbur (who looked like a stereotypical prospector with a leathery face, unkempt hair and a free-range beard) and Rych (my lovingly sadistic fishing buddy). Damn tricky place to leave. People kept buying us drinks and asking me about my trip. It was my open mic night. Three hours later Joleen and I made it back out the front door.

We sashayed toward her house to get my backpack and to call a cab to take me to the airport. I stopped halfway. The sky looked odd. A foggy patch drifted and undulated across the star-sprinkled blackness, as if someone was breathing on it.

"Can you see that? That's weird." I pointed up. "I might have had too much to drink."

"Oh, my God, Kristine!" Joleen squealed and shook my arm. "Those are the first northern lights of the year!"

Alaska waved goodbye to me.

Darkness in the sun

Key West, Florida

THERE WAS NO SUNSHINE in my state of being when I arrived in Florida. As I had sleeplessly flown through the night from Juneau to Seattle to Minneapolis to Tampa, my calm had grown brittle. I tried to shore it up by getting my bearings. I had enough money to last about six months. Dawn, my friend in Charlotte, said my cat Roxanne and I could crash at her place. I could probably stay with her for a few weeks until I picked a place to go.

Dawn and our other friend, Don, drove down from Charlotte to meet me at the airport. By the time I arrived to greet them, I was exhausted, mentally disheveled and less-than-pleasant smelling.

"You look great," they said. They seemed exactly as I remembered them. Don, as laidback as ever, was still the fittest man over 60 I had ever known due to his passion for bike riding. Dawn still shone with bubbly energy and a can-do attitude that had served her well in life and the military. At first there were easy laughs, warm hugs and playful banter between the three of us. But within days, after we drove to Key West, it was clear the trip was going south.

Many years later, I realized that I deserved most of the blame. As we drove along the flat roads in Florida, something inside me broke, something as powerful yet as delicate as the filament in a light bulb.

I felt an overwhelming need to spew out every detail of the trip. I talked endlessly as we rode bikes around quaint pastel-colored bungalows, touched a gold bar at the Mel Fisher Museum and petted six-toed cats at Ernest Hemingway's house. My monologue boiled down to, "I went there, and I saw this, and I did that, and I'll show you my photos." I talked at Don and Dawn, not with them. No doubt they could only hear so much before it became overwhelming, irritating and boring.

I could not connect with them. I had returned physically, but the version of Kristine they knew, the one who started the trip, was gone forever. When I said I felt like an astronaut at my goodbye party, I was closer to the truth than I knew. The first three astronauts who walked on the moon had suffered greatly when they returned to earth. No one could relate to what they had seen and experienced. The astronauts floundered in a great loneliness. They were outsiders. I had become an outsider, too.

While Dawn and Don were in Key West for a carefree vacation, I was ending a six-month-long travel-endorphin rush. When we biked over to see the famous Mile Marker 0 sign at the end of US Route 1, I choked up at its double meaning for me.

They were happy to eat every meal at restaurants.

"It's so great to have fresh seafood," Dawn and Don agreed as we sat at a waterside restaurant at sunset. "Why are you eating chicken fingers?"

I shrugged. Just like Tom Hanks' character in the movie *Castaway* had little interest in seafood at his welcome home party because he had been eating it for years, I had been feeding on halibut, crab and salmon for weeks.

I also found Key West's high prices distressing.

"Want another drink?" Dawn asked as we sat at the bar in the Hard Rock Café. I nursed my drink for at least an hour.

"No, thanks," I said, my thoughts drifting back to Tanzania. "When I was in Dar es Salaam, they were building a Hard Rock Café, and that's where I saw my first Maasai warrior. He was just hanging out on the front steps. He had this funky punk rock belt holding his red blanket in place. He even had a spear!"

I soon gave in to financial panic.

"This," I said at breakfast one morning, pointing to an English muffin topped with a square piece of luncheon ham, a slice of processed cheese food and a ring of canned pineapple, "cost more than five made-from-scratch meals in Laos."

My bearings cracked when Dawn mentioned, "I got a new roommate, but she's allergic to cats. You can still stay with us, on the couch or in the study, but Roxanne can't come."

I slid into an emotional abyss of depression on Aug. 21, my 40th birthday, as the signs of travel withdrawal began. I went from tears to whimpers to wailing. Fear and insecurity crushed me. I was lost. I was tired of being strong. Where was I supposed to go? What was I supposed to do? What happened to the epiphany that was supposed to show me the way when this trip was over? What had all that adventure gotten me? Nothing.

I only saw absence and darkness. I lost sight of all the intangibles I had gained, the lessons learned and memories bestowed.

Building baskets as a life raft

Charlotte, North Carolina

DAWN LEFT KEY WEST EARLY to visit her boyfriend, and Don and I drove to Charlotte, North Carolina. My need to talk incessantly about the trip petered out. There was nothing left to say. When Don pulled the car into the driveway, my trip officially came full circle. No one knew when I was due back, so there was no fanfare. That was just as well.

I walled up in Don's spare bedroom. It had briefly been my room for the weeks between selling my house and the day I left for my trip. Wearing my North Face jacket, I sat on the bed and, over the next couple of days, ate pints of Ben & Jerry's ice cream and read every page of my three journals. My handwriting varied from precise to loopy, depending on what I was doing at the time—riding a ferry or drinking too much with the hashers. My angst from the Florida days abated as I disappeared back into the trip.

I toyed with the wrist band from Club Sun and Sand, stroked the pink flamingo feather, laughed at the Lacto Fun candy label, smelled the box from a bar of Niva Ayurvedic Herbal Amala soap, and traced the edges of the dragonfly wing with my finger. Ferry ticket stubs brought back memories of screwy schedules. I laughed about the days I shared with Tom. I had seen and done so much, yet barely scraped the surface of so many cultures.

I had believed I could travel around the world, and I made it happen. I swelled with pride, jubilation, amazement, empowerment and bewilderment. I. Traveled. Around. The. World. Holy crap. I was powerful.

As I closed the last journal, sadness fell softly like a blanket of snow over my triumph. The trip was over. There was no going back.

"Okay, Miss Mighty, what's your next step?" I asked myself.

Roxanne was a deciding factor in any plan, so I decided to drive to Wilmington, North Carolina. If she had died while I was gone, I did not want to get the news over the phone, and I would want to reclaim her ashes.

The 200-mile drive came with a hitch. An hour into it, the alternator bolt fell out of my car, my car battery died and AAA refused to tow my car until I paid up my expired membership. Nothing a few hundred cherished dollars could not fix.

When I finally arrived at Lis' house, she was puttering around in the yard.

"Oh, I've been waiting for you to come back," she said with a salt-of-the-earth laugh. She hugged me tightly, then stepped back to look me over. "Looks like you came back in one piece, and I can't wait to hear all about it, but someone inside will be glad to see you first."

Tears in my eyes, I opened the sliding glass door at the back of the house. Across the room, Roxanne napped in a meatloaf pose in the center of a Papasan chair.

"Hello, Roxanne," I said quietly. Her eyes popped opened as her ears perked up. She jumped down to the hardwood floor and ran towards me, but stopped halfway. With her back to me, she leisurely cleaned her ears and sauntered back to the chair. I had left her, and it was time for me to pay.

For several hours, she punished me with aloofness. I waited patiently on the couch. When she finally relented, she curled up against my leg. She granted me permission to pet the tabby coat that I had adored for 16 years.

"I'm going to tell you about all the animals I saw," I said, gently pulling her pliable body up so I could nuzzle my face against her belly, inhale the familiar dusty smell of her fur. "I saw lots of kitties, but you are still the most beautiful."

DOORS OF OPPORTUNITY OPENED and gave me a brief reprieve. Friends Jim and Mariana had put their empty three-bedroom, ranch-style house up for sale in Charlotte and invited Roxanne and me to live in it until it sold. They left behind a single bed and a microwave oven. We moved in with a laptop computer, a litter box and a Boy Scout cook kit. I made a shrine on the fireplace mantel with a wooden giraffe from Kenya, a Buddha from Bangkok, a brass incense burner from Nepal and a cockleshell from Alaska.

I was going to stay in the house for only a month or two, so I did not move in my belongings from storage. When I did check on the storage unit, I could not remember what was in all the boxes. The stuff had once been important enough to justify the cost of a storage unit, but had since become insignificant. My pack had become my home.

With a place to stay secured, my next step was to find a job. When

I plotted my trip, I just penciled in that afterwards I would send out resumes, find a job somewhere besides Charlotte and get on with my life. I never considered how I was going to feel when I returned. After the trip's ultimate freedom, I hated the idea of suiting up in business clothes, forcing myself into a 9-to-5 schedule, wasting time in pointless meetings, and dealing with the power plays and pettiness of office politics. Been there. Done that. I half-heartedly sent out resumes for editor jobs, but I had little doubt that they included a few typos to sabotage the effort.

Kathi, who had trekked with me in Nepal, came to my rescue. She hired me as a full-time employee at her gift basket company for the holidays. It was the perfect first post-trip job. I wore what I wanted. I already knew my co-workers, genuinely sweet women who were happy to be entertained by my stories as we worked. Our jobs were simple, repetitive labor. Arrange the candies and muffins in the basket. Wrap the basket in clear plastic. Tie on a bow. Pack basket in a shipping box. Repeat.

One cold evening I sat in the empty living room with a red Maasai blanket around my shoulders and Roxanne curled in my lap. What a mess I had made of my life. Even though I had stumbled on a temporary place to stay and work, I still had no inner compass to guide my way forward.

As I gazed at my shrine and wished for a monumental "Go this way" sign, a wasp crawled out from under the Lord Vishnu carving I had hung from an old mirror hook. I had never seen a wasp with such an hourglass-shaped body and delicate wings. I opened the front door, and let it fly away. It was December. Where did it come from? The carving was solid teak.

And then I remembered something Ott said in Laos. "Seeing a snake is a good omen. It might be a god reminding us to be humble."

I emailed Alan, the professor I met in Kathmandu, who had since returned to Kentucky, to see what he thought the wasp might represent.

Alan checked with his Nepalese connections and relayed a stunning story. Sati, the daughter of Dakchhya Prajapati, married Lord Shiva against her father's wishes. One day her father arranged a religious ceremony and invited all the other gods but her husband. Sati crashed the ceremony and committed suicide because she could not bear her father's insult against her husband. As a result, Lord Shiva killed her father and then roamed the world with Sati's corpse on his back. To bring Lord Shiva back to normality, Lord Vishnu created a wasp to destroy the dead body of Sati.

Perhaps my wasp was a messenger of hope, a sign that my burdens were slowly easing, even if I could not feel it.

The 250-mile solution

Savannah, Georgia

AFTER THE HOLIDAYS, I escaped to Savannah on weekends to see my friend, Nykki, who lived there. She had the deft ability to mix upper-crust distinction with white-trash practicality. For example, she once set out a buffet of artisanal cheeses, hors d'oeuvres and crudités worthy of financier Donald Trump, yet served cans of PBR beer on ice in the nearby top-loading washing machine.

Savannah beckoned me. The architecture in its historical district reminded me of Luang Prabang. The expansive live oak trees, some almost 200 years old, reminded me of the married trees in Nepal. The historic squares burst with lipstick-colored azaleas in the spring. Confectionery shops sold pralines packed butter, brown sugar and pecans. The marshes and coastlines made me feel like I was poised at the edge of the world, that I could leave the United States any time I wanted.

Having spent my formative teenage years in Marietta, Georgia, I accepted Savannah's high humidity and palmetto bugs. Those two-inch-long cockroaches were not a sign that your house was dirty. They were a sign that you were in the South.

A month later, I asked myself why not move there? There was nothing keeping me in Charlotte. If I did not like Savannah, I could always leave.

Days after I told Jim and Mariana about my decision to move, they accepted an offer on their house. It felt like a sign that I was going in the right direction.

I rented a one-bedroom apartment on the top floor of a stately house in an older neighborhood, making sure the windowsills were wide enough for Roxanne to sunbathe on. Opening the boxes from my storage unit was like Christmas morning. Each item was a surprise and exactly what I liked. And yet they felt like mementos from a former life, the way high school keepsakes seemed after I graduated from college.

With rent and utility bills to pay, I decided to get a job waiting tables, so I applied at Moon River Brewing Co. I learned later that Gene, who was the general manager and co-owner, had tried to pawn me off to a friend who had a fine dining restaurant because he thought I was too qualified for the brew pub. The friend never called him back, so Gene hired me.

Forget working in an office cubicle. The restaurant was housed in a four-story brick building that opened as the City Hotel in 1821. The job's irregular hours and constant movement helped break up the shift work. Khaki pants were part of the uniform, so I kept wearing the pair I had worn during my trip.

The wait staff, about half my age, was both amusing and irritating as they struggled to be adults. Some suffered from partying too hard. Some panicked at the end of every college quarter because they were unprepared. Some seemed to change their sexual preferences as often as they changed their hair color.

"So let me get this straight, a couple of weeks ago she was engaged to a guy, but now she is dating Amanda," I asked. "Does she know Amanda is still sleeping with Katie?"

Besides the occasional rude customer, the main drawback to the job was Gene's militant management style. Wearing white Oxford shirts and blue Docker pants, he furrowed his brow, barked orders and stomped around.

"You. Wait. I've got four things to do first, and you're number five," he would say even if I just needed his storage room key to get toilet paper. I wanted him to at least say "please" as a sign of respect.

Seasons passed as I waited tables and wrote about my trip. I started to wonder if I would ever go back to my career. From the restaurant's front windows, I watched monstrous cargo ships glide by on the Savannah River. I toyed with the idea of leaving town on a cargo ship and watching Moon River Brewing fade in the distance.

I was not totally weaned off travel. Cousin Virginia generously flew me to Alaska for another visit. I went to England to visit a friend. My new Savannah friend, Scott, and I went to the weeklong Burning Man Festival, where 35,000 people celebrated artistic expression and radical self reliance in the Black Rock Desert in Nevada. People challenged land-speed records in the 400-square-mile dry lakebed.

"This sounded like such a good idea when we were back in Savannah," he mumbled as we sat on the floor of our tent, snorting saline to sooth the chapped skin inside our noses. We could handle the extreme temperature swings, but the aridity was daunting.

No amount of travel could have prepared me for the fantasy world the Burners created. Cars modified to look like giant bunny slippers, an Egyptian barge or a pirate ship. A lionfish with neon barbs that glowed at night. The back half of a VW van converted into a whole pig roaster. Barbie Death Camp and Wine Bistro. Panels of plywood arranged for roller skating. Arcing currents of electricity between a man and his Tesla coil. An igloo-shaped jungle gym where Goth warriors fought. Camps that gave away sake or clothes for playing dress up. The only commerce at the festival is the sale of coffee drinks and ice at the Center Camp Café. People came in every color, including red, green and blue, thanks to kiddie pools of vegetable dye.

Though everyone kept goggles and dust masks within reach due to dust storms, clothing was optional. Costumes ranged from Cirque du Soleil dramatic to winged vampires on stilts. Many men wore Utilikilts (canvas-like fabric versions of a traditional kilt) paired with combat boots. At Big Puffy Yellow Camp, a man named Lobster completed his manly ensemble with a flame-colored fur bolero jacket.

The pinnacle of the festival was Saturday night, when a 40-foot-tall, wooden effigy of a man was burned to the ground. Agile performers who spun balls of fire at the ends of chains entertained the giddy crowd until the fire began. Without prompting, we all started moving in a clockwise circle as if under the spell of a migratory pull.

When the Man slowly raised his arms, fireworks shot into the sky. Flames climbed his body as we sent cheers to the heavens. He burned throughout the night as we cast wild shadows on the bare ground. We were in the moment. We were alive. We were insiders.

EIGHTEEN MONTHS AFTER I MOVED to Savannah, Roxanne's kidneys failed. I spontaneously cried for days. I had lost my cherished pet, my live toy, my bedmate, my confidant, my family. Her unconditional love had been a grounding constant through so many evolutions of my life. I had her body cremated, but I could not bury the ashes. I did not know if I would stay in Savannah.

Without Roxanne to go home to, I started hanging out at Moon River Brewing after it closed at night while everyone finished their side work. One night, an impromptu game of strip poker broke out between Gene, a college student named Lois and me. Cards and beers went down smoothly. Lois raced along on a winning streak. Gene and I were soon down to our underwear.

"Okay, I'm done. I'm not playing any more because I still have to work with you," I said, putting my clothes back on, but not before I saw Gene for the first time as a person, not just a bossy manager.

He had a great smile, a witty sense of humor, and the broad shoulders/ narrow hips combination that I found sexy. He was two years older than me and divorced with no kids. He had a stunning work ethic and, the clincher, he loved to travel. Much later, he confessed that he had always found me attractive and that during the poker game he discovered I could be likable, not just an employee who was helpful to the point of irritation.

We started dating.

Within weeks, I nicknamed him Bear. Before his morning coffee, he could be as intimidating as an Admiralty Island grizzly. I enjoyed exploring his world as if it was a new country, discovering different sides of his personality. He was a rabid Tennessee Vols fan. He loved kayaking, college football, cooking from scratch and Lagavulin Scotch. Sometimes he acted like the same little boy who fell asleep with his body half way in the refrigerator next to a partially-eaten bowl of banana pudding.

The patience and flexibility I gained during my travels helped make our relationship thrive. I could accept him as he was, celebrate his triumphs, forgive his mistakes and support him when he was vulnerable. That perspective—and perspective is everything—helped me accept the ups and downs of daily life. Don't get me wrong. Sometimes he drove me crazy, like the time I asked him to pack an original watercolor we bought in Barcelona in his suitcase. Happy to please me, he did. What I did not learn until we got home was that he had folded it to make it fit. It took me a while to accept that it was not worth getting that upset about.

Our relationship did not change my hourly pay, but I always got the vacation time that I requested. Gene, my blue turtle sarong and I took vacations to other countries. My experience with flying came in handy when we missed a connecting flight in Amsterdam. Chubby snow flakes started cancelling flight after flight.

"There should be better way to manage this," Gene said as we stood in a line that looked at least 100-people long after our flight to Bologna was cancelled three times.

"You can make it better," I suggested.

"How?" he demanded.

"Don't believe you will get there until you arrive," I said, remembering the time when my plane landed at the wrong airport. "If you have no expectations, you won't be frustrated."

Somewhere along my travels, a part of me became Buddhist.

AFTER MORE THAN A YEAR of waiting tables, I was finally ready to get a career job. I wanted a salary, paid vacation, sick leave, health insurance and a retirement plan. In return, I promised myself that I would never wear pantyhose and would make monthly payments into a savings account dedicated to travel.

Savannah College of Art and Design hired me to be its web content producer. How great that the department was housed in a mansion built in 1870 and located a block from the 30-acre historic Forsyth Park. Some of my co-workers and I shared a former bedroom with three large windows, a fireplace and hardwood floors.

When I got cranky about the job, I reminded myself that it was better than trying to sell used flip-flops. Yet each day I worked, bowing to the demands of the office environment and slowly gaining 25 pounds, the farther I felt from the strong, independent woman I had been during my trip.

The banks were eager to loan money to anyone, so I bought an old two-story house with a spacious backyard. The kitchen and bathroom needed renovating. I had traveled around the world, so surely I could fix it up with the help of friends and people I could hire. Wrong. All my lessons about patience and acceptance went out the cheap windows, which I learned later were originally built for mobile homes.

Renovations triggered a cascade of demolition work and unexpected expenses. Difficulties were compounded by the idiot plumbers who used an upside-down cat litter bucket behind my hobby-size greenhouse in the back yard as a toilet. The basic construction of the Maasai and Samburu huts started to look better every day.

Sometimes when the work on the house got overwhelming, I sat by the fairy hut I built by the back fence. I struggled to believe that I was doing the right thing, that I was not over my head, that this was an adventure, that there would be the joy of accomplishment and investment when it was done.

When the house was finally back in working order, I grinned with pride. To take my trip, I had pried my grip off my first house and a secure job. Now I had a bigger house and a job that came with a priceless perk SCAD employees got one free class per quarter, so it was possible for me to earn an M.F.A. degree through the new contemporary writing program.

With tenacity that my trekking partner Kathi would admire, I spent five years taking one course after another. I found my voice and learned about the craft of storytelling.

Again, I looked at every trip photo with wonder and pride. When I had the best ones scanned and saw them on a 24-inch computer screen, I gasped. It was like looking through a window into a part of my life, it was so real.

I reread the journals and marveled at how each day of the trip was so different and had shaped me like water carving stone. When I added up the prime components of the trip—traveling alone around the world for six months, sacrificing my house and financial stability to do it, learning about myself, questioning my beliefs, and visiting such a spiritual place as Boudhanath in Nepal—I realized I had gone on a pilgrimage. And it had had profound consequences.

I have become more accepting when things do not work out the way I want. That is often life's way of lining me up for something better. I am more willing and confident about standing up for myself and making decisions. I am less influenced by other people's opinions and their definitions of beauty. I am more grateful. I applaud myself when I make mistakes because it means I have tried something new.

I GOT AN M.R.S. before I completed the M.F.A. degree. Gene proposed during a June trip to New Orleans, Louisiana, as we watched egrets in Audubon Park. I thought I might have been having a heat stroke, so I asked him to repeat the words before I said yes.

Gene had what I needed in a husband. He was strong enough that I felt safe leaning on him when I felt weak. And he was not threatened by my strong personality. He gave me what I wanted—excellent vacations (with my turtle sarong), kettle corn when we went to beer festivals and apple cider-cured bacon when I stopped by Moon River Brewing.

I was tickled when Gene delivered his bride price. Through Heifer International, he arranged for an Indonesian family to receive a water buffalo.

Five months later, we married in a small ceremony by the marsh in the backyard of a house we had bought together. Roxanne was buried at the base of the nearby live oak tree.

When it came time for him to slide the ring on my finger, Gene turned ash white.

"What's wrong?" I asked quietly, though the two dozen family members and close friends standing around us in a half circle could hear me.

"I forgot the rings," he confessed, looking at the ground. "We can go on without them."

"Where are they?"

"Upstairs in the dresser," he said.

"I've waited this long. I can wait a little longer."

Gene's brother, Forrest, ran to get the rings while everyone laughed and wiped away happy tears. It was a perfect moment for comic relief. I gently shook Gene's arms to loosen him up.

"I'm glad you forgot them," I said, nuzzling his ear. "It gives me a chance to ask why you're looking so serious? You're starting to scare me."

"I want you to know that I take our vows very seriously."

"Thank you," I said, touched by his devotion. "I love you, too. Now let's relax and celebrate that we found each other."

When he finally slid the ring on my finger, I wondered if the Baci Ceremony strings from Laos had brought me to that moment. Curious that I had traveled around the world, only to find a place and a man that I loved 250 miles from where I started.

About the Author

After graduating from Purdue University, Kristine K. Stevens took vacations to Costa Rica, Japan and France, which ignited her passion for travel.

"Travel gives me a sense of freedom and enlightenment," she says. "It frees me from the expectations of my own culture, and it shows me how intriguing and diverse life can be."

Kristine works at the Savannah College of Art and Design as the senior web content manager. She continues to have a weak spot for Snickers bars, Pringles potato chips and Fanta Orange sodas.

Although she thrives in Savannah, Georgia—despite its monstrous palmetto bugs, Kristine and her husband Gene Beeco are plotting another global adventure, this time focusing on the Pacific Rim.